# Mediation
# in the
# Campus Community

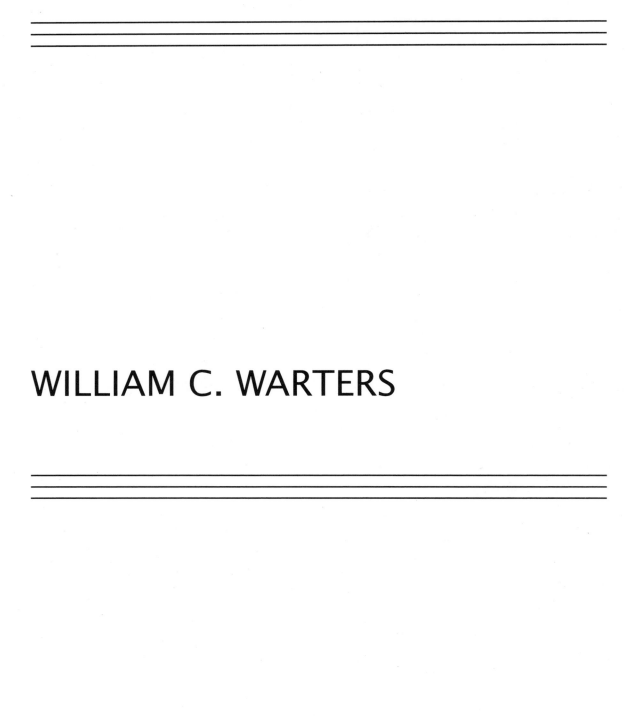

# WILLIAM C. WARTERS

# Mediation in the Campus Community

## Designing and Managing Effective Programs

Conflict Resolution Education Network

 JOSSEY-BASS PUBLISHERS ▪ San Francisco

Jossey-Bass books and products are available through most bookstores. To contact Jossey-Bass directly, call (888) 378-2537, fax to (800) 605-2665, or visit our website at www.josseybass.com.
Substantial discounts on bulk quantities of Jossey-Bass books are available to corporations, professional associations, and other organizations. For details and discount information, contact the special sales department at Jossey-Bass.

 Manufactured in the United States of America on Lyons Falls Turin Book. This paper is acid-free and 100 percent totally chlorine-free.

**Library of Congress Cataloging-in-Publication Data**
Warters, William C., 1959–
    Mediation in the campus community : designing and managing effective programs / by William C. Warters. — 1st ed.
        p.    cm. — (The Jossey-Bass higher and adult education series)
    Includes bibliographical references (p.    ) and index.
    ISBN 0-7879-4789-X (pbk. : perm. paper)
    1. Counseling in higher education. 2. Conflict management—Study and teaching (Higher) 3. Mediation. I. Title. II. Series.
    LB2343 .W37 1999
    378.1'94—dc21                                                                  99-6619

FIRST EDITION
*PB Printing*   10 9 8 7 6 5 4 3 2 1

The Jossey-Bass
Higher and Adult Education Series

# CONTENTS

# _____ FIGURES, TABLES, AND EXHIBITS

As anyone who has worked on a campus knows, conflict is relatively common in these complex settings. We also know that a college or university's response to conflict can have profound effects on students, staff, faculty, and the surrounding community. Dramatic and tragic shootings, lawsuits, and departmental feuds are only the most visible symptoms of conflicts gone awry. Most conflicts, however, remain "below the radar," woven into the daily experiences of students, staff, and faculty.

Campuses are clearly looking for new ways to handle conflict before it escalates, and one creative response has been the development of specialized mediation and conflict resolution services. Such programs have been appearing rapidly on campuses across the country, moving from eighteen programs in 1990 to some two hundred in 1999. Mediation services offer colleges and universities a flexible alternative for handling a wide range of conflicts. On some campuses mediation has been incorporated into the disciplinary code or grievance procedure as a first or optional step. On others, mediation is used to handle disputes in certain categories, such as staff, landlord-tenant, or roommate conflicts. At still others, mediation is offered to all members of the campus and to the surrounding community, covering the full range of conflicts experienced by people living and working together and interacting as group members, consumers, coworkers, friends, and lovers.

This book supports and encourages more effective handling of conflicts in the campus community through the increased application of formal and informal mediation. It is written to address the needs of student affairs administrators, residential life staff, student organizations, campus judicial officers, faculty committees, human resource staff, ombudspersons, academic programs, and community mediators who are interested in establishing or upgrading mediation services on their campuses. Although it has been designed with higher education settings in mind, the book will also be of interest to potential program designers working in other large organizational settings and to community mediation programs looking for a useful reference guide.

Pragmatic in focus and informed by theory, the book draws on my extensive experience establishing and running three very different campus mediation initiatives. It represents the next generation of a groundbreaking manual, *Peaceful Persuasion: A Guide to Creating Mediation Dispute Resolution Programs for College Campuses* written by Katherine Girard, Janet Rifkin, and Annette Townley in 1985. Much of that early work has stood the test of time and with permission is woven into this book. The book also reports and builds on some of the highly creative and pathbreaking work being carried out by campus mediation programs across the country.

The book is designed to provide all the basic information needed for programs to get started. General dispute resolution concepts are reviewed and explained, as well as a brief history of conflict management in higher education, and basic theories about colleges and universities as organizations to put the work in context. At the heart of the book is a ten-step guide to establishing a program that covers the full range of activities that program staff commonly engage in. Included are many sample documents and forms to increase the book's practical utility. And because mediation is not the "Swiss Army knife" of conflict, able to handle all circumstances of disagreement and dispute, the practical and ethical limits of mediation are examined as well. At the same time, a host of innovative nonmediation conflict management techniques is offered to encourage people to think creatively about the potential for conflict resolution on campus.

Chapter One begins by reviewing the basic terminology of conflict resolution; it presents core dispute systems design concepts and examines the growth of interest in mediation and conflict resolution on campuses. Chapter Two presents general theory on the organization of higher education settings and then examines arguments in favor of mediation from the perspective of various campus groups, providing sample case studies to illustrate the potential of mediation. Chapter Three begins the program development process, discussing the first six steps of basic program design in detail.

1. Developing a core planning group
2. Conducting a conflict management needs assessment
3. Deciding on the initial scope and focus of the program
4. Developing a statement of purpose
5. Developing a staffing and program coordination plan
6. Securing administrative and financial support and appropriate space

Chapter Four shifts the focus to training issues, examining strategies for selecting potential mediators, variations in mediation style and session formats, and what to look for in a training program. Also included is a set of mediation role-play scripts and a listing of training materials designed specifically for use in campus settings. Chapter Five examines the challenges of building awareness of a new initiative and presents a host of strategies for promoting a program and building systems of referral. Chapter Six focuses on the nuts and bolts of operating a program, examining intake and case management procedures, as well as the important topic of maintaining program quality and integrity and minimizing risks. Although the chapter presents general information on best practices, all program administrators are encouraged to consult their own legal advisers for specific advice on risk management. Chapter Seven looks at the role of research and program evaluation in program design. The extent of the literature on campus mediation is briefly sketched out, and a basic framework for evaluating a mediation program is presented. Also provided is a listing of useful resources for program evaluation purposes. Chapter Eight explores efforts to move beyond the mediation table using various training and prevention strategies, group-level interventions, development of culturally appropriate models, nonviolent activism, and community involvement strategies. The book concludes with a guide to resources, forms, and documents.

The extent and scope of campus mediation work is rapidly expanding. In society at large and on campus, alternative forms of dispute resolution have come of age. I hope that this book will become part of the movement to help build a stronger campus community through mediation.

## Acknowledgments

The work that the authors of *Peaceful Persuasion* did helped me and many others establish mediation programs at a time when few models existed and laid the foundation for this book. I also appreciate the staff at the National Institute for Dispute Resolution and the Conflict Resolution Education Network for encouraging and supporting the project through times of uncertainty.

Some early allies helped me learn about campus mediation development firsthand. These include Barbara Silverthorne, Gary Zimmerman, and Terry Amsler for their help at the University of California at Santa Cruz, and Neil Katz, Louis Kriesberg, Maggie McHugh, and Phil Moses at Syracuse University. These folks were good traveling companions and colleagues in exciting times. I also thank the various members of the Higher Education Committee of the National Association for Mediation in Education and the broader campus mediation network who worked together to end the isolation of campus dispute resolvers. And finally, I thank my wife, Loraleigh Keashly, and my son, Spencer, for their patience and caring support while I pulled this book together. It is good to be done and able to share it with others.

*May 1999*                                                                William C. Warters
*Harper Woods, Michigan*

# THE AUTHOR

*William Warters* is associate director of Wayne State University's Program on Mediating Theory and Democratic Systems and a part-time faculty member in Wayne State's master of arts in dispute resolution program. He holds a certificate in conflict resolution from the Program on the Analysis and Resolution of Conflicts, a Hewlett Foundation conflict theory–building center at Syracuse University, and he was the recipient of a Guggenheim Fellowship and Maxwell Dean's Award for his work on violence intervention.

One of Warters's primary areas of research, writing, and practice is campus conflict resolution. He served as the founding program coordinator of Syracuse University's campus mediation center and was director and faculty supervisor of the conflict resolution resource service at Nova Southeastern University, Fort Lauderdale, Florida.

Warters has helped found dozens of campus mediation programs by providing the initial mediation training or technical assistance. In 1990 he served as co-chair and host of the First National Conference on Campus Mediation Programs, held at Syracuse University. He also has served as chair of the Higher Education Committee and as a board member of National Association for Mediation in Education. In 1994 he established and began moderating an e-mail discussion list, CCRNet (Campus Conflict Resolution Network), that serves campus conflict resolvers. He maintains a Web site, Campus Mediation Resources (http://www.mtds.wayne.edu/campus.htm), that provides a wealth of information and resources for campus mediation program staff, volunteers, and advocates.

# Mediation
## in the
## Campus Community

# CHAPTER 1

# The Growing Need for Conflict Resolution Strategies in Higher Education

Higher education is a major enterprise in the United States. Approximately twenty-one hundred four-year colleges and universities and fifteen hundred two-year colleges provide a broad range of educational and research services. With faculty numbering about 900,000 and enrollments of more than 15 million students (including 2 million in graduate and professional schools), these institutions are at the center of our social system (Ausubel, 1998). And like all other kinds of communities or organizations, colleges and universities are regularly faced with conflicts that directly affect their quality of life and effectiveness.

Academia is built on the ideal of academic freedom and the vigorous discourse of ideas. Many good theories, innovative new practices, and well-prepared, critically thinking students have emerged from the crucible of campus conflict. Unfortunately, campus disputes, played out at many different levels, can become all too disruptive. Conflicts can bring in their wake a generalized sense of fear and disruption, bitterness, feelings of injustice or betrayal, reduced communication, and factionalism, not to mention expense.

Because of the costs associated with conflict, considerable effort and creativity since the late 1960s has been devoted to improving the general processing of campus-based disputes. Important innovations have included the development of campus ombudsperson offices, new peace and conflict studies programs, employee assistance programs, diversity training and sexual harassment prevention programs, and revised and improved campus judicial and grievance procedures. One particularly important trend, and the focus of this book, has been the significant increase in the use of mediation on campus since the early 1980s. There were fewer than twenty campus-based mediation projects in North America in 1990 (Warters and Hedeen, 1991), but now the number exceeds two hundred and continues to grow.

The existing programs are diverse in design, due in large part to the wide range of potential campus environments, each with its own unique characteristics. Fortunately, this also means that many diverse examples of program design are available for emulation. Effectively functioning mediation programs exist across the full spectrum of higher education settings, in public and private institutions, large research universities, small liberal arts colleges, community colleges, and unionized and nonunionized environments (Warters and Hedeen, 1991; Holton and Warters, 1995). These programs can be found in a variety of campus locations:

- Counseling centers
- Ombudsperson's offices
- Student government organizations
- Academic programs
- Research clinics
- Employee assistance programs
- Human resource departments
- Residential life programs
- Deans of students offices
- Campus judicial systems
- Off-campus housing offices
- Faculty committees
- Student cooperatives

The types of cases handled by these programs vary widely as well:

- Student-student disputes
- Organizational or intergroup disputes
- Neighborhood conflicts
- Staff peer and supervisor-supervisee conflicts
- Sexual harassment disputes
- Student, staff, and administration disputes
- Internal and interdepartmental faculty conflicts
- Town-gown conflicts
- Student protests and occupations

The goal of this book is to limit the destructiveness of campus conflict and to maximize its potential as a learning opportunity. To that end, this chapter sets the stage for the in-depth review of program development strategies and procedures that follows. It provides a brief introduction to core conflict resolution concepts and some of the history of campus conflict management innovation.

## Basic Orientations to Conflict

There will always be hot political or moral topics that will energize campus controversy. There are also ongoing disputes that arise out of the daily interactions between members of any campus community. These conflicts are based on some combination of lack of experience (by newcomers or people changing roles), stress or boredom (or both), miscommunication, destructive patterns of interaction, and differing needs and interests of community members. Regardless of the initial source of the dispute, however, the outcomes of conflict (either positive or negative) often hinge on the way the dispute is handled.

People who respond to campus conflict are inevitably faced with the challenge of clarifying their own underlying beliefs about the place and role of conflict. Perceptions of what constitutes a significant conflict and how best to respond to it are greatly influenced by one's role and location within the organization, as well as prior socialization, personality, and past experience. Generally conflict can be viewed as negative and destructive (to be settled or eliminated) or positive and potentially productive (to be nurtured and explored), or something in between. Indeed, it can be argued that conflicts are neither inherently good nor bad but simply facts of life.

The larger field of conflict studies also grapples with questions regarding its basic orientation toward conflict. Conflict scholars and practitioners have used a variety of basic terms, including *conflict management, conflict resolution,* and *conflict transformation,* to describe their general frameworks for addressing conflict. In a relatively young academic area such as this, definitions and distinctions remain somewhat fuzzy. Nevertheless, the terms are frequently used. Familiarity with the general orientations they represent and different interpretations of them is useful, if only to help one get a sense of one's own point of view.

*Conflict management* is perhaps the most commonly chosen phrase. It reflects a belief that conflicts are an ongoing part of life and that many in fact will not be ended but can at least be managed constructively. Disputes are handled on a case-by-case basis.

A range of intervention techniques known as alternative dispute resolution (ADR) are used to minimize the destructive aspects of conflict, and considerable emphasis is placed on the parties' quickly reaching a settlement. Critics of the term *conflict management* are concerned that this orientation tends to place too much emphasis on controlling or managing the individual parties involved in a dispute, focusing on peace, as in "peace and quiet," rather than peace as in "justice." A major concern is that the opportunity to address underlying social or structural inconsistencies or inequities that are driving the dispute are too often suppressed or lost along the way.

Advocates of the *conflict resolution* term and approach argue that rather than always dealing with the symptoms of conflict and applying essentially Band-Aid responses, we should focus on the underlying causes. The approach suggests that individual disputes and larger ongoing conflicts can be ended successfully by using techniques that address and resolve the root causes of the conflict. Critics of the term *conflict resolution* are concerned that the phrase is too idealistic and may often overstate what is possible. There is a myriad of underlying structural sources of conflict in most areas of social life, and many practical and political difficulties lie in the way of truly eliminating them. For instance, a true conflict resolution approach may require drawing more participants than the initial disputing parties into the process in order to build enduring and just solutions. Sometimes this is difficult or impossible to accomplish. Given the challenges, the actual resolution of conflict may be hard to attain and maintain.

Recently a third term, *conflict transformation,* has gained currency. Proponents of this perspective note that the meaning of *conflict* is socially constructed and reconstructed through interaction. They argue that both conflict management and conflict resolution approaches, although valuable, focus too intently on settling conflict issues. In the process they pay too little attention to the nature of the relationships between the parties and the learning opportunities inherent in most conflicts. Transformationalists argue that if the process supports it, positive changes in parties' basic understanding of the meaning of their dispute, their understanding of their choices and options, and the nature of their relationship with the other party and their community may occur while a conflict is being worked through. Critics of this approach argue that the facilitative, nondirective approach that transformationalists advocate is inappropriate in many situations that require a firmer hand and is unrealistic when the issue is not the relationship or people's perceptions but rather some question of distribution of scarce or contested resources.

All of these general perspectives have validity and utility depending on the kinds of conflict in question. However, given the highly interdependent nature of the campus community and the importance of ongoing relationships, a general transformative orientation to many kinds of campus conflicts seems to make the most sense.

## Alternative Dispute Resolution and Dispute Systems Design _____

The traditional methods for resolving escalated disputes have been litigation and adjudication. These formal processes are governed by specific rules or laws that result in a judgment handed down by a judge or jury, which is then enforced by the state or institution.

The term *alternative dispute resolution* (ADR) is now frequently used to identify alternative nonlitigious conflict-handling methods such as mediation, arbitration, and principled negotiation. Recently ADR advocates have begun substituting *appropriate* for *alternative*. This change reflects a desire by ADR practitioners to move away from the inferred shadow of the law and focus attention instead on their role of supporting appropriate dispute-handling options and choices across the board.

Within the larger ADR field, increasing attention is being paid to both the formal and informal approaches that entire organizations use when dealing with conflict. A systemwide perspective that looks at how the various conflict-handling mechanisms interrelate, rather than viewing and responding to conflicts on a case-by-case basis, comes highly recommended. The general process has been given the name *dispute systems design*. Advocates of this approach (Ury, Brett, and Goldberg, 1988; Costantino and Merchant, 1996; Slaikeu and Hasson, 1998) argue that there are serious inefficiencies built into most current organizational dispute-handling designs. A dispute systems review and redesign is used to help establish a more fully integrated system able to respond to the entire range of conflicts in the most effective, satisfying, and least costly manner.

At the center of this analysis are three conceptual elements, known as *interests, rights,* and *power*. According to the basic framework, people within an organization who are involved in a dispute have certain *interests* at stake that can be discovered and articulated. At the same time certain *standards* or rights may exist that may provide guidelines toward a fair outcome. And finally, there is always some kind of *power* relationship between or among the disputants that can affect the outcome.

The parties and the organization can choose (consciously or by default) to focus on one or more of these basic elements when working to resolve a dispute. They can strive to resolve the dispute by reconciling underlying interests, determining who is right according to some standard, or who is most powerful, or through some combination of approaches. The various conflict management mechanisms available emphasize different basic elements. Methods for handling the conflict can thus be categorized as being interest-based, rights-based, or power-based forms of conflict management.

## Interest-Based Approaches to Conflict Management

Interest-based methods of resolving disputes involve the parties in identifying their basic concerns, needs, and issues as the starting place for building a mutually satisfying agreement. The most common methods in this category are interest-based problem solving, negotiation, and mediation. In all these circumstances the parties retain ultimate control over the outcome of the process.

**Negotiation.** The most basic interest-based conflict management approach is *negotiation,* a process of voluntary problem solving or bargaining. The disputing parties seek to work out their concerns by themselves, using direct discussion and other forms of communication. It is the most informal method and can take place spontaneously whenever people talk out their differences. Depending on the setting, negotiation can be made more formal through the use of agreed-on ground rules and procedures. An important strength of negotiation is that the power to control both the process and the outcome remains in the hands of the primary parties. There is no third party involved to influence the process or render judgment on what should occur.

**Mediation.** *Mediation* is generally a voluntary, semistructured process where a neutral or impartial third party assists the disputing parties in identifying, and hopefully satisfying, their individual and mutual interests relative to the dispute. Mediators try to help the parties create integrative or so-called win-win resolutions. They do this by listening to both sides and helping the parties communicate with each other in productive ways. Although the mediator has some power stemming from the role of managing the process, the parties still retain control over the substance of what will be discussed and any outcomes that result. Exhibit 1.1 provides an overview of the basic mediation framework that I have used for years, which is similar in most respects to other basic models. (Note that this model does not reflect more transformative models that downplay discrete stages and phases.)

I. Setting the Stage

*Mediator's Role:* Prepare environment, do introductions, explain process and ground rules, share expectations

*Participant's Role:* Arrive, get settled, review expectations, agree to ground rules, ask questions to clarify process

II. Uninterrupted Time

*Mediator's Role:* Listen to each party; manage process

*Participant's Role:* Describe conflict in own terms; speak of both content and emotions in conflict

FOCUS ON THE PAST

III. Focusing the Issues

*Mediator's Role:* Summarize and clarify main issues; ask for verification that these are the issues to be discussed

*Participant's Role:* Agree or modify summary of issues; agree on list of issues to be discussed

FOCUS ON THE PRESENT

IV. The Exchange

*Mediator's Role:* Encourage dialogue on issues, encouraging parties to speak to each other; listen for points of agreement and nonmediatable issues

*Participant's Role:* Speak to each other about selected issues; provide questions and information to help dialogue

V. Generating Potential Solutions

*Mediator's Role:* Summarize mediatable issues; facilitate brainstorming and problem solving; perhaps caucus to support movement toward agreement

*Participant's Role:* Accept responsibility for conflict choices; generate potential solutions; consider interests, not just positions

FOCUS ON THE FUTURE

VI. Agreement Building and Writing

*Mediator's Role:* Specify points of agreement; provide a "reality check" when necessary; write down terms of agreement in clear and specific language; wrap up

*Participant's Role:* Negotiate in good faith; work toward a mutually agreeable solution; develop written agreements if appropriate

Exhibit 1.1. The Process of Mediation: An Overview

### Rights-Based Approaches

Rights-based methods, grounded in fixed rules or principles that may or may not be codified, seek to determine which party's rights should prevail. The most common methods in this category are judicial proceedings, grievance hearings, arbitration, and litigation. The third party, a judge, arbitrator, or tribunal of some sort, seeks to determine who is right in a particular dispute, as measured against the code, contract, accepted practice in the field, or applicable law. In rights-based methods, decisions of equity or justice are supposed to be reached without resort to the use of power plays or power struggles. Formal student disciplinary processes still tend to be patterned on this judicial model, although their methods also incorporate student development concepts.

**Arbitration.** In *arbitration,* the most common rights-based ADR method, the third party takes control of both the process and the outcome. The disputing parties present and justify their case to an agreed-on impartial third party or panel, who then provides an advisory or binding settlement based on their assessment of the case. In most cases the settlement is enforceable through some form of legal or administrative means. In *binding arbitration* the parties agree ahead of time that the arbitrator's judgment will settle the dispute. In *nonbinding arbitration* the parties take the judgment of the arbitrator under advisement as they work to reach their own settlement agreement or a decision to pursue other more formal methods.

It is still relatively common to find processes that are essentially arbitration being mislabeled as mediation. For instance, many faculty grievance procedures listed in campus handbooks include referral to a so-called mediation committee. Rather than truly mediating, however, most of these committees in practice function instead as a panel of arbitrators. The panels review the case and find in favor of one side or the other in a dispute, or they issue a recommendation to the president based on their review. The important distinction is that whenever the third party, instead of the parties, determines the outcome in the conflict (or uses his or her power to advocate for a particular outcome), he or she is essentially arbitrating rather than mediating.

### Power-Based Approaches

Power-based methods of resolving conflict hinge on who has more power. Examples of this approach include outright warfare, coercive or punitive violence, some forms of nonviolent social protest, and the use of strikes and lockouts. Decision-making procedures that ultimately come down to a majority vote are also power-based models, if somewhat more subtle in their application. In previous periods of campus conflict and unrest, some activists and campus law enforcement personnel in fact used varying degrees of violence to wage their conflict. In contrast, the outright violence reported on campus today is primarily limited to fights, tragic shootings done by disgruntled students or employees, and sexual violence or prejudice-related incidents of ethnic violence. These forms of violence and assertions of power over others, while destructive, may or may not be directly related to ongoing conflicts. Other common power-based methods used in campus conflicts include threats, strikes, votes of no confidence, and unilateral decision making.

## Hybrid Approaches

As the ADR field has advanced, hybrid approaches have been developed that combine elements of the different basic processes. Exploring the full range of these methods takes us beyond the scope of this book. Fortunately, the methods have been described well by others (see, for instance, Goldberg, Sander, and Rogers, 1992) for those interested in more details on specific models.

## Informal Approaches

Many approaches to solving conflicts have the same basic structure as the processes already described but involve less formalization of roles. For instance, a mutual friend or colleague who assists two or more principals in communicating more calmly or effectively is providing informal mediation or conciliation services. Rather than having the parties meet face to face, this may often involve a kind of shuttle mediation, where the third party goes back and forth between parties until some kind of resolution can be found. Informal versions of arbitration, when both parties present their case to a neutral person who then decides what should be done, are often provided by supervisors or administrators in the regular course of their work. Direct negotiation between parties may be supported through informal means as well, for instance, through conflict management coaching provided by colleagues who help disputing parties prepare for a meeting. Supporting and enhancing existing informal (and preferably constructive) conflict-handling networks is an important part of any campus conflict mediation initiative.

### Campus Ombudspersons

Any discussion of a systems approach to dispute resolution on campus must include reference to the campus ombudsperson (also called ombuds). On campuses that have them, ombuds are often the most broadly experienced members of the campus community when it comes to conflict handling. Campus ombuds offices serve as a visible point of contact for people with a wide range of concerns. They are flexible services, providing various formal and informal conflict-handling functions based on the parties and issues. They are available to discuss in confidence the concerns and questions that parties who approach them may have. They help by listening, explaining common interpretations of university regulations and customs, exploring possible avenues for problem resolution, offering options, and making referrals. As appropriate, ombuds may also work with all the parties in a conflict, serving informally as a conciliator and less frequently in the capacity of formal mediator. Ombuds have no formal decision-making power and thus do not function as arbitrators or policymakers. The role is instead firmly grounded in the principles of objectivity, independence, accessibility, confidentiality, and justice (see University and College Ombuds Association Ethical Principles, 1999). A basic tenet of the ombuds is that an aggrieved party who approaches this office for assistance is the ultimate decision maker as to what approach, if any, he or she wants to take in attempting to resolve the dispute.

Cooperation between mediation program developers and ombuds is key to the success of most new initiatives. Although the two are functionally somewhat different, the work of campus ombuds offices and formal mediation programs is closely related and often overlaps. In fact, a growing number of ombuds offices have sponsored mediation programs as one activity or offshoot of their office. Sources of additional information on campus ombuds program development are referenced in the Recommended Resources section at the end of this book.

## Integrating the Different Conflict Resolution Approaches _____

Conflict-handling approaches focusing specifically on interests, rights, or power are believed to vary considerably in the degree of party satisfaction provided and their costs to the organization. When compared with rights-based methods such as arbitration or adjudication, interest-based methods (such as mediation) are considered better methods of dispute resolution because they result in lower transaction costs, greater satisfaction with outcomes, less strain on the parties' relationship, and lower recurrence of disputes. In turn, rights-based approaches such as arbitration are thought to be less costly and more satisfying than many power-based approaches such as the strike or lockout or hostile takeover.

The most basic dispute systems design principle is to try to create a coordinated system that makes appropriate use of the various dispute-handling methods based on their overall cost and likelihood of satisfying the parties. This approach moves away from a "one-size-fits all" method of handling conflicts and focuses instead on "fitting the forum to the fuss." It is understood that before settling their conflict using an interest-based method such as negotiation or mediation, some parties may need or wish to assess how their rights stack up compared to those of the other party or to assess how much power they have in comparison to the other party. Well-designed integrated systems are thought to channel people toward interest-based approaches first (thought to be the least costly and most satisfying), but still support the use of lower-cost rights-based approaches (such as advisory or nonbinding arbitration), or low-cost power-based approaches (such as votes of confidence or straw votes) as appropriate and desired by the parties. Channels leading from one type of method to another are often referred to as *loops forward* (from interest-based to rights-based or power-based methods) or *loops back* (from power-based or rights-based to interest-based methods). Integrated systems gives disputing parties a low-cost way to get more information on the likelihood of winning a rights-based case or power-based struggle (looping forward), while keeping alive the possibility of going back to the bargaining table or back into mediation (looping back) to settle the dispute. The system should be designed to be flexible, resolving disputes at the lowest and least costly level possible based on the case and the parties' wishes.

Mary Rowe, long-time ombudsperson at the Massachusetts Institute of Technology, has written extensively on general dispute system design principles. Based on her observations of a broad range of organizations, she notes that an effective internal dispute resolution system embodies the following general characteristics:

- The system is taken seriously (strong support from the top).
- The system provides significant evidence of change (including reversal of some management decisions) as a result of complaints and disputes.
- The system provides options—and choice—for pursuing most complaints.

- The system provides loops back, from adjudicative options to problem-solving options, and also loops forward.
- The system is available to everyone, managers and employees alike, for every type of problem.
- The system provides in-house designated neutrals.
- The system provides, if possible, more than one available neutral.
- The system guarantees confidentiality to all who approach an in-house, designated neutral off the record, except in the rare case where there is a duty to protect (i.e., a danger to self or others) (Rowe, 1991, pp. 355–356).

It is unlikely that most mediation program designers will have the kind of influence, organizational buy-in, or energy necessary to effect an entire systems redesign. However, those who keep these basic design principles in mind can make more reasoned arguments when discussing long-term project plans with representatives from other campus dispute-handling mechanisms and higher-level administrators. (For more information on dispute systems design, see the Recommended Resources.)

## Dispute Resolution on Campus: A Brief History

Procedures for dealing with conflicts in the college and university environment have varied considerably over time, based on prevailing norms, societal conditions, and available resources. (Readers interested in specifics of the history are encouraged to consult a more detailed working paper on this topic [see Warters, 1998b] or the time line posted at the Campus Mediation Resources Web site [see the Recommended Resources] that chronicles some of the specific events that have marked the emergence of formalized mediation on campus.)

### Increasing Regulation and Legalization of the Campus Environment

University student enrollments and number of personnel expanded dramatically when the post–World War II baby boomers started to matriculate. During the 1960s and 1970s college administrators developed a seemingly ever-increasing number of rules and regulations in an attempt to manage the rapidly changing campus environment. Numerous changes were underway that directly or indirectly influenced campus dispute-processing procedures. For instance, whereas previously the courts had been highly reluctant to get involved in campus issues, during the 1970s they began to hear more campus-related disputes, and federal courts established guidelines relating to internal grievance procedures on campus. Students began to demand increased involvement in running their educational institutions. During the same period, a larger proportion of university personnel joined unions and collectively bargained over contracts.

One significant response to these pressures was a "due process explosion" during the mid-1970s. Many new policies were developed providing detailed grievance and disciplinary procedures aimed at protecting individual rights and checking administrative discretion (and hopefully fending off possible lawsuits). Although the focus on fairness and due process was valuable as a means of limiting mistreatment, it also took its toll on the general campus environment. As evidence of this shift, an article in *Change* magazine (Ryor, 1978) argued that the era of collegiality was being replaced by the era of liability. Other observers of the legal climate on campus described the environment of the late 1970s as follows:

> The heterogeneous, impersonal and at times, almost alienated quality of the academic climate fosters the utilization of law to assert individual rights and settle grievances in academic situations. Students more and more come to view themselves as "consumers" of education, faculty operate under rules and regulations with regular contracts, and administrators work under a complex web of legal guidelines [Marske and Vago, 1980, p. 168].

A common perception at this time was a feeling that just about any issue could end up in court. Other indicators of the legalizing of the campus climate can be found in the increase beginning in the late 1970s of prepaid legal services (funded through a student fee) available on campus for students. Legal resources also became more readily available to faculty as the American Association of University Professors (AAUP) began offering a liability insurance policy tailored to the needs of faculty. The National Association of College and University Attorneys (NACUA), founded in 1961 by a small group of attorneys providing legal advice and services to campuses, experienced its greatest period of growth during the late 1970s. NACUA grew as university administrators, no longer able to function with occasional use of the expertise of a lawyer sitting on their board of directors, moved to establish in-house legal counsel. By the late 1970s an annual conference on law and higher education was established to help university administrators keep up with the rapidly changing legal climate. The Association for Student Judicial Affairs (ASJA) was formed in 1987 as an offshoot of this conference to promote and support professionalism in the increasingly complex student judicial affairs area.

By the late 1970s changes in the external environment, such as decreasing enrollments and a tightening up of the economy, spurred additional conflicts related to the allocation of scarce resources. One 1978 review of higher education trends predicted that

> presidents and other top administrators...will become increasingly involved in managing conflict among competing interest groups. Top level administrators will be required to serve as a "court of last resort" in settling disputes among various schools, divisions, departments, interest groups, entrepreneurs, superstars, research institutes, special program directors, and students. There is no way to resolve this dilemma, because conflicts are going to increase, no matter what methods people use to reduce them [Baldridge, Curtis, Ecker, and Riley, 1978, p. 228].

## Development of Alternative Dispute Resolution on Campus

As the laws surrounding higher education became more numerous and more complicated, students became more vocal consumers of education, and the number of lawsuits brought against universities by students and faculty increased, interest also began to grow in the use of alternative methods to resolve or reduce conflicts. This trend mirrored the growth of interest in ADR that was occurring within the larger society.

The formal ombuds role emerged on campus in the late 1960s and early 1970s as a new approach to dealing with campus conflict and unrest. Ombuds offices were established to respond to demands for a neutral, confidential, and safe place to discuss concerns and voice complaints. The earliest programs primarily handled student complaints. The majority of campus ombuds offices today have expanded their focus to include faculty, staff, and administrative problems as well (Stern, 1990). The ombuds office has become a well-established part of many campus communities. Nationally the University and College Ombuds Association provides networking and professional development opportunities. A conservative estimate of the current number of campuses with formally established campus ombuds offices is about two hundred, and the number appears to be growing.

An early example of experimentation with formal mediation on campus began in 1979–1980 when the New York branch of the American Arbitration Association sponsored a new entity, the Center for Mediation in Higher Education. The center, now defunct, functioned for a number of years, encouraging the use of mediation to resolve disputes involving university administrations and staff or faculty. In 1980, the journal *New Directions in Higher Education* published a special issue on conflict management in higher education that was edited by Jane McCarthy, director of the Center for Mediation. In the lead article McCarthy (1980) describes some of the thinking emerging at the time:

> Many educators appear concerned about the prospect that the educational communities' commitment to collegial governance and decision-making will be threatened as institutions are forced to choose between conflicting constituencies as competition for scarce resources escalates. Mediation can foster collegiality by encouraging disputants to identify common interests and work supportively to achieve mutually acceptable solutions [p. 4].

The fledgling University of Massachusetts Mediation Project, also described in the special issue (d'Errico, Katsch, and Rifkin, 1980), served students and community members, and was one of the first of a growing number of distinct mediation efforts located on a campus. Other early efforts occurred at the University of Hawaii and Oberlin and Grinnell Colleges (Warters, 1991).

Student grievance-handling procedures established in the 1970s began to include the use of third-party procedures as well. A 1981 study of 741 colleges and universities (Folger and Schubert, 1985) found that over half of the surveyed institutions had implemented some kind of third-party procedure (formal or ad hoc) for responding to student-initiated grievances.

The mid- to late 1980s witnessed the significant growth of publications addressing campus conflict resolution methods and increased experimentation with mediation. In 1985, the predecessor to this book, *Peaceful Persuasion: A Guide to Creating Mediation Dispute Resolution Programs for College Campuses* (Girard, Rifkin, and Townley, 1985), was published by the University of Massachusetts Mediation Project and the National Institute for Dispute Resolution. Information on mediation also began to appear in specialized publications for student affairs personnel (Knechel, Moore, and Moore, 1984; Engram, 1985; Beeler, 1986) and for campus human resource professionals (Cunningham, 1984).

In the 1990s campus mediation efforts began to blossom. Growing interest in and use of mediation on campus resulted in the first National Conference on Campus Mediation Programs, hosted by the Campus Mediation Center at Syracuse University in the spring of 1990. Three additional independent national campus mediation conferences were held in subsequent years at other locations. In 1994 the campus mediation network merged with the National Association for Mediation in Education (NAME), which expanded its previous K–12 focus by establishing the Committee on Higher Education. By 1996 NAME merged with the National Institute for Dispute Resolution (NIDR), becoming the Conflict Resolution Education Network (CREnet). NIDR/CREnet continues to host an annual conflict resolution education conference, at which school-based mediation programs is a core component.

ADR approaches are becoming more accepted in areas of campus life that have become quite legalized. For instance, campus judicial affairs programs began incorporating mediation more formally into their processes in the 1990s. The Association for Student Judicial Affairs (ASJA) passed a formal resolution in 1994 supporting the use of mediation within student judicial affairs, and by 1997 it had established an On-Campus ADR Committee, which hosts an annual mediation training institute for ASJA members. Similarly, the National Association of College and University Attorneys (NACUA) now has a separate Litigation and ADR Committee and has sponsored a number of mediation training programs designed specifically for college and university legal counsel. A growing number of sessions on mediation are now appearing at the annual conferences on law and higher education.

Generally the scope and complexity of campus mediation work increased dramatically during the 1990s, evidenced by increased experimentation with mediation as a response to diversity disputes (Volpe and Witherspoon, 1992; Hartzog, 1995; Avery, 1990; Wing, 1994) and sexual harassment and sexual assault cases (Gadlin, 1991; Gadlin and Paludi, 1990; Sisson and Todd, 1995; Weddle, 1992; Cloke, 1988), and disputes involving the Americans with Disabilities Act.

We are now seeing the spread of mediation techniques to previously undeveloped areas such as community colleges, and the increased use of service-learning models that move conflict resolution services off campus (Moses, 1997). There also appears to be increasing institutionalization of campus mediation as signified by campus grievance policies that now write mediation into their basic procedures. On a broader scale, entire state systems, such as the University of Georgia, are adopting ADR initiatives in an effort to improve dispute processing systemwide.

The campus mediation story continues to unfold as new ADR applications are developed for the campus community. Readers of this book may become active participants in this process.

The next chapter looks in more depth at some of the unique and challenging aspects of working in the college and university environment and explores arguments supporting the use of mediation in the campus community. This material is particularly helpful for people unfamiliar with university organizational theories and those who will need to make the case for mediation as they propose a new campus initiative. Readers who are already well versed in campus organizational theory or are already sold on mediation and want to get started can jump to Chapter Three, which sets out the initial program development steps in detail.

# CHAPTER 2

# Why Mediation Makes Sense for Academic Organizations

Theorists have struggled to describe adequately the essential features of colleges and universities (Birnbaum, 1988; Bergquist, 1992), in the process characterizing them as complex bureaucracies, collegial communities of scholars, political environments made up of competing interest groups, and even "organized anarchies" (Cohen and March, 1974). Depending on size, age, or mission, an individual college or university may resemble one model more than others, but few campuses fall unambiguously into a single category. Individually these models only partially capture the higher education experience; considered together, however, they offer a valuable window into campus life, providing interpretive frameworks that can help mediation practitioners function more effectively amid the complexity.

## Bureaucratic Model

The bureaucratic model of universities (Stroup, 1966; Blau, 1973) was popularized at a time when colleges and universities were growing rapidly. A bureaucracy is essentially a large-scale organization that relies on rules and procedures and a carefully contrived hierarchy of authority to carry out its functions in an impersonal (and thus hopefully unbiased) way (Weber, 1947). As organizations grow, the number of subunits does as well, with each subunit becoming increasingly specialized, and administrative structures become more complex, and thus more bureaucratized. Functions of various offices are codified in rules and regulations, and officers are expected to relate to each other more in terms of their roles than personalities (Birnbaum, 1988). Bureaucratic institutions value rationality and structure, putting a lot of emphasis on organizational charts. They tend to exhibit explicit attempts to relate means to ends, plans and the allocation of resources to institutional objectives, and goals to mission statements. It is assumed that rationality prevails and that organizational goals are clear and shared by most members.

In a bureaucratic organizational structure, supervisors are expected to handle the bulk of conflicts that come up, applying established procedures and using various forms of discipline and control over the distribution of rewards. The source of most conflict from a bureaucratic perspective is thought to be a failure of the institution's leaders to organize appropriate structures properly, design correct tasks, or effectively delegate authority. Conflict may also mean that communication of goals, plans, and decisions has broken down on its way through the chain of command. Or it might mean that individual members of the organization were not properly selected, trained, or supervised.

Universities and colleges feature many classic bureaucratic characteristics, such as a formal division of labor, an administrative hierarchy, and clerical, registration, and grade processing systems. However, they lack other key bureaucratic attributes, including, most notably, direct supervision of the work of a major group of employees, the faculty, and detailed rules governing the performance of most academic responsibilities (Blau, 1973). The bureaucratic model is thus not applicable holistically; although some campus units clearly are bureaucratically organized (for example, purchasing departments), it is equally clear that other units are not (for example, academic departments).

## Collegial Model

Aware of the limitations of the bureaucratic model, some theorists have moved to reject it in favor of other frameworks, such as the community of scholars or collegium. For example, in *The Academic Community* (Millet, 1962, p. 27), John Millet points out the inaccuracy of bureaucratic models and argues that anyone who uses these will most certainly "misconceive the nature of the institution of higher education." Millet is particularly adamant about the inappropriateness of hierarchical models:

> I do not believe that the concept of hierarchy is a realistic representation of the interpersonal relationships which exist within a college

or university. Nor do I believe that a structure of hierarchy is a desirable prescription for the organization of a college or university. I would argue that there is another concept of organization just as valuable as a tool of analysis and even more useful as a generalized observation of group and interpersonal behavior. This is the concept of *community* [emphasis added] [Millet, 1962, p. 234].

The basic premises of community and collegiality that Millet and many others before and since have called forth are deeply engrained in the fabric of university culture. The concept of a community of scholars has been traced back to the medieval universities and to the English colleges of the fifteenth and sixteenth centuries (Duryea, 1986). In these early settings, governance and decision making was often informal, with faculty coming together as necessary to handle emergent concerns, and the role of rector or provost was rotated among the faculty. These apparently nonhierarchical European traditions of higher education were transferred to America and have influenced our thinking and traditions, but they have also gone through considerable adaptation to the new environment and changing circumstances.

Millet, in his call for a community framework, acknowledges the growing specialization of university structures, but prefers to focus attention on fostering a set of diverse and yet interconnected functions that work cooperatively rather than coercively to achieve their goals:

> The concept of community presupposes an organization in which functions are differentiated and in which specializations must be brought together in a harmonious whole. But this process of bringing together, of coordination if you will, is achieved not through a structure of superordination and subordination of persons and groups but through a dynamic of consensus [p. 235].

In theory, conflict should seldom be a big problem in a collegial college or university, since it is assumed that all members of the community accept the institution's goals and are steeped in the academic tradition of shared governance. It is assumed that all participants are well-educated individuals, working in good faith to accomplish agreed-on goals, and that reason will prevail after full and open discourse. When conflict does arise, it should be resolved through consultation and consensus, with all members of the academic community given opportunity to be heard and to participate in a collective decision-making process.

Unfortunately, the "dynamic of consensus" that Millet advocates has many obstacles to overcome. For one thing, at the root of the collegial model is a belief that faculty are the key actors in the life of the campus community. However, they are also understood to be professionals with expert knowledge and thus represent the kind of employees who do not fit well into a traditional bureaucratic structure, creating an ongoing source of tension with administrators who have responsibility for many of the systems of the campus. Beyond this, university faculty are an atypical professional group, unlike doctors or lawyers who have well-developed systems of professional self-regulation. Burton Clark (1963), a higher education researcher, has this to say:

> The campus is not a closely-knit group of professionals who see the world from one perspective. As a collection of professionals, it is decentralized, loose, and flabby. The principle is this: where professional influence is high and there is one dominant professional group, the organization will be integrated by the imposition of professional standards. Where professional influence is high and there are a number of professional groups, the organization will be split by professionalism. The university and the large college are fractured by expertness, not united by it [p. 41].

Advocates of the collegial model do not naively assume that the modern collegium is exempt from conflict and power struggles. Millet (1962) notes, for instance, that conflict is "characteristic of all organized societies" and that it is simply evidence of a "dynamic process of growth and decline" (p. 224). Although some campus conflicts may be normal, Millet blames much contemporary conflict on the power and control issues characteristic of bureaucratic models: "Many situations of conflict which arise in an academic community are fundamentally conflicts about hierarchical relationships" (p. 231).

This potential for conflicts between bureaucratic administrators and professionals is widespread on today's campuses, going well beyond the faculty. Student affairs personnel, human resource managers, financial specialists, lawyers, labor negotiators, management information specialists, and fundraising experts are all examples of the broad range of professionally trained campus employees who consider themselves experts in their subject area. This proliferation of experts can quickly blur the lines of authority on campus, potentially making life difficult for bureaucratic leaders. This situation also makes the establishment of shared values and common ground quite challenging for leaders desiring a collegial approach.

## Political Model

Clark (1970, p. 23), in a review of the higher education environment, notes that the contemporary university is in fact "a conflict-prone organization, [with] many purposes [that] push and pull in different directions." A third general framework, known as the political model (Baldridge, 1971; Hobbs, 1974), focuses intently on these pushes and pulls of campus life.

Victor Baldridge, a primary proponent of this model, dismisses both the bureaucratic and collegial models as inadequate and inaccurate. In *Power and Conflict in the University* (1971), he acknowledges that there are many bureaucratic elements in the university that cannot be ignored; nevertheless, he dismisses the bureaucratic paradigm as falling short as an analytic tool. Although it describes authority relations, for example, it does not address other more informal forms of power and influence, including power based on expertise, mobilization of constituencies, and appeals to emotion and sentiment. And although it describes formal structures found on organization charts, it does not address the dynamic processes that occur when people attempt to get things done.

Baldridge (1971) also criticizes the community of scholars concept, in this case for being overly ambiguous and conveying a misleading simplicity. He suggests that talk of community and collegiality on campus is more of a lament for paradise lost than a description of reality. He believes that consensus-based decision making among equals is an inaccurate depiction of current practice at most levels of the university outside the academic departments and argues instead that colleges and universities can best be understood as essentially political environments. According to Baldridge (1971), "Rather than a holistic enterprise, the university is a pluralistic system, often fractured by conflicts along lines of disciplines, faculty sub-groups, student sub-cultures, splits between administrators and faculties, and rifts between professional schools" (p. 107).

In the political model, conflict is ever present; it is normal and to be expected. Conflict is managed through bargaining, negotiating, and exercise of influence. Power blocs form and re-form around different issues, in ways unrelated to the organization's formal structure. The organization's goals are perceived as diffuse, ambiguous, and often themselves in direct conflict. Personal goals may be in conflict with organizational goals. From this perspective, those who seek to manage campus conflict effectively are better served by studying and applying conflict theory, community power studies, and theories about interest groups in organizations rather than focusing on bureaucratic management theories or vague notions of collegiality and decorum.

Walter Hobbs (1974) agrees that the political model articulated by Baldridge "speaks to our condition" (p. 570) at universities. However, Hobbs argues that the model is hampered by focusing primarily on disputes waged over policy. In an effort to refine the model, Hobbs conducted a study of other types of conflicts among five categories of campus disputants and found a consistent "pattern of conflict among university personnel analogous to the operation of a defective pressure-cooker: unsuccessful suppression is followed by unpredictable eruption—producing, more often than not, a genuine mess" (p. 569). Noting the political nature of campus disputing and the existing lack of useful mechanisms for addressing midrange conflict, Hobbs (1974) called for new institutional channels for the processing of both interest- and value-based disputes.

## Complex Systems Model

All three of the organizational models discussed thus far paint a picture of a complicated university environment, at least in comparison to other more "rational-purposive" organizations such as businesses or even government bureaucracies. Researchers from the Stanford Project on Academic Governance have summarized some of the unique qualities of academic environments:

> Academic organizations have several unique organizational characteristics. They have unclear and contested *goal* structures: almost anything can be justified, but almost anything can be attacked as illegitimate. They serve *clients* who demand input into the decision-making process. They have a *problematic technology*, for in order to serve clients the technology must be holistic and nonroutine. As a result, academic organizations are important instances of *professionalized organizations* where professionals serving the clients demand a large measure of control over the institution's decision processes. Finally, academic organizations are becoming more and more *vulnerable to their environments* [Baldridge, Curtis, Ecker, and Riley, 1978, p. 25].

This acknowledgment of complexity is broadly shared. In *How Colleges Work,* Birnbaum (1988) provides an even more extensive list of aspects that set higher education apart from other large organizations. These complications have prompted many higher education theorists to move beyond the more traditional bureaucratic, collegial, and political models, seeking yet additional ways to describe the university experience. Weick (1976) suggests that universities are better described as "loosely coupled systems," while Birnbaum (1988) proposes use of a cybernetic model. Researchers Cohen and March (1974) prefer the descriptive term *organized anarchies* to emphasize the unclear goals, problematic technology, and fluid participation that are common on campus. Millet (1978), who espouses a collegial model, does not take to the organized anarchy imagery and prefers to describe university life as "organized autonomy" (Millet, 1978). Nevertheless, all of the theorists of complex systems agree that describing colleges as essentially making decisions and solving conflicts rationally or politically or even collegially may not be accurate. James March has described campus structures as being much more fluid and less predictable. Painting an interesting picture of university decision making, he states:

> Imagine that you're either the referee, coach, player, or spectator at an unconventional soccer match: the field for the game is round; there are several goals scattered haphazardly around the circular field; people can enter and leave the game whenever they want to; they can throw balls in whenever they want; they can say "that's my goal" whenever they want to, and for as many goals as they want to; the entire game takes place on a sloped field; and the game is played as if it makes sense [James March, cited by Weick, 1976, p. 1].

Anarchical or loosely coupled organizational models are thought to flourish in times of abundant resources and decline in times of diminishing resources. During times of financial restriction, the accompanying addition of more hierarchical controls is expected to bring on increased levels of conflict.

Conflict management and problem solving is complex and unpredictable in the loosely coupled university in which various subunits have their own cultures and patterns of decision making. For university-wide issues that affect multiple groups, a so-called garbage can model (Cohen, March, and Olsen, 1972) of decision making is frequently operative. Decision-making opportunities such as specially appointed committees, budget meetings, and faculty senate meetings are easily bogged down as numerous unresolved conflicts and unsolved problems are thrown into the can, complicating and diverting focused efforts at problem solving. Cohen, March, and Olsen (1972) observe that typically problems are not resolved and choices are instead made by flight or oversight. In addition, the quality and rationality of decision processes vary considerably according to the load on the system, and the interpretation of decisions that are made is continually changing. From this vantage point, life on campus is complex indeed.

## Conflict Management Challenges and Opportunities _____

The organizational models of college and university life reviewed thus far serve to highlight a variety of the challenges that face campus inhabitants, especially those whose job it is to offer leadership or attempt to solve problems. In all of the models, the campus response to conflict seems to be less than what could be hoped for.

## Challenges Posed by the Basic Frameworks

The bureaucratic framework is fraught with challenges. Near the top of the list is the seeming impossibility of consistently codifying, applying, and regulating the diverse aspects of university procedure and clarifying and enforcing individual, group, and organizational rights. The lines of communication that bureaucracies rely on to ensure that goals, plans, and decisions are appropriately communicated across the system appear to be easily jammed by conflicts over authority and values. Supervisors are relied on to manage conflicts, whether or not they have the time and training or accepted authority to do so.

The collegial model also highlights conflict, though more often by way of contrast. A frustrating dissonance between the desired collaborative community ideal and the reality of campus life leads to considerable internal conflict. Cherished beliefs in shared governance, reasoned persuasion, and collaborative decision making run up against daily reminders that university schedules and patterns of interaction do not often support careful and respectful deliberation. Economic constraints and pressing new opportunities strain the often fragile relationship between faculty and administrators, and faculty department chairs who straddle the administrative-faculty line puzzle over how best to respond. Faculty departments and university senates, thought to represent the best opportunity for collegial decision making in action, too often appear to be unskilled in problem solving or easily fractured along the fault lines of methodological, disciplinary, or political differences.

The political model, seemingly conflict savvy, directly acknowledges the many and changing divisions of a pluralistic university system. However, proponents too often seem to fall victim to power-based methods of influence and decision making that leave bitterness and confusion in their wake. Adversarial modes of negotiating, which some praise as realistic and necessary, may leave unrecognized value on the table or create unnecessary costs, and in the process alienate those who still cling to hopes of a collegial campus experience. Unresolved conflicts also make coalition building more difficult when issues change, and restrict regular communication between campus subgroups to lobbying and crisis-response situations.

The complex systems models paint a picture of an environment that is loosely connected, unpredictable, and heavily reliant on symbolism and administrative theater. Role playing and cynicism replace genuineness and hope as feelings of being able to control and influence the environment are lost. Valuable decision-making opportunities turn into "garbage cans" where all sorts of unresolved issues are dumped. Solutions to problems that do emerge are unclear, subject to many different interpretations, and too often unrelated to initial needs and concerns.

## Strengths of the Basic Frameworks

The campus experience may not be as gloomy as I have portrayed it, but clearly there is room for improvement. Fortunately the collegial, bureaucratic, political, and complex systems models, for all their flaws, also present valuable frameworks for thinking about organizational dispute management. Well-developed campus mediation initiatives will work to acknowledge and enhance the underlying strengths of these models, and perhaps in the process become part of the fabric of campus life.

A major strength of the community of scholars model is its emphasis on addressing underlying interests through collaboration and problem solving, and the focus on separating disagreements over ideas (acceptable) from antagonisms between individuals (undesirable). The bureaucratic model's strength includes paying good attention to individual and organizational rights and the careful development of fair due process procedures. The political model does not fear conflict but rather accepts it, recognizing the significance of power relations and group processes and the hazards of tests of strength and imbalanced negotiations. The complex systems models, with intellectual roots similar to those of dispute systems designers, are strong insofar as they help us move consciously and holistically toward more optimal forms of decision making and conflict management. Attention is paid to the interrelations of the campus units, and the overall system is understood to be more than the simple sum of its parts.

Campus mediators, as quintessential boundary spanners, have the potential to help weave together loosely coupled, politically charged, and bureaucratically bogged-down campus systems in ways that reduce destructive conflict and encourage reasoned problem solving. Beyond being a useful service for resolving day-to-day conflicts, campus mediation programs may serve as a vital bridge or link among different campus domains and perspectives. It may also provide a way to maximize the educational opportunities inherent in conflict, helping universities to become better learning organizations.

## Mediation and Community Building on Campus

The feeling that life on campus has become increasingly fractured and "uncivil" is widespread. Current concerns about incivility in the classroom (Boice, 1996; Schneider, 1998) are part of a much longer trend. In *The Campus as Community,* Stamato (1992) noted that over the course of three years, incidents of intergroup conflict had occurred on several hundred college campuses. A 1980 survey of higher education professional organizations (Bolding and Van Patten, 1982) found that six of the top seven faculty concerns dealt with a lack of humaneness and justice within higher education. The number and cost of lawsuits also appears to have increased (Gose, 1994), with average legal defense costs for private colleges and universities nationwide rising some 250 percent between 1992 and 1997 (Casper, 1998). As Ernest Boyer's report *Campus Life: In Search of Community* (1990) makes clear, there is a growing sense among university leaders that something must be done to counter these negative trends. The report notes that 85 percent of chief student affairs officers surveyed indicated that the provision of conflict resolution workshops was an important campus priority, and 77 percent felt that the development of better procedures for handling complaints and grievances was an important priority.

North American colleges and universities are not without models of community-sustaining methods of conflict resolution. The practice of using local, informal approaches for solving community problems is in fact fairly well established in the United States. Many communities in early America developed local informal conflict resolution forums (Auerbach, 1983) such as town meetings, clearness committees (that is, Quaker decision-making assistance committees), and community-controlled mediation and arbitration boards to help preserve the unique values of their community, values that could be damaged by the imposition of adversarial methods and external standards. In ways similar to these early communal groups, college campuses represent a definable community with relatively clear boundaries and the possibility of shared social norms and a strong sense of belonging. What are needed are more mechanisms to bring the community together. Mediation is certainly one of them.

Promoting civic values is an important function of colleges and universities, and campus mediation programs provide both a tangible mechanism and a symbolic means to support important values within the larger community (Slaton, 1994). The following list of five values, based on those espoused by the San Francisco Community Boards Program (Shonholtz, 1984), a neighborhood justice project, is an example of the positive values that a campus mediation program can encourage:

• *Conflicts are part of life's experiences and have positive value.* Conflict is the norm; it is familiar to everyone. Conflicts have meaning and purpose. When disputants understand this meaning, they have an opportunity to understand their own goals better and find nondestructive means of achieving them.

• *The peaceful expression of conflict within the campus community is a positive value.* Perhaps the easiest way for a campus community to assist in the resolution of conflict is to advocate for its early and peaceful expression, rather than wait until it has escalated and can no longer be avoided before taking action.

• *Combining individual and campus or community acceptance of responsibility for a conflict is a positive value.* The campus community can demonstrate its willingness to share responsibility for conflict resolution by making available to persons in conflict a team of competent and trained community mediators. However, the mediators place the final responsibility on the disputants for the actual expression and resolution of the conflict, because it is their dispute. By building a new structure like a mediation center on the campus, the community signals support for the direct expression and reduction of conflicts, as well as providing a hedge against people's tendency to want to find someone more powerful to handle their conflicts for them.

• *The voluntary resolution of conflict between disputants is a positive value.* The advantages of cooperation and mutual responsibility taking are modeled when program participation is kept voluntary and emphasis is placed on working toward jointly constructed agreements that address the needs of both parties.

• *Campus diversity and tolerance for differences are positive values.* The mediation process and the program itself can be used to model respect for diversity and help provide a space where disputants can learn acceptance of differences. This is possible only when the university itself publicly honors and supports a diversity of perspectives.

## Using Mediation

The complex systems models imply that leaders must work to develop methods that make the most of campus loose coupling rather than trying to control the environment tightly. They should attempt to lead in both symbolic and managerial ways, attending to inputs and outputs, roles and relationships, peer networks and webs of influence, symbols and rituals. As the political model makes clear, the existence of strong organizational subcultures, in addition to differences based on sex, race, and ethnicity, makes campuses unique "conflict laboratories" in which individuals with great perceptual and value-based differences must coexist. This growing awareness of university complexities has fueled considerable interest in understanding the various organizational cultures of universities (Bergquist, 1992; Harman, 1989; Peterson and Spencer, 1990; Warters, 1995a) in the hope of working more effectively within them.

Higher education researcher William Tierney (1988) reiterates the importance of attending to organizational culture in higher educational settings. As Tierney reports, when film star Spencer Tracy was asked for his advice on acting, he remarked, "Just know your lines and don't bump into the furniture." Tierney elaborates, suggesting that

> on the stage of organizational culture, such advice is wholly inadequate. Participants within collegiate cultures have few if any written scripts prepared by an author to go by. And as for the furniture, the most visible props—role and governance arrangements—are not the ones we tend to bump into. Rather, we most often trip over perceptions and attitudes, the intangibles that escape our attention even as they make up the fabric of daily organizational life [p. 2].

As Tierney implies, understanding campus subcultures and the norms and values of the people working within different domains is important to reduce awkwardness, miscommunication, and conflict. Paying attention to perspectives of different campus constituencies can be particularly important to the success of campus mediation program development efforts. In fact, the primary job of most programs in their early years is to build credibility and trust with a wide variety of campus actors coming from different perspectives and operating methods. This is especially true of broadly based mediation programs that serve multiple groups on campus. The kinds of groups and problems that a mediation program can creatively address, highlighted in Figure 2.1, can be very broad indeed.

Some reasons that mediation may make sense on campus from the point of view of various campus constituents are reviewed next, along with some case examples from *Peaceful Persuasion* (Girard, Rifkin, and Townley, 1985) to show how mediation can work in actual practice.

## Administrative Effectiveness

From the point of view of an administrator, mediation may be useful for a broad variety of reasons. An important one is that internal, low-level resolution of disputes is clearly preferable to more costly options, such as internal upheaval, bad publicity, or litigation. Well-coordinated systems for resolving issues internally may be desirable on both philosophical and practical grounds. On the philosophical level, a stated goal of resolving conflicts in-house

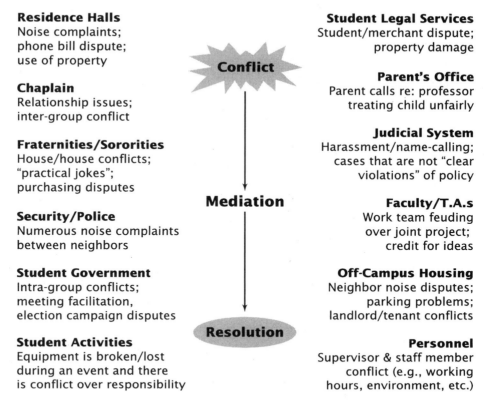

**Residence Halls**
Noise complaints;
phone bill dispute;
use of property

**Chaplain**
Relationship issues;
inter-group conflict

**Fraternities/Sororities**
House/house conflicts;
"practical jokes";
purchasing disputes

**Security/Police**
Numerous noise complaints
between neighbors

**Student Government**
Intra-group conflicts;
meeting facilitation,
election campaign disputes

**Student Activities**
Equipment is broken/lost
during an event and there
is conflict over responsibility

**Student Legal Services**
Student/merchant dispute;
property damage

**Parent's Office**
Parent calls re: professor
treating child unfairly

**Judicial System**
Harassment/name-calling;
cases that are not "clear
violations" of policy

**Faculty/T.A.s**
Work team feuding
over joint project;
credit for ideas

**Off-Campus Housing**
Neighbor noise disputes;
parking problems;
landlord/tenant conflicts

**Personnel**
Supervisor & staff member
conflict (e.g., working
hours, environment, etc.)

Conflict

Mediation

Resolution

**Figure 2.1. Examples of Potential Cases from Various Domains**

may express the institution's belief in its duty to protect the rights of its members from unfair institutional or individual policies and practices. On a practical level, adding mediation and other informal channels for conflict management may better serve the desires of campus constituents (Rowe, 1990, 1997). The internal adjudication forums found in most grievance procedures, when combined with mediation options, can provide a fair and flexible means of resolving conflicts within the institution, making successful resolution more likely.

The legal environment for mediation and ADR seems to be improving as well. Federal and state law increasingly support ADR, creating a better legal environment for the growth of programs. For instance, the Federal Civil Rights Act of 1991 and the Americans with Disabilities Act of 1990 endorse ADR to resolve discrimination and equal access disputes. The Administrative Dispute Resolution Act of 1990 strongly suggests enabling settlements at the lowest level. Similarly, in May 1998, President Clinton issued an executive order requiring all federal agencies to take steps to promote greater use of mediation, arbitration, agency ombuds, and other ADR techniques, and promote greater use of negotiated rule-making. Within the legal profession, an American Bar Association poll (Reuben, 1996) of a representative sample of lawyers revealed that 51 percent of those polled favored mediation over litigation; only 31 percent preferred litigation. Recently ombuds practitioners have begun pioneering work on establishing confidentiality shield laws for campus ombuds that, if successful, will most certainly benefit mediation program efforts as well.

During times of decreasing enrollments or increased competition for college-bound students, concern among campus decision makers about retention of students also often increases. Less than 15 percent of all student departures result from academic dismissal (Tinto, 1987). Instead most students leave college voluntarily due to a variety of concerns that include conflict or feelings of isolation. Nationwide, only about 50 percent of all doctoral students complete their graduate programs. Conflicts with faculty are cited as one of the two most important reasons that they leave their graduate programs (the other reason is financial concerns, which may also be influenced by conflict with faculty) (Nerad and Miller, 1996). Mediation provides an additional tool for preventing students from leaving due to unresolved or painful conflict experiences by facilitating the airing of concerns that need to be resolved. Folger and Schubert (1985) found in their study of student grievance mechanisms on twenty colleges and universities that mediators addressed a much wider range of student issues than did other dispute resolvers, helping to get at disputes that might otherwise fuel attrition.

Mediation can also help provide broad support for the educational goals of the organization, permitting community members to address breaches of the social contract in a structured, cooperative, and educational manner. Disputants of any age often learn important lessons from conflicts that are handled appropriately. In contrast, resolution in terms of winning or losing within the framework of the rules (such as is found in many campus judicial or grievance processes) can lead to manipulation of the rules to win instead of an examination of the situation by all involved parties so as to understand responsibilities, fairness, and concerns from different perspectives.

Exhibit 2.1 is a case where mediation may have made a difference with respect to a potential attrition risk and as a means to address a breach of the social contract that may have otherwise gone unaddressed.

Mediation programs are also being recognized as important contributors to an efficient and effectively run university, winning

A gay male student, named Jim, had taken some positive assertive steps in coming out to other students in his residence hall. However, the reactions of the other students were by no means totally positive, and in fact, Jim was thinking of filing harassment charges against some of these students, all male. There had been no physical incidents up to this point, but there had been plenty of verbal insults and some snide anonymous notes concerning Jim's sexual preference. For a variety of reasons, including the fact that he did not seem to have a very good case as far as the university disciplinary system was concerned, Jim did not take out charges against the men he felt had harassed him. But the atmosphere was so bad that he decided, unwillingly, to move to another residence hall. While this situation was developing, Jim had consulted with Paul Andrews, assistant director of residence halls. Paul was helpful but, according to Jim, not very supportive. Jim wrote a letter of complaint to the director of residence halls and complained to other students about Paul. When Paul Andrews heard of Jim's actions, he was infuriated.

The director of residence halls referred the case to the campus mediation program. Her reasoning was that the neutrality and objectivity that the program could provide were essential in resolving this situation and that she, as supervisor, could not provide it. On the one hand, Jim might feel that she would back her staff member and not listen to him; on the other hand, her staff member would expect her support against what he called the "unfounded complaints" of an angry student.

The case between Jim and Paul Andrews was successfully resolved through mediation. The agreement included these points:

1. A statement of support for the student by the staff member
2. A promise by the staff member to help the student with some specific educational activities around homophobia and heterosexism
3. A promise by both parties to be clearer in their communications
4. A formal apology by the student to the staff person for his remarks about him

In this case the neutral and nonjudgmental presence of the mediators enabled the conflict to be resolved. Administrative actions are necessarily rule bound and hierarchical, and the administrator in this case realized that she could not provide or would not be perceived as providing the support to both parties that they felt they needed. Because mediation acts outside the normal administrative procedures, Paul Andrews had a chance to express his anger and to explain his actions without worrying about how his boss would interpret his actions and statements. Jim got a personal affirmation from Paul, and the institution got a chance, through the staff member's promise of help with educational activities, to take action against harassment of gay students.

Exhibit 2.1.  Student-Staff Case

*Source:* Girard, Rifkin, and Townley (1985). Used with permission.

top cost-savings awards from the National Association of College and University Business Officers (Academe Today, 1998). As administrators know, campus conflicts can often escalate and lead to lengthy and costly disputes that tie up valuable time and sap energy (Casper, 1998). Management studies have found that between 25 and 30 percent of the typical manager's time is spent responding to conflict (Dana, 1984). Unresolved conflicts between employees can also be costly in terms of employee turnover, subtle sabotage, and low productivity. Mediation is a method that resolves many disputes at considerably less cost (in terms of money, emotional distress, and time) than existing adversarial methods, including arbitration (Brett, Barsness, and Goldberg, 1996).

Mediation can also help maintain cooperative working relationships among individuals and groups on campus, reducing the complexity of implementing new campus initiatives that otherwise might founder due to grudges and resentments. Mediation allows for the clarification of issues in a private setting, thus reducing the potential for public exposure of the dispute and public postures on issues and demands. And by guiding disputing parties to find their own mutually agreeable resolution, the parties experience (or reexperience) their ability to work together, an outcome that has an important effect on reducing the tensions that often persist even after a dispute has been settled. Exhibit 2.2, although it is somewhat dated in terms of subject matter, provides a good example of a case in which mediation helped resolve a potentially debilitating dispute among parties who required a cooperative ongoing relationship.

College administrators are also concerned about the quality of relations that they maintain with the surrounding community. Neighborhood associations near universities have become quite vocal, often expressing feelings of being encroached on by a growing number of students who rent and share homes or apartments in residential areas near campus, and blaming the university for not providing enough on-campus housing. A survey (London, 1991) of twenty-seven college towns identified concerns over student housing and shortages of parking as top problems. Mediation and other creative initiatives can help reduce bad feelings that may otherwise fester. Exhibit 2.3 provides an example of an off-campus conflict that mediation helped address when few other means were available.

## Student Development and Satisfaction

Conflict is essentially a fact of life for most students. They experience the daily problems of living and working together and interacting with people who are different from themselves and perhaps

With the national attention on hazardous materials, the college administration had begun to investigate their use on campus. They quickly discovered that the lining of many of the pipes contained asbestos. The administration realized it would be critical to hold educational programs on the dangers of working with this material because the campus plumbers' normal activities involved working with asbestos. Lectures and workshops emphasizing the development and implementation of proper procedures for handling asbestos were scheduled. Workers received time with pay to attend.

However, when the plumbers became aware of the dangers they informed the administration that they no longer would perform jobs that required working with asbestos. The college was upset by this response for they felt they had acted in good faith and in return the information was being used against them. As far as the plumbers were concerned, working with hazardous materials was outside their job description. The administration's position was that handling asbestos was part of the job of being a plumber.

There was a stalemate and the administration and union asked the mediation program to help them in resolving this complicated problem. Despite its complexity, the issues were resolved after a lengthy process. The outcome included the following points:

1. The college would provide new and specialized equipment that would significantly reduce the risks of working with asbestos.
2. Jobs involving asbestos would command a higher pay rate.
3. Working on jobs involving asbestos would be voluntary.

Mediation afforded the college the opportunity to settle the conflict in-house, and saved them from a potentially complex lawsuit which would have been costly for all parties involved. It also eliminated the need for and likelihood of numerous individual grievances which would have been time-consuming for all parties and which might have undermined the plumbers' bargaining position as a united group.

Exhibit 2.2.  Administrative–Employee Group Case

*Source:* Girard, Rifkin, and Townley (1985). Used with permission.

different in race, culture, sexual preference, ethnicity, or religion from people they have known before; fears rooted in their stereotypes and fears of confronting those stereotypes may surface. They face personality conflicts and conflicts stemming from testing boundaries and learning the real meaning of independence and personal and group responsibility. They test drinking, smoking, drugs, and sex as a way of learning—often through conflict—what is acceptable behavior for themselves and for others. They face conflicts with landlords, merchants, and roommates that arise from errors in managing finances. And in the academic realm, they find

Mary and Paul Pratt recently moved into a neighborhood in which a fraternity was located. Previously, they had lived in the country, but decided to move into town because their child would be entering school in the fall and they were impressed with the local school system. They found the street on which they lived quiet and friendly, but when the college students returned to the fraternity in the fall, the tone of the neighborhood began to change. On weekends beer cans were strewn on the street and loud music was a common occurrence. One Saturday night their child, Anne, was sick and the music was disturbing her. They called the campus police and were told it would be taken care of; however, the situation became worse as the fraternity members strolled down the street drinking and singing. Mary became very angry and went out on the porch and told the students to get away from the house. A verbal fight ensued. Meanwhile, Paul called the campus police again. The police came and told the boys to get back to the fraternity house which they did. Things seemed to settle down.

The next morning Mary and Paul found the windshield of their car smashed in. They called the town police explaining what had happened the night before and expressed their belief that fraternity members had broken the windshield of their car. The town police referred them to the campus police. Because there was no evidence, the campus police felt there really wasn't anything they could do.

Mary and Paul felt angry and frustrated. They decided to call the college's Dean of Students Office feeling that office should be responsible for students' behavior. Again, because there was no evidence tying the fraternity or an individual to the incident, the Dean of Students Office felt it wasn't an appropriate case for the college judicial system. However, the office suggested that they might want to go to the mediation program with representatives of the fraternity to try to resolve the tension. The Dean's Office said they would ask the program to contact the fraternity to indicate that there seemed to be a problem. Seeing no other alternative, the Pratts decided to try this suggestion.

Although the Pratts did not receive compensation for their windshield, they and the fraternity students were able to arrive at an agreement which included:

1. A promise by the fraternity not to leave beer cans around the neighborhood.
2. A promise by the fraternity to try to be considerate about the playing of music.
3. A promise by the Pratts to contact the fraternity directly if they were having a problem.

In this case, the mediation program provided a recourse when it appeared none was available. It helped to create an atmosphere for dialogue and further communication. Most important, it was the college that provided a forum for the Pratts to resolve a conflict that, in their minds, was connected to the college. If this situation had been settled in the college's judiciary system or the courts, the end result would probably have been in the fraternity's favor due to the lack of evidence, and the future relationship between the Pratts and the fraternity would most likely have been a hostile one.

Exhibit 2.3. Town Members–Fraternity Case

*Source:* Girard, Rifkin, and Townley (1985). Used with permission.

out whether their standards for work are acceptable—in both content and honesty.

In all of these categories, students learn lessons about how to handle conflict from the institution and from their peers. Since few eighteen-year-olds have developed good conflict resolution skills, using each other as models of how to manage and solve conflicts is often ineffective. Research on roommates in conflict (Rodgers, 1983) suggests that typical first- and second-year students are often not developmentally ready to negotiate interpersonal conflicts with roommates on their own. As a result, the ways an institution handles conflict must serve not only to maintain rules and order but also to teach conflict resolution. Mediation is equipped to do this. Exhibit 2.4 provides an example of a student case that went to mediation and offered students a valuable learning opportunity while addressing a potentially volatile situation.

From a student's point of view, the option of using mediation to resolve conflicts can be important for a number of reasons depending on their circumstance:

- Students often do not want to have to get other students (roommates, coworkers, classmates) into trouble with "the system" in order to address interpersonal problems.

- Students appreciate having someone else (for example, mediators) available to assist when they need to address a problem with a staff or faculty member who is older, more experienced, or more powerful.

- Students appreciate services like mediation that can address off-campus as well as on-campus life, providing tangible support in solving troubling problems involving summer sublets, landlords, and neighbors.

- Being in conflict with someone who shares an academic major or social circles can be very uncomfortable and can persist for years. Mediation can help prevent the escalation and prolongation of conflicts that disrupt students' social and academic lives.

- Many students are involved in intimate relationships that eventually break up. Mediation can help former romantic partners who must still live or work or go to class together to clarify and realign their relationships.

- Mediation provides students with a new way to approach each other and deal with disputes. This can mean a second chance for friendships that might otherwise have been lost due to the negative effects of unresolved conflict.

Kathy, who was white and a returning sophomore, had requested a single. Because she had to work twenty hours a week and carry a full academic load she wanted to live in as quiet an environment as possible. To get a single, Kathy had to transfer to a residence hall in which she didn't know anyone.

Andrea and Paula were black women who lived next door to Kathy. They were active in campus politics, and their room was often a hub of activity with people from both the residence hall and outside the residence hall participating in frequent meetings. Kathy had been finding it difficult to concentrate when the meetings, which often turned heated, were held. Three weeks ago she left a note for Andrea and Paula asking them to move their meetings to the lounge, but nothing came of it.

Last week Kathy had a big test coming up and again there was a meeting going on. She felt the noise was intolerable and went to find the resident advisor or head of residence who she hoped would break up the meeting. The resident advisor was out and the head of residence was in a meeting so Kathy called up a couple of her friends to complain. They told her they would be right over to take care of the situation. When they arrived they said, "those people have no right using their room for meetings. They have plenty of other places to go like the Afro-Am building. Besides, dorms are for living and studying and not for plotting a black revolution." At that point Kathy was exhausted from working and studying, and her only aim was to get the people out of Andrea and Paula's room. Her friends suggested they call the campus police with a disturbing the peace complaint.

The police arrived and knocked on Andrea and Paula's door telling them of the call. An ethnically diverse group of people looked back at the police in shock and anger. The police sensed the situation was not what was presented and said a few words about keeping it down and left. Paula, Andrea, and some of their friends went next door and a verbal fight took place. The head of residence was alerted and after an hour she was able to quiet things down. However, since there were still many unresolved issues, she referred them to the mediation project.

At the end of the mediation process there was still some tension between Kathy and Andrea and Paula, but they all felt that with time the agreement they reached would help to dissolve the tension. Among the points written into the agreement were:

1. A schedule would be set up so that Kathy would go to the library to study at times that meetings were planned to be held.
2. That whenever possible meetings would be held when Kathy was working or at class so as to minimize the need for Kathy to always go to the library.
3. When impromptu gatherings were held, Kathy would be told and if possible the meeting would be moved to the lounge.
4. An apology by Kathy and her friends to Paula and Andrea for the call to the campus police and for their underlying racist assumptions.
5. An attempt on both parties' part to make some personal contact with each other.

This experience allowed these students to find a resolution to their own conflict, one that they could live with rather than one they felt imposed upon them. It also opened up a channel for communication and understanding among people from different cultural backgrounds, an important part of the educational experience.

Exhibit 2.4.  Student-Student Case

*Source:* Girard, Rifkin, and Townley (1985). Used with permission.

- An increasing number of students enjoy and benefit from learning opportunities available as a volunteer or intern at a mediation center.

On many campuses students have been the most vocal supporters of mediation programs (Rule, 1993). Numerous peer mediation programs are being run as student organizations, relying primarily on student volunteers. Scott Pence, one of the founders of the Student Dispute Resolution Program at the University of Michigan, noted, "I had been trained as a mediator in high school, and learned what a valuable resource the process could be for people in conflict. I expected to serve as a mediator in college, however, when I arrived at the University of Michigan, I could not locate a firm to which I could offer my services" (Pence, 1996, p. 1).

As more and more students come out of high schools that have mediation programs, student support and interest in campus mediation is likely to increase.

## Faculty Autonomy and Productivity

Faculty members are central actors in any university system, and most endorse a collegial rather than bureaucratic model of interaction and decision making. However, the graduate training of faculty may not have prepared them, or their most significant colleagues, to handle conflicts collaboratively. Often dissertation research and writing is an isolated experience, and skills for working with others are not essential. In fact, the graduate experience may have made faculty more prone to act critically and unsupportively of the ideas of others, while clinging unreasonably to beliefs of their own that are subject to criticism (Leal, 1995). Processes such as mediation and group facilitation can help increase faculty members' effectiveness as participants in a collegial, consensus-building environment.

The existing style of university governance and administration can also affect the faculty's experiences with conflict. Walter Gmelch (1995) from the Center for the Study of the Academic Chair notes:

> In anarchical institutions of higher education, where faculty have a great deal of autonomy, the potential for *inter*personal conflict increases since roles and expectations become less clear and more difficult to monitor and supervise. On the flip side, this autonomy also reduces faculty's potential *intra*personal conflict. The key is to capture the energy from autonomy and synergistically transform it into productive ideas for the department [p. 38].

When budgets shrink and competition and expectations expand, many universities move in response to a more bureaucratic and tightly coupled approach to management. If the university system is tightening up its coupling to control costs, resulting in increased levels of hierarchy and supervision of faculty, mediation will make sense, particularly for conflicts between faculty and administrators, which are likely to increase. On the other hand, if the organization remains loosely coupled and the autonomy of faculty is rather great, mediation can perhaps be most valuable for disputes between faculty members or between faculty members and university staff.

In either case, mediation services for disputes involving faculty can be appealing to faculty for a variety of reasons:

- When conflicts between faculty members are resolved appropriately, the need to involve administrators drops, maintaining higher levels of faculty autonomy.

- Faculty department chairs report that dealing with interpersonal conflict among the faculty is second only to bureaucratic red tape and paperwork as the major source of dissatisfaction with this position (Gmelch, Carroll, Seedorf, and Wentz 1990). The availability of designated faculty mediators can reduce this strain on faculty chairs and prevent them from having to make decisions that may haunt them when they return to the faculty and must deal with the "losers" in other contexts.

- Faculty engaged in joint research or writing projects or team-teaching efforts can be more productive when conflicts that arise are managed directly and in ways that preserve the possibility of future working relationships.

- Faculty members often have limited access to various kinds of valued staff support. If these relations go sour due to unresolved conflict, it can have negative impacts on the kind and quality of support that is forthcoming.

- The relationship between faculty and their student assistants can be complex and fraught with potential conflict and misunderstandings. Mediation can provide a private, informal way to address problems that might otherwise escalate to more formal campus grievance systems or lead to withdrawal or delayed graduation of students and/or damage to faculty reputation.

Exhibit 2.5 is an example of a faculty and student dispute that shows how mediation might be helpful in this delicate arena of interaction.

Susan was in the Ph.D. program in English and had just completed her comprehensive exams. Due to a job offer in another part of the country, she had given herself six months to write her dissertation. Her committee and the chair of the committee had agreed to this schedule. The area in which she was working was a highly specialized field and required frequent consultations with Professor John Sterling, the chair of the committee. Susan chose John because of his expertise in the subject matter.

Recently, unbeknownst to Susan, John had separated from his wife. When Susan met with John to arrange a meeting schedule, John mentioned that they might have to have a dinner meeting in town occasionally because of scheduling problems created by the accelerated timetable for her dissertation.

They did meet once for dinner, but then John began asking Susan to his house for dinner. Susan was not comfortable with this arrangement, particularly since she had just learned of his separation. She told John that she would prefer to keep the meetings during office hours. He responded by saying that it had become impossible for him to meet with her during the day and that she would have to come to his home. Susan felt he was forcing her to make the relationship more personal than she wanted and she told John of her discomfort. He became indignant and angry and informed her that he was just trying to accommodate her ridiculous schedule. Susan soon realized that there was no reasoning with him and decided to take the situation to the mediation program.

Susan and John did not come to an agreement on the intent of John's invitations, but they were able, through mediation, to arrive at a clear definition of their working relationship. This included:

1. Regularly scheduled meetings during office hours.
2. An acknowledgment by Susan of how valuable John's contributions have been to her work.
3. An effort to diminish the overload for John by finding another committee member to share responsibility for overseeing Susan's dissertation.

Mediation was able to provide a neutral non-judgmental forum that defused the power imbalance between Susan and John, focused on Susan's dissertation, and recognized the value of their relationship.

Exhibit 2.5. Student-Faculty Case

*Source:* Girard, Rifkin, and Townley (1985). Used with permission.

## Expanded Staff Options

Mediation can serve those who staff a college's offices and support programs in two ways. First, it can provide additional resources for handling conflicts that are brought to them—whether those conflicts involve students, community members, or supervisees. Second, it provides resources for resolving conflicts in which they themselves are involved. Some of the benefits of mediation for staff vary based on the role the staff member plays on campus.

Residence hall staff, when supported by their supervisors to do so, often appreciate the option to refer appropriate cases to mediation. It can free up their time for working on educational programs and other tasks and educate students about the availability and value of nonhierarchical, self-directed conflict resolution.

Student counselors or employee assistance program staff often hear about interpersonal conflicts in which they cannot intervene due to their lack of access to the second party. Although both parties to the dispute may be needed to solve the problem, because of the confidential nature of their work and the limits of their mission, they may have no mechanism for creating a neutral forum. The availability of mediation services can remedy this concern.

Campus police and security personnel often appreciate being able to refer recurring conflicts to mediation rather than waiting for them to escalate to the point at which it has become serious enough to warrant an arrest. This is often true with respect to noise complaints.

Staff members in conflict with other staff members may not feel comfortable taking their disputes to someone in the same supervisory chain or may be reluctant to let these others know about all the problems in the dispute. They may be uncertain as to the neutrality of the supervisor, concerned about confidentiality and the impact that revealing oneself may have on future actions of the supervisor, power and authority imbalances, and the perceived skills and temperament of the supervisor. Mediation is often seen as a welcome confidential and informal means for resolving disputes.

There are also staff conflicts that, without mediation as an alternative, have no place to go on most campuses. A typical example is a supervisor who hears second-hand that an employee is talking negatively about the supervisor or the office. Loyalty is not an explicit part of most job descriptions, and personnel and grievance structures are not organized to handle such problems until the supervisor finds a way to get back at the employee—usually through performance review reports—and the employee files a grievance. Mediation is well suited to handle such conflict anomalies prior to their escalation.

The final case in this chapter, in Exhibit 2.6, provides an example of what this process might look like in practice.

Bob, the supervisor of a small administrative office on campus, recently decided to sell his old car so that he could buy a new one. While he didn't want to put any more money into it, he felt the car would provide good, reliable transportation for someone willing to do the repairs that an eight-year-old vehicle would need. He let his office staff know that the car was for sale in case they had friends who might be interested in a good used car.

One of the newer typists in his office responded enthusiastically, test drove it, and asked Bob some questions about its repair record and current condition. Satisfied that the car was in good shape and that the price was a bargain, Helen bought Bob's car.

When Helen took the car for the required state inspection, she found that two new tires were needed. Helen bought the new tires. When Helen told her coworkers this they sympathized and one mentioned that she thought Helen had legal grounds for getting Bob to pay for the tires. Her closest friends in the office advised her not to say anything since she would need Bob's recommendation for a promotion to Betty's position when Betty retired in another 6 months.

Two weeks later, driving to work, the car died. A major transmission job was required and the estimate was over $400. At this point Helen began implying to her coworkers that Bob had been dishonest in describing the car's condition. Again, there was the suggestion that if he weren't her boss she could take him to court. Two coworkers suggested that maybe it was Helen's fault for not checking out the car thoroughly. The argument became polarized and the staff became quite divided. While productivity remained fairly even, morale dropped.

When word finally got to Bob he was furious that Helen had been saying that he was dishonest. He called Helen in to tell her that he was upset with her behavior and to suggest that she bring her complaints to him directly.

The interview did not go well as Helen and her friends thought Bob was using his authority to keep Helen from talking about what he had done.

Bob went to his supervisor and asked for help. His supervisor suggested that since the problem had to do with a personal matter, Bob should try to get the conflict mediated.

The case between Bob and Helen was mediated and the agreement included:

1. Bob would pay the cost of the two new tires.
2. Helen would apologize to Bob for talking about him behind his back and for thinking he had been dishonest.
3. Helen would speak to her coworkers about Bob's willingness to be fair in dealing about the car.
4. Both parties acknowledged that the transmission problem could not have been anticipated.

Mediation was effective in part because it was conducted in an atmosphere of impartiality due to the fact that the mediators knew neither Bob nor Helen and that they had no connection to their office. Also, by using various mediation techniques the mediators helped to diminish the role differences between Bob and Helen so that they could discuss and resolve the dispute as equals rather than as employee and boss.

Exhibit 2.6. Staff-Staff Case

Source: Girard, Rifkin, and Townley (1985). Used with permission.

As the case studies illustrate, mediation can be used in a variety of ways to handle a wide range of individual and social problems and needs. Its actual application varies tremendously from one campus to the next, based in part on the organizational culture and the type of campus populations involved. In some places, mediation is incorporated into student disciplinary codes as an option for handling specified code violations, while on others it is structured to handle conflicts in which no code violations are involved. It can be used as an intervention tool for short-term crises that over the long term may require counseling or structural changes. Or, conversely, in a violent dispute, separation and containment may be used to control the immediate situation, with mediation part of the longer-range solution. In a broad context, mediation (or one of its close variants) has the potential to provide a forum for addressing most any conflict involving personal, institutional, or policy differences.

Perhaps the best gift that mediation has to offer educators is a model for promoting individuals' capacities and responsibilities for making decisions about their lives, building a sense of community, fostering mutual respect and cooperation, and developing the use of fairness rather than power as a basis for resolving disputes—skills everyone needs in addressing the complexity of individual and collective lives.

# CHAPTER 3

# First Steps in Building a Program

Establishing mediation services on a college or university campus requires considerable planning. Each campus is different, and each planning group has different goals or motivations for establishing mediation services, making it impossible to rely on simple formulas or one standardized model. Nevertheless, there are certain core concerns that every effort should address. The following ten-step process is designed to assist mediation services in getting off to a good start (the steps are also relevant to organizational settings outside academe):

1. Developing a core planning group
2. Conducting a conflict management needs assessment
3. Deciding on the initial scope and focus of the program
4. Developing a statement of purpose
5. Developing a staffing and program coordination plan
6. Securing administrative and financial support and appropriate space
7. Identifying and training mediators
8. Publicizing the program and building referral systems
9. Operating and maintaining the program
10. Implementing evaluation and feedback mechanisms

The first six steps are covered in detail in this chapter, and steps 7 through 10 are addressed in subsequent chapters.

The speed and sequencing of the basic steps reviewed here may vary somewhat, but experience shows that programs that skip essential planning tasks risk instability and unnecessary confusion. The Campus Mediation Program that I helped found at Syracuse University moved forward rather quickly once we got underway, taking about seven months to get up and running. We began with preliminary meetings in the summer (a less stressful time for many campus staff), continued planning and development work during the fall semester, and held our first mediator training at the beginning of spring semester, with the pilot project beginning in late January. Our relatively rapid pace was made possible due to a variety of factors, such as the availability of in-house trainers and an existing academic program in conflict analysis that made the conditions ripe for the pilot project. Depending on the scope of the program, it is perhaps more reasonable to assume that a group would spend a year or more in the planning stages.

# Step 1: Developing a Core Planning Group _____

Development of any kind of program in a community requires working with as broad-based a group as possible to gain essential support and assistance. Frequently the perception that a mediation program would be valuable comes from an individual or a small group. Developing a program as an individual can be exhausting, isolating, and ultimately unsuccessful if burnout, unexpected resistance, or suddenly being saddled with other responsibilities arises. A program developer who is working alone should find allies on campus who share this interest in ADR and are willing to share some of the initial work necessary to get a program off the ground. Working with others helps prevent burnout, expands contacts and available skills, and builds group investment in the success of the initiative.

## Finding Allies

Finding other campus people interested in mediation can be surprisingly easy at some universities. There may be faculty who are interested based on their research or teaching in conflict resolution or other staff who have a background in mediation. The campus ombudsperson may be able to identify possible interested individuals as well. On other campuses it can seem more difficult, with people apparently too busy or distracted or cautious about new initiatives to come forward, or the program developer may not know where to look. One useful approach is to invite a knowledgeable guest from outside the campus community to speak on the topic of campus conflict resolution, perhaps for a lunch presentation. When word of this talk spreads broadly, it may ferret out interested colleagues. Having someone from the outside can also help build early credibility for this effort and permit people to come to a "no-commitment-necessary" session where they can consider getting involved. As an example of this method, at Syracuse University, we invited an experienced ombudsperson from another campus in the region to speak on lessons learned from campus conflict. This presentation drew together a number of people we would have guessed were interested in the topic, and it surfaced a couple of people with campus mediation experience from previous jobs whom we otherwise may not have discovered.

## Considering Group Composition

An initial core working group of mediation supporters should have three to five people at a minimum; a dozen is probably too big without subcommittees. The first few meetings should provide time for group members to get to know one another and establish a shared sense of purpose and begin to develop a needs assessment and program justification strategy. However, this initiating group should also consider expanding soon to include key people needed for early planning—for example, those who are part of the population to be served, those who might be involved in the administration or funding of the program, those who need to approve or support the program through referrals, and interested faculty who can help build the program's legitimacy and increase options related to internships or course credit for trainings.

Another important consideration is finding ways to involve people who might feel threatened by the initiative due to budgetary or space concerns, philosophical differences, or a feeling that this effort may intend to usurp an area of their responsibility or prerogative. For example, if a mediation program is set up within student services, is there a law school or labor relations program that will feel a mediation program should be under their supervision or initiated at their discretion? These groups can be included in planning meetings, interviewed as part of a needs assessment, or through brief presentations about the project given to their group and inviting their thoughts afterward. If you completely neglect potential naysayers, you may be in for some unwelcome surprises later.

The choice of who to involve will revolve somewhat around the program's intended scope, but any effort should at least consider involving these important groups in the process:

- Residence life staff
- Dean of students and university judicial system representatives
- Student activities staff
- Campus police or security officers
- Fraternity and sorority councils
- Student government groups
- Campus religious leaders
- Counseling and guidance staff
- Academic programs, department heads, and faculty senate
- Chancellor's or president's office
- Student legal services
- Ombudsman's office
- Human resources or personnel
- Union representatives
- Off-campus housing staff
- Representatives from local community mediation service

The core group may also wish to seek official sponsorship for the committee from the president's office, perhaps the ombudsperson, or the designated head of the division that the group hopes to provide services for. This sponsorship can help facilitate selling the idea of mediation throughout the campus and helps give legitimacy to the group. Again, this decision will vary based on the politics of the campus.

The list of people in the planning group will change over time as the scope and focus of these efforts become clear. Although the initial planning group is often fluid, over time it is useful to formalize membership in this group for symbolic and political reasons and to help keep the positions filled as original members move on. This typically is done through personal contact with potential board members, followed by a formal letter of invitation explaining the role of the committee and expected time commitments. Keep in mind that committee members may need to get approval from their supervisors prior to accepting the position.

## Making the Most of Meetings

An early issue is to spend some time with the group establishing how it will function: meeting times and place, meeting facilitation, responsibility for the minutes, decision-making procedures, and style. Clarity about the process can make the group's work much more effective and keep people coming back to meetings.

## Step 2: Conducting a Conflict Management Needs Assessment ___

You may already have a pretty clear idea of where you want to start using mediation, but it is valuable to do a more general assessment to get a sense of where mediation may be most needed and thereby most successful. Because this issue relates to students, it requires reviewing available information on the campus judicial processes and disciplinary systems at the college- or university-wide level and within particular schools and organizations (such as fraternities and sororities, student clubs, and student government). With regard to staff or faculty, it means attending to the grievance procedures as described in handbooks and orientation materials, as well as more informal conflict-handling procedures, such as common practices by deans or department heads.

Often annual reports summarize some of this information, including usage statistics, but you will also need to gather your own information. Members of the advisory group can help check the "conflict management pulse" within areas where they are most familiar by identifying sources of useful information or by directly gathering desired data. These initial explorations often identify particular types of conflicts in most need of better handling.

### Informal Methods

There are a variety of ways to conduct a needs assessment, and they vary in terms of their comprehensiveness and degree of formality. For instance, many program planners begin with informal conversations with key decision makers or frontline staff to get a sense of the current campus climate and readiness for change. In addition to being a sign of respect, informal consultations can help identify potential conflict areas ripe for a change. They may also uncover political or organizational issues currently on the agenda that might affect attempts at innovation, both positively and negatively.

As you develop your data-gathering approach, be sure to take the opportunity to elicit the needs and interests of the people you are talking to. University members will help make mediation a success if they perceive the program to be in their own interests or in the interest of their superiors, peers, or students. Respectfully asking people what might be helpful to them and then listening is vital. People can be initially quite cautious when asked to talk about conflict, especially if they fear criticism or potential harm to themselves or their programs if they reveal the existence of or particular patterns of conflict within their areas. They may feel relatively free to talk about patterns of student conflict but much more reticent when it comes to discussing conflicts among staff or within and between various departments.

## More Formal Methods

Another way of assessing campus conflict management needs involves more standardized surveys and questionnaires. These can be helpful as a way to introduce the concept of mediation to parts of the community, determine if there is a perceived need for mediation, and get a quick sense of how much support exists for mediation. Information gathered from these surveys can provide a focus for discussion during meetings and elicit important design information about possible procedures or means of case development. In addition, the process of asking for information, if done respectfully as opposed to investigatively, demonstrates to respondents an interest in their needs and invites their participation.

Surveys can be taken from the point of view of students, employees, administrators, or other campus dispute handlers. They can be done through interviews or distribution of a questionnaire, by hard copy or e-mail.

## Family Student Housing Example

At the University of California, Santa Cruz, our initial focus was on providing mediation services to people living or working in the family student housing complex. At the time there was no designated support staff similar to the resident assistants, hall directors, or night watchmen found at other more traditional campus residences. Early in the planning process, we conducted a general survey of all households in the complex. Our questions, included as part a longer survey used for general campus programming purposes, explored the types of problems or conflicts most troubling or annoying to residents, the kinds of support services they commonly used, and services they found to be lacking or that they wished were available. Survey results indicated that conflict was common in the complex, including acts of vandalism and incivility, and access to and support from conflict intervenors was generally lacking. The survey also established that residents, who were paying a student fee like all other students, desired more tangible signs of support for their community. The results helped the planning group make the case that certain types of conflict commonly found in the community (problematic behavior by children, parking, noise) were amenable to mediation and that a pilot project was in order.

## Community College Example

Donald Cleveland, director of the Office of Academic Intervention Services at Broward Community College in Florida, was aware that community colleges have been slower to develop mediation programs compared to other institutions, and he thought that a survey might help his program get off to an informed start. To move things forward he administered (with the help of two students studying conflict resolution at a neighboring university) a short survey to a convenience sample of students (students who were passing through the student center) at one of the community college campuses. He used a one-page questionnaire that would be quick and easy for busy students to complete. The questionnaire was designed to gauge the predominant conflict management style among students (using a short styles inventory), assess common areas of conflict in students' lives, alert participants to the idea of conflict resolution services on campus, and query their thinking as to whether they might use a conflict resolution service should it become available. The survey was also used as a way to begin gathering a list of students interested in conflict resolution skills–training seminars. Students who might be interested in potentially attending training were asked to provide contact information and some optional demographic information.

The questionnaire results (Cleveland, 1995) ($n = 146$) indicated that the largest category of disputes concerning these community college students were family related (58 percent), followed by boyfriend-girlfriend (42 percent) and workplace disputes (31 percent), and only then followed by school-related conflicts (15 percent). Although most of the reported conflicts dealt with the students' nonacademic life, Cleveland was aware that when students were distracted by conflict in their lives, it was often reflected in the quality of their work and their ability to focus on school. Students who were surveyed expressed strong interest in conflict skills training, and about half felt that they would use a conflict resolution service if the campus provided it. This preliminary information helped the program planners decide to focus on providing conflict skills training and conflict coaching useful at home or on the job in addition to mediation services. To reflect this emphasis, the program that was developed is called the Program for Peaceful Problem-Solving.

## University-wide Examples

Sheila Hale, while a graduate student at the University of Oregon, did much of the groundwork that led to the successful creation of the Mediation Program there. In her master's thesis Hale (1987) describes the interviews she conducted with deans responsible for the grievance process in each department or school. She prefaced the interviews with a brief description of their purpose, stating that interest had been expressed in the possibility of a mediation program for students and that neutral, third-party facilitation had proved useful at a number of other universities. She acknowledged that careful analysis of need at the University of Oregon would be necessary and that a personal response to the following questions would be very helpful (Hale, 1987, pp. 78–79):

1. Do you ever have misunderstandings in your department?
2. Do any of these problems seem to have recurring themes?
3. Who is responsible for handling grievances?
4. Would you describe your procedures?
5. Is there someone on your staff with a particular talent for achieving informal resolution?
6. Can you think of circumstances in which a neutral mediator might be useful to you?
7. Will you please share your reservations or any suggestions with me?
8. Is there someone else you think I should talk to?

Hale reported that the interviews were very helpful. Of particular value were the questions about people who were already performing effectively as neutrals within the departments because they had interest, experience, and lots to say about shortcomings in the system. She also learned about some of the boundaries on what would be considered appropriate for mediation, such as a strong bias against mediation of grade grievances.

Hale's research helped her identify important concerns among student grievance handlers while building awareness and support for her initiative, which eventually resulted in a jointly funded (half administrative, half student government) mediation service that is still functioning today.

As a second university-wide example, the mediation planning committee for Indiana University at Bloomington, dubbed the Mediation Task Force, used their committee members as their initial source of data. The committee included representatives from the Office of Affirmative Action, residence halls, residence life, the Intensive Freshman Seminar, the graduate school, the health center, the Office of the Registrar, the Student Advocate's Office, and Student Legal Services, among others. Each committee member was asked to take an eight-question survey back to his or her department, completing it with the help of their colleagues or on their own. The basic questions were these:

1. What kind of disputes do students bring to your organization?
2. How often are you (or your staff) asked to resolve student disputes?
3. How are student disputes resolved in your operation?
4. What kind of staff training do you use—does it involve mediation?
5. Would mediation training be beneficial to your operation?
6. Would it be helpful to your organization to have a central mediation center to refer students to?
7. Would it be more beneficial to have mediation training for your staff instead of utilizing a centralized service?
8. How do you see a mediation center operating on this campus? What would its parameters be?

The answers to these questions were collected and put into a report that helped focus the planning committee's discussions.

## A Systemwide Example

This final example of needs assessment strategies looks at a larger initiative involving multiple campuses. Bruce Barnes (1998) and his colleagues are part of the Program on Conflict Resolution at the University of Hawaii at Manoa, where a campus mediation service has existed sporadically for many years. Barnes and a planning group were interested in the establishment of a systemwide ADR initiative in Hawaii, similar to what has occurred within the University of Georgia system. Their goal was to support increased use of mediation and other collaborative ADR methods across all ten campuses. Drawing on the dispute systems design literature, Barnes and his colleague, Karen Cross, developed a five-step planning approach based on Costantino and Merchant (1996):

1. Identify the stakeholders.
2. Assess the current conflict management system in four areas:

    the organization (mission, culture, and customers), the disputes (types, number, and nature), the resolution methods (procedures, who uses, how chosen), and the results (time, cost, durability, satisfaction).

3. Clarify conflict management goals (for example, "earliest point" or "lowest level").
4. Get buy-in.
5. Set a date to design a conflict management system.

To assist with the assessment phase, a graduate student who was visiting Hawaii on a summer internship was given the assignment of interviewing key dispute handlers on each of the ten campuses. She interviewed thirty complaint handlers systemwide using the following questions:

1. What types of conflicts or problems do you handle?
2. What options are currently available to someone when they come to you with a complaint (formal and informal)?
3. What seems to be working well in the existing system?
4. What are symptoms or examples of what is NOT working now?
5. What are the contributing factors as to why the current system doesn't work optimally (if any)?
6. From your point of view, what are the objectives that a good conflict resolution system would/should meet?
7. What would you suggest as ways to build a better system?
8. Can you suggest ways to motivate or reward grievance handlers, dispute managers, and disputants such that conflicts will be handled fairly and efficiently by those closest to the conflict?
9. From your perspective, is there the appropriate degree of emphasis on "legalistic" aspects of the problems and conflicts you see?
10. In a general way, please provide a breakdown of the numbers of cases handled in one year by your office. If possible, estimate the total value of staff time in hours or dollars that is used by the university to manage or process each dispute and all those disputes during the year. [No one attempted to estimate the costs involved in dispute resolution.] [Barnes, 1998, p. 5].

Although this information was very helpful for planning purposes, the results are not without their limitations. The researchers noted that participants' definitions of conflict varied, with some respondents focusing on all complaints that come forward, while others limited their discussion to formally filed grievances. Also significant, but not surprising, was a general reluctance to share such information due to concerns over confidentiality, fear of airing dirty laundry, and at times poor or absent record keeping. These factors made assessment of the accuracy of findings difficult.

As an example of the kind of useful information that initial data-gathering efforts can uncover, the cost of a grievance arbitration was estimated to be about $10,000 to $12,000 per side (Barnes, 1998). In addition, the researchers discovered that the percentage of grievants making use of the arbitration option (available after a two-step internal grievance process) varied considerably across campuses, despite similarities in procedures. These data suggest that organizational cultures on the different campuses vary considerably, with strong support for the use of the rights-based process of arbitration at some locations and more support for internal interest-based or combined interest- and rights-based resolution options existing at others. Any effective dispute systems design will of necessity have to take into account the different prevailing cultures, if or when new systems are proposed and tested.

A needs assessment can provide valuable information for the decision as to whether there is sufficient support and enough potential need to move a project forward. If the president or other significant campus leaders indicate that they will not support the effort, and in fact may oppose it, or if the current system seems to be working well, you may decide to devote your energy to other efforts. Generally deciding how much support is enough depends on the instincts of members of the planning group and the depth of their commitment to implementing a new program. There will always be some resistance to starting a new service, and developing support for mediation services is a slow and steady process. If the level of energy or commitment is low in your group, perhaps it is best to stop at this point and reconsider the question at a later date or under different circumstances.

## Step 3: Deciding on the Initial Scope and Focus of the Program ____

Campus mediation services around the country vary tremendously in their design and emphasis (Warters and Hedeen 1991; Warters, 1995b). A quick review of the over 130 campus mediation-related Web pages currently linked to the Campus Mediation Resources site reveals the true diversity. Some of the basic differences among programs involve the target populations served, the types of cases deemed appropriate, and the range of auxiliary services offered in addition to mediation.

### Initial Target Populations

Some campus mediation programs meet educational and direct service needs for all groups. These programs open their doors to cases from all parts of campus and often from the surrounding community as well. As an example, at Syracuse University, our planning group eventually made the decision to cast a broad net, providing service to any dispute involving a university member (broadly understood to be students, faculty, and staff—both cases between university members and between a member of the university community and someone from off-campus).

Other campuses focus on a single conflict area (such as off-campus housing disputes) or a single population (such as faculty, students in residence, or fraternity members). This narrower choice may provide the focus for initial activities, with a gradual phasing in of additional populations over time.

Among the various populations that current campus mediation programs seek to serve include the following:

- Students who live in university-affiliated residences
- Students involved in fraternities and sororities
- All students (graduate and undergraduate, on and off campus)
- Staff (nonunionized only or both union and nonunion)
- Faculty members
- The entire university population: students, staff, and faculty
- Members of the university community and people from the off-campus community with whom they interact—landlords, merchants, or residents of close-by neighborhoods
- Cases referred from local courts
- Services to local groups—for example, high schools, neighborhood associations, housing projects, and juvenile detention facilities

Choosing which population to focus on should be easier with needs assessment information in hand. This decision may be influenced by which referral sources on campus are most supportive, the kinds of cases that seem to be most in need for a changed approach, services that will help fill gaps in existing dispute-handling mechanisms, or practical reasons that will help ensure the program gets funded and underway with minimal resistance. Many programs start out with a pilot project approach, declaring the early efforts to be experimental and subject to review and change as appropriate in the future.

## Types of Acceptable Cases

In addition to making some decisions about target populations, the planning committee needs to begin considering the kinds of cases that are most appropriate for mediation in their setting. Generally mediation has been found to be particularly effective in situations where the individuals involved are likely to have ongoing relationships or are interdependent in some way, and the situations involve miscommunication, misinformation, or misunderstanding. Figure 2.1 provides some cases in point.

The decision about appropriate cases invariably includes a discussion about the kinds of cases that should be considered out of bounds for the program, at least in its early stages. This is important so that the program coordinators can respond to inquiries appropriately and feel supported when they need to turn down inappropriate requests for service. A variety of factors may influence this kind of choice, including perceptions of turf, duplication of service, anxiety about liability, existing contract agreements, current campus controversies, ethical issues, safety of participants and mediators, and the level of mediator preparation and training. (Chapter Six provides a deeper discussion of these kinds of concerns.) After program coordinators and mediators gain some experience and develop their campus networks, the range of services offered often expands.

The following list contains cases that on occasion are mediated on some campuses but can be complex or may raise challenging ethical or policy-related issues:

- Grade grievances
- Vandalism and minor property damage
- Various forms of harassment
- Inter- or intragroup conflicts
- Violence (fights, relationship violence, assault)
- Problems related to the use of drugs, including alcohol
- Student protests
- Conflicts related to race, ethnicity, and culture
- Date rape situations
- Family disputes, if residents of married student housing are part of the population
- Student-faculty conflicts (undergraduate or graduate)
- Disputes between faculty members, inter- and intradepartmental conflicts
- Coworker disputes among unionized staff members
- Staff and supervisor conflicts (unionized or not)
- Off-campus landlord-tenant cases
- Nonpayment-of-funds disputes brought forward by local merchants
- Policy-related disputes

Cases involving relationship violence and significant imbalances of power are most often considered inappropriate for mediation, but sometimes special arrangements are made and mediation of some form is conducted.

Decisions about the kinds of cases to accept are often difficult to make, especially for new initiatives. Anxiety levels within a planning group can quickly increase to nonproductive levels as a host of perplexing or threatening hypothetical cases are raised. The discussion of case management and quality control in Chapter Six looks more carefully at some possible criteria to help the group decide what cases are appropriate for mediation. The important point at this stage of the process to come to some kind of general agreement with the planning group as to the particular focus of these efforts, the kinds of cases to seek out, and what the broadly sketched boundaries are for this program's efforts. The day-to-day running of the program and the process of case screening is really the job of the program coordinator or intake person, and they will need some discretion to function within broadly agreed-on parameters. Sample mediation policies are available on the Campus Mediation Resources Web site. Exhibit 3.1 shows the general case parameters that the Syracuse University program settled on after gaining some experience through their pilot project.

Agreement on the range of target case types is also important in order to produce a reasoned mission statement, another important program development task.

## Range of Services Offered

Some programs primarily offer mediation on demand; others offer a whole host of services, including skill training, meeting facilitation, process consultation, neutral observation of campus protests, moderation of strategic planning processes, debate moderation, town hall meeting sponsorship, conflict resolution curriculum design assistance, and others. (We explore these nonmediation possibilities in more detail in Chapter Eight.)

The range of services offered, either now or in the future, can have a variety of implications, including the choice of a name for the service. In his article "What's in a Name: Capturing the Essence of Campus Mediation" (available on-line at the Campus Mediation Resources Web site), Neil Katz (1995) addresses this concern directly. Katz, faculty supervisor of the Campus Mediation Center at Syracuse University, explains why in retrospect he wishes that the program had chosen a name using a term other than *mediation* to capture better the breadth of its services and mission.

*Peaceful Persuasion* (Girard, Rifkin, and Townley, 1985, pp. 31–33) provided some additional strategic considerations related to choice of scope. Exhibit 3.2 reviews these pros and cons of broadly versus narrowly focused services.

Determining how broad or narrow the focus and goals of a program should be comes back to the assessment of the institution's conflict management needs. There are other considerations as well: the current campus climate, knowledge of which administrators might champion mediation services, and some strategic

The Campus Mediation Center is designed to address and help resolve interpersonal disputes between two or more people in an interdependent living or working situation. Examples include roommate, family or neighbor, coworker, landlord-tenant, student group, and consumer or debtor situations. At least one party to the dispute must be a student, staff, or faculty member at Syracuse University. The Center staff reserves the right to refuse to assist in the mediation of any case that is deemed by Center staff to be inappropriate for mediation due to a range of issues such as inappropriate timing, significant imbalances of power between parties, involvement by the parties in other dispute resolution mechanisms, and perceived inability of one or both parties to function appropriately in the mediation context. The Center will refer out cases that are more appropriately handled by counseling services or existing formalized grievance procedures.

The Center does not handle cases involving felonies or cases involving a continuing threat to person or property. The Center is not designed to investigate alleged violations of university rules and regulations, and will refer these types of cases to the university judicial system or other appropriate venue for resolution. In these types of cases, in the event that findings of guilt (or innocence) and the laying of sanctions has already occurred in the appropriate judicial forum, mediation may be made available for parties who wish to address future-oriented relationship concerns.

Exhibit 3.1.  Sample Policy on Appropriate Cases

*Source:* Syracuse University Campus Mediation Center Policy Statement (1989). Used with permission.

thinking about potential funding level, current available human capital, and long-term plans. (Some campus mediation program summaries are available on-line at the Campus Mediation Resources Web site.) Program developers might look for campuses that are similar in size and type to their own to see what their program structure looks like. (These on-line descriptions, which also include other nonmediation initiatives, were developed based on research conducted by Susan Holton and myself [Holton and Warters, 1995], which was later summarized in *Conflict Management Programs in Higher Education* [Holton, 1996], on-line.)

## Step 4: Developing a Statement of Purpose

The statement of purpose helps focus the activity of the planning group and makes it easier to explain to other members of the campus community what campus mediation is all about.

---

### Advantages of a Broadly Focused Program

- Opportunity to meet institutional community-service goals
- Opportunity to provide training in mediation skills to people at all levels and in all sectors of the institution
- Flexibility in program focus, allowing for changes in response to changing conditions and needs within the institution
- Opportunity for research and contributions to the field of mediation or ADR
- Ability to attract and maintain volunteer mediators' interests due to the varying nature of disputes handled

### Disadvantages of a Broadly Focused Program

- Requires a larger pool of mediators
- Demands considerably greater outreach and education efforts as part of case development
- Makes the establishment of credibility more challenging given different needs of various potential users
- Often requires greater resources to develop and maintain

### Advantages of a Narrowly Focused Program

- Ability to monitor and document the effect of the program on a group or conflict area increased
- Opportunity to institutionalize the use of mediation in specified circumstances
- Opportunity to maximize the impact of resources
- Case development is easier given clearly focused target audience

### Disadvantages of a Narrowly Focused Program

- May impede later expansion due to identification with one conflict area or group
- Makes it difficult to maintain interest of volunteer mediators over time
- Results in lack of cases if focus is not well chosen

---

Exhibit 3.2. Issues to Consider Regarding Program Scope

---

*Source:* Adapted from Girard, Rifkin, and Townley (1985). Used with permission.

Purpose statements often include a mission statement (a concise, broad expression of the purpose of a conflict resolution program) and a statement of specific goals (manifestations of the mission, aspirations, and intentions of the program). Some purpose statements also incorporate belief statements expressing fundamental convictions and tenets that the program's developers hold to be true (such as that conflict is a natural part of university life). As part of their annual planning, many programs also include a list of specific objectives that they hope to carry out to accomplish their goals.

Section A in Resources, Forms, and Documents contains purpose statements developed by other programs. Statements like these, commonly posted at program Web sites, are useful for program publicity purposes and as a key part of any formal proposal put forward to justify the program. Some of the statements are quite brief, while others are more elaborate, including lists of specific goals and references to important university values. Georgia State University Peer Mediation Center's Goals and Objectives is provided in Section B in Resources, Forms, and Documents as a good example of a document that combines many of the basic elements for a useful planning tool.

## Step 5: Developing a Staffing and Program Coordination Plan _____

The method of mediation service delivery varies widely.

### Program Models

Gene Zdziarski (1998), in his discussion of the use of mediation in student affairs, categorizes services into three different basic approaches: peer mediation, a mediation service, and a campus dispute resolution center. I add a fourth model to examine here: the clinical model. Although some services defy categorization in this way, this framework is useful as a sketch of what is currently being done. And although this scheme relates to student dispute-handling mechanisms, the basic organizational models can be logically extended to serve other campus populations as well.

**Peer Mediation Program Model.** Peer mediation programs are those in which trained volunteer mediators (in this case, students) who are at more or less the same level in the organization as the disputants mediate the conflict. These programs may be totally student operated (Rule, 1994), or they may get support from a member of the university staff who serves as supervisor or intake coordinator. These programs may be affiliated with residential life, student judicial affairs, or student government or student organizations. The Haverford College Communication and Outreach Program and the Student Mediation Services at the University of Michigan are examples.

**Mediation Service Model.** The mediation service model uses a separate office or center offering mediation. There may be one or two professional staff members trained in mediation (and often certified by whatever state or local agency that may exist) who coordinate the activities of the office and provide a majority of the mediation services themselves. Sometimes the mediation duties are shared by the staff coordinator and volunteer mediators from across the campus or local community. The Syracuse University Mediation Center office is staffed by a program coordinator (a graduate student on assistantship) and a cohort of volunteer mediators. In this type of setup, the mediators assigned to the case may or may not be peers (that is, on the same level) of the disputants. The program at the University of Oregon is another prominent example of this type of service.

**Campus Dispute Resolution Center Model.** The campus dispute resolution center model integrates its mediation services with other dispute resolution services already available on campus to create a renamed campus dispute resolution center. This approach is based on the so-called multidoor courthouse model: individuals with a dispute or grievance can go to the center and meet with a trained intake worker, who then reviews the situation and makes a referral to the process most appropriate for their case. Centers taking this approach might incorporate judicial affairs, legal services, and an ombudsperson in addition to mediation. This centralized model may help reduce the sense of being given the runaround. Texas A&M University uses this model in student affairs.

**Clinical Model.** In the clinical model, an academic department, say in communications, psychology, social work, or conflict studies, develops a mediation service that uses students in training who are supervised by or co-mediate with a faculty member. Faculty or staff with a research agenda who use the cases to further their research efforts can also staff clinics. The service may or may not have its own separately designated office and may rely on a very specific referral system (often involving off-campus disputes) to ensure a steady flow of cases. As an example along these lines, the mediation program I was involved with at Nova Southeastern University in Fort Lauderdale uses family therapy and dispute resolution doctoral students to mediate child dependency cases. The program is conducting a special pilot project addressing cases that involve family violence. The Center for Mediation at James Madison University affiliated with the faculty from the department of speech communication is another example.

Clinics are also becoming more common in law schools. Many law schools now offer course work in ADR combined with a clinical practicum. A roster developed in 1994 by the American Association of Law Schools (McDonald, 1994) listed over thirty law schools that had or were developing clinics mediating cases referred from local courts, police, or other sources, and the number continues to grow.

## Program Coordination Strategies

Developers need to consider how to manage program coordination and oversight. A common approach is to find someone already on the campus payroll and provide that person release time from other activities, essentially writing mediation into the job description. On some campuses, particularly those using a peer mediation model, the work of coordinating a service is often a labor of love that an interested faculty member or staff person takes on with minimal additional compensation. This is perhaps an unfortunate situation, because the more active and involved the coordinators are able to be, the more impact the service can have on the campus community. On campuses that have set up a separate mediation center, it usually becomes necessary to hire (and appropriately compensate) a designated program coordinator. It is also possible to divide the coordination responsibilities among two or more individuals or to assign various volunteer subcommittees to the primary tasks. The Campus Mediation Center at Syracuse University uses a graduate assistant from the academic program in conflict resolution who works approximately twenty hours per week under the supervision of a faculty member. Job descriptions for these and one additional position are found in Section C of Resources, Forms, and Documents.

It is very important that the coordinator of the program be a skilled communicator who can embody conflict resolution principles. Implementing a new program almost inevitably causes some conflict, and the coordinator must be able to respond creatively, calmly, and nondefensively to avoid alienating potential program supporters.

The coordinator may be responsible for a range of functions—for example:

- Coordinating publicity and public education efforts
- Overseeing solicitation and selection of volunteer mediators
- Arranging or providing mediation training
- Coordinating mediator availability

- Designing program forms
- Accepting and making referrals
- Explaining mediation process to parties and encouraging them to try it
- Scheduling mediation sessions
- Assigning appropriate mediators for each session
- Mediating cases when necessary
- Helping mediators improve their skills
- Recruiting new mediators
- Coordinating the advisory council process
- Following up on cases and keeping records
- Coordinating or conducting evaluations
- Preparing reports, budgets, and funding requests as needed

Depending on the design, scope, and caseload of the program, coordinators can work anywhere from just a few hours weekly to full time. As the list of tasks above suggests, however, most coordinators end up doing a lot more than just scheduling mediation sessions. Especially in the early phases of a program's life, a lot of time may be spent on developing forms, establishing referral protocols, and doing outreach and public education work to make the service known to the campus community.

Given this reality, many programs also make use of student interns or volunteers, such as retired faculty or recruits from a local community mediation center, to help build the program's momentum. To assist you in your thinking about the various tasks commonly associated with running a new campus mediation center, Exhibit 3.3 depicts a hypothetical duty roster that includes volunteer committees and some already skilled in-house mediator-trainers.

It is important to determine to whom the coordinator is accountable so that complaints about the program or the coordinator, should any arise, can be responded to constructively. As the program gets underway, often the planning committee or some other similar body becomes a formal advisory group responsible for overview and evaluation. In other cases primary supervision of the program coordinator falls on the administrator under whose jurisdiction the program resides. In some settings, programs are given considerable autonomy based on a trust in the program's coordinator and the need for perceived neutrality. Work done by the planning committee to establish clear operating guidelines in the early stages can go a long way in preventing struggles or misunderstandings later.

Advisory committee tasks

Developing short- and long-range plans in cooperation with staff
Assisting in securing stable funding base for program
Supporting program staff in decision making
Assisting program through networking and referrals

Program coordinator tasks

Coordinating public relations and program development
Selecting mediators from a trained pool
Screening cases
Conducting intake interviews
Keeping records
Matching mediators to cases
Coordinating and "care and feeding" of volunteers
Drafting administrative policies and reports
Evaluating of mediators
Following up on mediation cases
Supervising interns and volunteer projects

Office support staff tasks

Scheduling hearings
Assisting with record keeping
Handling correspondence
Preparing needed training manual, handouts, and flyers
Mailing of referral follow-up letters
Mailing of evaluation forms at proper time

Training team tasks

Developing basic training design
Gathering materials for training packet or manual
Identifying and securing appropriate space for training
Assisting in initial screening of potential mediators
Conducting twenty- to forty-hour basic training for mediators
Providing feedback on readiness of various trainees
Coordinating in-service workshops for volunteers
Developing additional short workshops for campus groups

Exhibit 3.3. Campus Mediation Program Coordination Plan

---

Trained volunteer mediators' tasks

Attending complete basic training

Conducting actual hearings on rotating volunteer basis

Attending additional in-service workshops

Assisting with program outreach and mini-workshops

Publicity and outreach team tasks

Identifying target groups

Making presentations at appropriate staff meetings and training sessions

Integrating the campus mediation center into new student orientation

Distributing posters, brochures, and cards

Securing press and radio coverage

Developing and maintaining a Web page

---

Exhibit 3.3. (Continued)

## Step 6: Securing Administrative and Financial Support and Appropriate Space

Once the need for and focus of a program has been determined, a physical and administrative location needs to be chosen. In some cases, the administrative home of the program has already been determined by the administrator who convened or sponsored the planning group, but in many cases the fine points of how the program should be administered and where it should be housed are open and negotiable. The question of where to locate the service within a college's or university's structure can often be a thorny one because of the symbolism these kinds of decisions convey to the community at large. The choice of location—within the administrative structure, physical location, and location based on association stemming from financial or other support—has implications for how the program is perceived by various campus constituencies, which in turn may have an impact on program usage and referrals. For instance, if there have been recent conflicts between students and the office of the dean of students over political or student rights issues, and students are the primary population to be served, it might be a good idea to avoid directly connecting the program administratively to the dean's office. Similarly, if conflicts between the president and the faculty are at a high level and trust is low, locating a faculty mediation program administratively under the president's office may negatively affect faculty perceptions of whose needs the mediation program serves, who controls it, and how impartial it is.

In the light of the importance of perceived impartiality, it makes sense to begin the process of seeking financial support only after clearly determining the population to serve. Using this approach, the program developers can consider the possible impact the funding source or administrative home may have on referrals to and usage of the program.

The more specialized the target population, the easier it is to select an appropriate location that will provide perceived impartiality, credibility, and referrals. Usually the organizational division that one population sees as fair or "for them" can be readily identified. Finding the administrative unit that will be seen as appropriate and neutral by a combined audience of students, staff, faculty, and community people is harder and requires more careful analysis and assessment.

When multiple populations are to be served, physical distance from a single administrative unit to which the program is accountable may be important. In other words, when locating within a particular organizational division creates a problem in perceived impartiality, it may be best to obtain space in a neutral part of the campus rather than in the administration building. For example, if a program were accountable to the office of the dean of students but intended to serve faculty and staff as well as students, it might be important to have an office that by its physical location deemphasized the student-oriented administrative line of accountability. A mediation program located within a residence hall might create a great deal of credibility among the student population but would probably not gain respect and trust as a forum for faculty and staff concerns. Clearly it is important to establish a program in a place that creates an atmosphere of acceptability and trust for those whom it intends to serve and for those on whom it relies for referrals.

It may be helpful to consider each potential target group separately in terms of how they might perceive various potential administrative locations. You may wish to try constructing a chart like the one in Exhibit 3.4 for your campus and your target populations based on what you know about local norms and expectations.

Although it is useful to think carefully about the symbolic and political implications of an administrative home, in many cases the choices will be limited, or an offer may be too good to pass up. In any case, the committee should try to avoid getting too tied up in knots when making this kind of a decision. If there are multiple potential sites, the committee may wish to prioritize them and approach the best potential sites first, then work down the list until there is a reasonable arrangement.

| Target Population | Possible Administrative Locations | | | |
|---|---|---|---|---|
| | Student Services | President's Office | Academic Affairs | Counseling Center |
| Students | + | * | − | * |
| Professional staff | − | + | + | * |
| Faculty | − | * | + | * |
| Union employees | * | − | * | * |
| Administrators | * | + | + | * |
| Community residents | * | * | * | * |

Perception of possible location
+ Good
* Neutral
− Negative

Exhibit 3.4.  Preference Analysis Chart for Administrative Locations

*Source:* Girard, Rifkin, and Townley (1985). Used with permission.

Programs have been successful using a wide range of organization formats. To help illustrate this diversity and relieve concerns about making the absolute "right" choice, the characteristics of a number of programs from my 1991 survey (Warters and Hedeen, 1991) are presented in Table 3.1.

## Potential Sources of Funds

Mediation programs may be funded from many different campus budgetary units. Where multiple populations are to be served, multiple funding sources may also be appropriate. Funding for campus mediation services around the country has come from these sources:

- Presidents' or chancellors' offices
- Personnel office
- Student governments
- Student affairs office
- Counseling centers
- Off-campus housing
- Student activities

**Table 3.1. Examples of Program Arrangements**

| Campus | Location | Funding | Staffing | Case types |
|---|---|---|---|---|
| **Grinnell College** | Student Affairs | Student Affairs Office | Hall director and student adviser | Student-student |
| **Haverford College** | Student Council, Communication Outreach Program | Student Council | Thirty student volunteers | Roommate problems, anything involving student groups |
| **James Madison University** | Own office near Speech Communication Department | Faculty senate | Three faculty, thirty student volunteers | Landlord, fraternity, roommate, merchant |
| **Northeastern Illinois University** | Counseling Office | Release time | Program coordinator, students, faculty, staff volunteers | Students, faculty, staff |
| **Oberlin College** | Residence Life | Dean's Office | Twelve to fifteen faculty | Roommate |
| **Pennsylvania State University** | Center for Conflict Management | Division of Campus Life, Student Services | One conflict management specialist, volunteer intake coordinator, volunteers | Student, faculty, or staff; special discipline cases. |
| **State University of New York, Albany** | Residence Life | Division of Student Affairs | One administrator, some help | Roommate, academic |
| **University of California, San Diego** | Student Legal Services | Student fee | Nine volunteers, mainly prelaw students | Cases involving students |
| **University of Alberta** | Office of Secretariat | President's Office, Office of Secretariat | Four each: undergraduate, graduate, academic, support staff | Anything involving a university community member |

*continued*

**Table 3.1. Examples of Program Arrangements (continued)**

| Campus | Location | Funding | Staffing | Case types |
|---|---|---|---|---|
| **University of Maryland** | Professional building near campus | The university and city council | Three administrators, twenty-five volunteers | Small claims, landlord, student-faculty, roommates |
| **University of Nevada, Reno** | Student Services | Through state-appropriated budget | Director, management assistant | Grades, faculty relationships, harassment, roommate, international student issues |
| **University of Waterloo** | Ombuds Office in Student Centre | Federation of Students, Graduate Student Association, University Admin. | Advisory committee, student coordinators, twenty-five volunteer mediators | Landlord-tenant, roommate or sublet, lifestyle conflicts |
| **West Virginia Wesleyan** | Counseling and Wellness Center | Counseling budget | Counseling staff, five students | Roommate, student, faculty, staff |

- College deans
- Academic departments
- Omnibus student fees

Most of these sources of funds can provide relatively stable and long-term support once the program has established itself and becomes a regular part of the budgeting process.

Additional potential sources of funds that may be of shorter duration include federal, state, or county grants; private foundation grants; gifts from individuals or companies; money gathered at fundraisers conducted by volunteers or program advocates; and project cosponsorships by a local municipality, court, or community mediation center. Grants are particularly appropriate in the first few years of a program's life, when programs need the most support (to cover start-up expenses like training and initial printing of promotional materials), and the time when grantmakers are most interested in being involved.

## Determining How Much Money Is Needed

The amount of money needed to run a campus mediation program varies tremendously based on the scope and ambitions of the program and its already available resources. Budgets range from a few hundred dollars to well over $100,000 per year.

Generally there are five categories of expense to consider:

- Compensation for the coordinator(s)
- Training expenses
- Operating expenses
- Publicity
- Evaluation expenses

The new money needed to compensate a coordinator can be minimal if an existing staff person's duties are redesigned to incorporate the role of coordinator or if the role is performed by a volunteer. More expensive options include hiring part-time staff or a graduate assistant and hiring a full-time person, whose duties may be full time with the center or may also provide assistance in other areas beyond the role as mediation coordinator. The rates of compensation vary by campus, job grade, and geography. Usually by looking at comparable types of positions on campus, the program developers can come up with a reasonable estimate of how much it would cost to find a quality coordinator.

Training expenses vary depending on the strategy used. (We look more fully at training issues in Chapter Four.) Hiring an outside consultant specializing in higher education mediation might cost something in the neighborhood of $2,500 to $3,500 for twenty-five hours of basic training provided on-site to a group of mediators, plus any additional expenses related to food, travel, lodging, space rental, and training materials. Another option is to work with a nearby community mediation program (check the Yellow Pages under "mediation," or contact the National Association for Community Mediation). These centers, located in most major cities, can often offer training at somewhat lower rates and without the expenses associated with an outside consultant.

An alternative to bringing a trainer in is to send trainees to a training session being conducted elsewhere by a local mediation center or a nationally recognized training institute. Fees for these sessions can range from a low of about $150 per person for a local effort to over $1,200 per person at some of the national trainings. If travel and lodging are required, the costs can increase dramatically.

It is wise to consider budgeting money to establish in-house trainers over time. This can involve hiring someone with mediation skills for the staff or sending core program staff who have participated in a basic training to a training-for-trainers course where they develop the skills necessary to train others. Programs should also consider budgeting some discretionary professional development money so that the program coordinator can travel to a regional or national conference and build his or her knowledge base and contacts.

Finally, some campus programs already have in-house trainers available on the faculty or staff who are willing to donate their time or do the work for a small fee.

General operating expenses can be relatively small, especially if the service is being integrated into an existing office. Typical expenses include telephone use, postage, printing of forms, copying, flipchart paper and markers, and the development of a reference library. Additional discretionary expenses include providing lunch for advisory committee meetings and bookstore gift certificates to reward hard-working volunteers. Hardware needs may include an answering machine, computer hardware and software to manage intake information or to assist in developing and giving presentations, easel stands for presentations, and a locking file cabinet to hold program records.

Publicity-related expenses can include fees to run advertisements in student or local newspapers, development and printing of posters and brochures, production of video or audio promotional pieces, and such additional items as keychains, pens, and refrigerator magnets that can build awareness about the program.

Evaluation costs are often minimal (mainly postage and printing and data input and analysis time), especially if the program is evaluated by the coordinator or by someone else at the university who donates time to carry out the project. Some programs choose to hire an outside or more objective firm or office to evaluate their work, and thus include budget expenses related to this effort.

## Securing Financial Support

University libraries or development offices can usually provide considerable assistance with grant writing. Although a small number of funding sources now include terms like *conflict resolution* as one of their goals (among them are the Hewlett Foundation, the Surdna Foundation, and the U.S. Institute for Peace), most do not. Thus, the program developers must search more broadly for granters that fund higher education initiatives that might logically be interested in supporting this work. The job is to present the mediation service in terms that a potential funding source can understand. If the foundation is interested in violence prevention, for example, the developers can highlight how mediation supports the early expression of difference, before it escalates to violence. If the funder is interested in campus civility, they can stress the quality of dialogue that occurs in mediation sessions and the essential democratic nature of collaborative problem solving. If the funder is interested in innovation in higher education or on improving the teaching and learning climate, they can stress the way that mediation can help resolve conflicts that emerge in times of change or ways that mediation can reduce the level of tension on campus that may be interfering with the educational process. They may also want to stress to funders that they do not intend the program to be dependent on this seed money indefinitely. The committee members may show how the costs of the program will decrease over time as initial start-up costs are no longer necessary and highlight plans to get the university to underwrite greater portions of the program expense as the program matures.

The process of securing internal funding varies on each campus and within different divisions. Gaining some awareness of how the budget process works for potential funding units can help the program developers avoid missing important yearly or quarterly deadlines. In most cases they will need to prepare a proposal justifying the project and outlining anticipated activities and expected expenses. Similar to grant applications, proposals should demonstrate the need for mediation, the degree of support that exists for the program, and the benefits expected from implementing it.

To help us approach funders at Syracuse University, we wove our mission statement into a short proposal explaining and justifying the program. In this one and a half page document, we did the following:

- Acknowledged the existence and normality of conflict on campus and the value of early identification, expression, and resolution
- Briefly explained what mediation was and who would provide it
- Referenced the growth of mediation on campuses nationally
- Noted the local resources that could help our effort be successful
- Briefly stated our goals and objectives
- Acknowledged our commitment to evaluation and review

We used this short document to approach a variety of campus funding sources that jointly contributed to the pilot project.

## Physical Space Needs

In addition to securing financial and administrative support, the program needs physical space to do case intake work and conduct mediations. As is true on most campuses, space may be at a premium, so the program developers may have to settle for whatever space is currently available, with a longer-term goal of locating more suitable accommodations.

Where a program fits into the institution's physical structure may have some impact on the number of referrals it receives, although a host of other factors are important as well. Being out of sight and out of mind is certainly not ideal. A location with visibility and centrality or proximity to other frequently used services can be beneficial in leading to cases. A physical location that will enable program staff to reinforce referrals, build important relationships, and conduct the educational and public relations activities can also help gradually increase case referrals.

Knowing the ideal location and the specific conditions that make it ideal can be useful in negotiating for space. In the best-case scenario, a mediation service has an office of its own for conducting intake interviews and confidential telephone conversations, and a locking file cabinet. It also has a private conference room to conduct mediations that has a rectangular table and space for at least four movable chairs, and two different comfortable waiting areas so that parties can be separated during mediator caucuses or if tensions are running high. It should also not be obvious to passersby that parties in the waiting area (should it be visible) are there for a mediation because this visibility can make parties uncomfortable. When possible, the mediation room should probably be distinct from the traditional disciplinary offices to set a different tone and expectation.

Good space for conducting mediations has these basic characteristics:

- Privacy (both visual and auditory)
- Maintenance of confidentiality
- Relatively quick scheduling access (scheduling a session is harder to manage if a separate call or waiting period to confirm the conference room's availability is necessary)
- Access to a telephone if parties or the mediators need to consult with someone not at the table
- Access to a copying machine to make copies of any agreements reached in the session (preprinted tripart forms is another option)

- Nearby bathrooms and a smoking area
- Handicap accessible
- Available for evening or weekend sessions
- Safe and available nearby parking
- Not too isolated, should the potential for violence exist

Planning groups that have accomplished the early objectives examined in this chapter are well on their way to establishing a successful program. In subsequent chapters we will look at the later-stage tasks necessary to get a program off the ground once its basic parameters have been decided on and support has been established:

Step 7: Identifying and Training Mediators (Chapter Four)

Step 8: Publicizing the Program and Building Referral Systems (Chapter Five)

Step 9: Operating and Maintaining the Program (Chapter Six)

Step 10: Implementing Evaluation and Feedback Mechanisms (Chapter Seven)

The next chapter addresses the issues related to selecting potential mediators and arranging for the required basic training. If training is not an immediate concern, you may wish to go on to Chapters Five and Six for information on promoting a program and managing its basic operations.

# CHAPTER 4

# Identifying and Training Mediators

All the work that has gone into organizing a mediation effort begins to bear fruit when the first group of mediators is identified and trained. The mediators form the core of a campus mediation effort. Not only do they mediate cases, but they can be major resources in terms of building a referral network, publicizing the program, and evaluating and refining operating procedures. Thus, the mediation project organizers must give significant consideration to choosing the training group and ensuring that this group has a positive initial training experience. Most people who go through a mediation training program leave the experience feeling tired but exhilarated and excited about helping move the program forward. Nothing can take the wind out of a new program's sails faster than a poor training experience.

## Selecting Potential Mediators

An important preliminary decision for any program is determining who will do the mediation. Primary choices for mediators are:

- Paid staff (often also the program coordinator)
- Campus volunteers: Students, staff, and faculty
- Local community volunteers (trained on campus or on loan from the local community mediation center)

*Significant portions of this chapter are adapted from material that appeared in Girard, Rifkin, and Townley (1985). Used by permission.*

- Paid professional mediators from off-campus (on retainer or paid on a case-by-case basis)

If the decision is to rely on a pool of volunteer mediators (a common practice on campus) or to choose among a number of potential staff mediators, a prime consideration is how to select and screen possible candidates. If the choice is to use trained volunteers from a community mediation program or a paid professional mediator, much of the screening has already occurred, but a consideration of the characteristics wanted in your mediator remains important.

Mediation is a complex process requiring a range of skills by those serving as third-party neutrals. These skills are necessary whether one is an ombudsperson or a mediator, whether the dispute involves two parties or twenty, and whether the dispute involves property, behavior, or policies. *Peaceful Persuasion* (Girard, Rifkin, and Townley, 1985, p. 60) listed ten basic mediator skills:

- Establishes rapport and trust with the disputants and between the disputants
- Facilitates communication such that disputants are able to state and hear positions, feelings, and perceptions in ways that promote communication and lead to new options for resolving the conflict
- Clarifies issues, perceptions, and information for each disputant and between disputants
- Recognizes and interrupts communication patterns that prevent dialogue and resolution
- Sees and helps others to see both self and mutual interests
- Helps people moderate positions while saving face
- Minimizes the effects of power imbalances on negotiations
- Determines when negotiating is not in good faith
- Acts impartially
- Maintains confidentiality

Although the specific use of these skills might vary from program to program, they represent the essence of what is seen as a good mediator who functions as a neutral third party.

## Criteria for Selecting Trainees

Within the field of mediation, there are different perspectives on who should be acting as third-party neutrals, given the above set of skills. Some groups believe that anyone can be trained to mediate successfully and that the process of training a cross-section of the community is empowering for the community as a whole. These groups often train and develop a pool of mediators based on a "first come, first taken" basis. Others make a case for selecting from certain groups of professionals (lawyers, counselors, family therapists, labor negotiators), those demographically related to likely disputants, or those who meet certain preexisting skill requirements.

Programs that handle a range of cases often try to select a pool of mediators that reflects the age, sex, sexual preference, ethnicity, and economic and job classification characteristics of the population served. Typically disputants do not know anything about the third parties until they arrive at the mediation session. This matching of characteristics between third parties and disputants is seen as a way of establishing initial trust and credibility. The degree and emphasis of matching varies greatly from program to program. For instance, some programs that mediate landlord-tenant disputes may insist on having landlords in the mediator pool. Other similar programs, fearing inherent bias on the part of people in the role of landlord, may substitute age as the essential criterion, letting the age of the mediator serve as a primary way of connecting to disputants rather than job description or background.

Most programs use some model of preselecting potential mediators for participation in a training program and then later select mediators for assignment to actual cases based on their performance during training. At the preselection stage, the following criteria may be useful to consider:

- Contributes to demographic and cultural diversity: age, sex, sexual preference, race, town of residence (if the program serves many towns), socioeconomic status, job classification, years until graduation.

- Has clear personal communication style: listens closely, showing attention and demonstrating understanding; speaks clearly with understandable syntax.

- Has valuable personal skills and abilities (in addition to good communication skills): has respect of peers, self-confidence, empathy, leadership or trainer potential, ability and experience speaking in front of groups, previous training, and experience as a neutral.

- Has specific knowledge in areas relevant to the program's target population: applicable laws, university procedures, student development theories, family dynamics, domestic violence issues, grievance procedures, sexual harassment policies, and so on.

- May increase useful political connections within the university structure (for example, ties to key parts of the administration, counseling center, judicial program, union, board, academic departments, or campus police).

- Has good availability: some mediators may only be available in the evening, while others have the flexibility to be available during the day. Some faculty are only on campus certain days of the week, due to a long commute or responsibilities elsewhere. Some applicants may already be heavily committed to other time-consuming activities or heavy course schedules. Student programs also want to consider training sophomores and juniors as well as seniors, to avoid having a mass exodus of mediators at graduation.

- Shows a high level of commitment: Agrees to attend training and attend in-service trainings and to work one evening a month as needed (or whatever other expectation is deemed necessary).

## Basic Steps in Setting Criteria

Although the criteria used to select potential trainees will vary based on the program's focus and intended target population, there are some basic steps to take in choosing the criteria:

- Determine the likely characteristics of disputants based on the populations or conflict areas to be addressed.

- Determine the degree of similarity to be used to match disputants and neutrals, and identify characteristics needed in the mediator pool to allow for that level of matching.

- Determine the level of communication skills, types of life experience, knowledge and awareness, and other skills desired in those who will be trained.

- Determine the necessity for specialized knowledge that disputes will require.

- Determine the level of commitment in terms of training and volunteer work that will be required.

## The Process of Soliciting Potential Trainees

Once the criteria have been determined, advertising or recruiting candidates for the training can occur. There are a variety of ways to select the trainees, some of which involve significant prescreening, with others that are more open-ended.

**Training an Existing Group.** Perhaps the easiest approach is to train an existing group such as all students registered for a particular class, all third-year resident assistants, members of a particular student club or committee, faculty and staff serving on an employee relations committee, or all members of the staff serving certain functions (for example, associate deans or sexual harassment liaisons). Although this process may perhaps be efficient, especially if these groups are already diverse, there is often less control over the characteristics of people already in these roles. Also the program may be training the already engaged core of active and assertive students or staff, rather than bringing in less involved students or staff, who are less likely to receive special attention and training. The mediation project developers may also miss discovering some excellent mediators if they do not open up the process using a broader invitation.

**Soliciting Recommendations or Nominations.** This method has the benefit of involving more of the college or university community in program development, which can be good for building awareness of and investment in the program. The solicitation process can be informal, based on conversations with key administrators, staff, faculty, and students (depending on the program scope), or it can be more public, involving more people. For instance, there might be presentations to appropriate groups at orientations or staff meetings, or an advertisement in the campus newspaper describing the initiative, in each case providing a nomination form that outlines the qualities sought in mediators. Managers can recommend staff from within their areas, or faculty or residence hall or student organizations staff can recommend students. Ideally, participation in the training should remain voluntary. If there is concern about limiting the size of the potential pool, a requirement might be that someone must have at least two nominations to qualify for an invitation to participate. The program coordinator or the planning committee could then decide to invite all nominees or some subset that fit other basic characteristics the program was looking for. A sample nomination form is provided in Section D in Resources, Forms, and Documents.

Although this approach has benefits related to increased levels of involvement and program outreach, it may also mean considerable work on the part of the program coordinators, who in their first year may feel swamped with a host of start-up tasks. Also names will be submitted of a number of nominees who are not interested in participating when asked directly, so the mediation developers need to invite more than they expect to train in the end.

**Making an Open Invitation.** Another approach, once there is a decision on the category of people who will serve as mediators (solely staff, solely students, or some combination), is to do an open invitation to the appropriate group. This can be accomplished using an ad in campus publications and through flyers, posters, and other information distributed through various campus channels. Interested individuals are asked to fill out an application or self-nomination form to participate in the training, which may then be used for further screening as deemed necessary. Section E in Resources, Forms, and Documents provides an example of an application form used for this purpose.

## Screening Potential Trainees

Once potential participants have either applied or been nominated, some kind of additional screening usually occurs. Some programs train anyone who applies, allowing individuals to determine for themselves whether they are right for the program after receiving a full explanation of what will be expected of them. This might involve hosting a preliminary meeting for nominees or applicants, where the process, time requirements, and other commitments are spelled out. Other screening methods include having a telephone conversation or interview with each applicant or holding face-to-face group or individual interviews. Interviews may also be scheduled with a subset of applicants, using the information provided on the application forms as the first level of screening. The process of screening applicants can be time-consuming, especially if a large number of individual interviews are required. However, information gained in these interviews can help select a strong initial group of mediators, and thus be well worth the effort.

Another method of selecting trainees is to have the mediation training be available after participants have met a series of other training prerequisites. For instance, at the University of Minnesota's University Mediation Program (UMP), staff and faculty serve as the mediators. They are eligible to participate in mediation training only after they have attended two day-long trainings: one on basic negotiation skills and the other on advanced negotiation and conflict resolution skills. The program offers day-long training sessions every few months, building on an agreement from the deans and department heads to give staff and faculty release time to participate in these trainings. Having initially attended a training program on negotiation skills, perhaps for personal reasons like the desire to negotiate for a raise or better laboratory space, participants become curious and return for the advanced training, and eventually many sign up for the more intensive mediation training that is offered less frequently. Depending on the focus of the program, other potential prerequisites include having taken certain academic courses, taken sexual harassment training, or having been through two previous residence adviser orientation trainings.

In addition to or as an alternative to using interviews and some kind of ranking system, some programs have used a lottery system. An advantage, especially when choosing student mediators for a peer mediation program, is that students typically perceive the lottery process as an opportunity rather than a personal risk of rejection. More students may apply to become mediators if the selection criteria are random than if judges make the selection using strict criteria. The feeling of being rejected from a program is never pleasant, and finding ways to minimize it can help keep good feelings about the program alive among the student body. Whatever method is used, the program developers must be sure to find a way to thank applicants who are not chosen, so as not to alienate them from the program early in its existence.

The lottery process can be adapted to meet program diversity goals by doing a controlled lottery—actually a series of lotteries. For example, to generate gender balance, the candidates can be separated into male and female groups, with an equal number drawn. To reflect the college's racial composition, the program can first draw from the minority pool the minimum number of candidates to guarantee a representative group. Then all remaining minority candidates can be placed in the general pool and drawn from until the total number of mediators is determined. In a similar fashion, the pool could be divided by other desired criteria (such as freshman, sophomore, junior, senior, graduate student) to ensure other types of diversity.

## Additional Selection Considerations

There are a few additional matters that are useful to keep in mind in selecting a group. For example, the value of having as diverse a group of trainees as possible participate is important. But the goal is to have the actual training experience to be positive rather than alienating. Thus, the program developers may want to strive to include at least two of each "type" of student or staff in the training. Participating in the various training exercises involves taking some risks, and if a trainee is the only representative of his or her self-identified group (for example, the only Hispanic, freshman, union person, or clerical staff person), that trainee is more likely to feel isolated and uncomfortable. Having a similar other in the training can help ease the initial discomfort until other relationships can be built during the training. If space is limited, making this criterion difficult to meet, there should be at least an attempt to avoid having the singularly unique person be someone with multiple characteristics that set him or her apart—for example, being the only freshman *and* the only African American in the training. Each additional kind of difference can magnify a participant's discomfort.

Another issue has to do with the size of the group invited to participate. Most mediation trainings include fifteen to twenty-five participants, a workable group size. If the goal is to have twenty participants, remember that it is common to have a couple of people drop out of the training at the last minute for whatever reason. To compensate for this shortfall, a good practice is to develop a waiting list of alternates who can attend the training if a space opens up. In terms of the final pool, a safe assumption is that about 85 percent of the training group will be adequately prepared and appear suitable after the training to provide mediation services. Because of this and the dropout factor, it is wise to invite a few more people than the final mediator pool will contain.

Another consideration has to do with incentives, if any, that may be offered to students and staff to encourage them to participate. Often it is unnecessary to offer incentives because many people are now interested in being trained as mediators, but it can be a nice touch and can help attract good-quality or highly committed trainees. Possible incentives include course credit, certificates of completion, letters to their personnel file, awards, and release time. If the hope is to involve disadvantaged or at-risk students in the pool, one choice is to consider offering student participants stipends, like the UCLA program has done using grant money, for their involvement in the program. Otherwise, if students have to take time off work to participate, it may limit their ability to be part of the program.

The University of Michigan combined a number of suggestions incorporated in this chapter in developing its staff and faculty mediation service. Exhibit 4.1 describes its approach.

## Choosing the Mediation Format

Among the most basic operational decisions that need to be made are deciding what format the program will use to conduct the mediation sessions and determining session characteristics.

### Format Choices

The basic choices are single mediators, co-mediation using teams of two mediators for each session, or panel mediation using three to five mediators. There are some pros and cons to each format. Given the various strengths and weaknesses of the different models, programs may wish to settle on a standard operating procedure to train their mediators in, with acknowledgment that this

The University of Michigan's Consultation and Conciliation Services was developed to serve staff and faculty (Johnson, 1996). The services to be offered were defined as confidential consultation: private and off-the-record conversations with any faculty or staff person to explore their concerns and assist in identifying potential courses of action and related policies, and third-party-neutral conciliation services of a trained mediator to conduct private, interest-based negotiations to resolve a dispute. Services would be available to both faculty and nonbargained-for staff on the main campus in Ann Arbor (not including the hospitals)—a population totaling some twelve thousand people. Some issues were deemed inappropriate for conciliation, including faculty peer-reviewed issues such as tenure, and instances of severe discipline or discharge for serious misconduct. Within these limits, the intention during the pilot period was to test the appropriateness of the new procedures for as wide a variety of issues as possible. The program established two program coordinators who were responsible for the consultation work and sought out a pool of volunteer staff and faculty mediators who would provide the actual mediation services.

The project mediators were to be drawn from existing faculty and staff. Using the help of the Association of Black Professionals and Administrators and the Academic Women's Caucus on campus, the planners sought faculty and staff suggestions (nominations, so to speak) for individuals who would be recognized by their peers as neutral, confidential, and fair. The committee also established some criteria to help them sort through the nominees. The final criteria settled on by the planners indicated that appropriate mediators must be:

- Long-service, mature individuals already in established positions
- Perceived as neutral by the staff or faculty member
- Perceived as neutral by management
- Easily accessible at convenient times and places
- Demographically diverse, including representation of both faculty and staff
- Not likely to experience mediation as conflicting with their regular responsibilities

In addition, the mediators must possess these qualities:

- Ability to remain objective
- Sense of humor
- Excellent listening skills

From a list of more than one hundred names that were suggested, a diverse group of fifteen individuals was identified and invited to participate in an intensive professional mediation training. Eight of this group accepted the invitation and undertook the training. They were joined by a number of staff whom the planning committee identified as important to involve in the project, including five affirmative action staff members, six employee relations specialists, three human resources administrators, the employee rehabilitation manager, and the campus sexual harassment program coordinator. Although it was understood that affirmative action and employee relations specialists, because of their responsibilities to guide and staff formal grievance processes, would not often be appropriate as neutral mediators, they were included in the training so that they would be familiar with mediation and could recommend it when appropriate.

Exhibit 4.1. Staff and Faculty Mediation Program Example

*Source:* Johnson (1996). Used with permission.

format may be modified as need or circumstance dictates. The program I developed at family student housing, with its emphasis on community building, relied on a panel process, whereas the Syracuse University Campus Mediation program uses co-mediation.

**Single Mediator Format.** The main arguments in favor of using a single mediator are that it is easiest to schedule, and it increases the parties' sense of privacy because only one intervenor is involved. Single mediators may be deemed acceptable by disputants due to their visibility, reputation, and credibility on campus. Programs in which mediators are not known to the disputants and identification between clients and mediators is important may be better served by at least two mediators. One-person interventions are limited in that there is no second person with whom the mediator can clarify complex and difficult issues, check out their perspective on the case, or explore alternative strategies for bringing the dispute to resolution.

**Co-mediator Format.** Co-mediation is the standard on most campuses. This format provides additional educational opportunities for the mediators and disputants. Mediators learn cooperation and the art of teamwork. This makes the model particularly appealing for programs interested in training student mediators. The model has these primary benefits:

- Permits greater levels of quality control when using volunteers
- Increases learning opportunities for mediators (through mentoring with a more experienced mediator and by permitting more volunteers a chance to work on cases)
- Creates the possibility of matching mediator team characteristics to disputants' characteristics, which can help with rapport building
- Reduces mediator fatigue by giving a mediator the chance to think, collect thoughts, review notes, and organize while the co-mediator is speaking
- Provides support for one's partner when necessary (as when one loses one's train of thought or briefly goes blank)
- Increases the range of skills provided by mediators
- Permits the modeling of cooperation by the two mediators

Scheduling two mediators is more difficult than one, however, and there is the possibility of personality and style conflicts between mediators.

**Panel of Mediators.** The panel process is used less frequently than the others because it is the most difficult to schedule and requires increased levels of coordination and teamwork between mediators. Nevertheless, panels are particularly useful for community disputes or cases with multiple parties, because the mediator panel can reflect the diverse parts of the community structure involved in the case or its resolution, helping to build rapport, make sure all views are aired, and increase people's sense of the fairness of the process.

## Sessions

Another consideration in selecting a structure for mediation is the emphasis placed on using joint sessions exclusively or combining them with individual sessions. A joint session gives the mediators an opportunity to understand the situation by having all the parties present and giving each person a chance to explain what brought him or her to mediation. Mediators use this time to build trust by listening carefully and well and to obtain information by asking neutral, clarifying questions. Individual sessions with each party, typically referred to as caucuses, are used to further trust, gain clarity on what each person wants, and sometimes move the parties toward agreement. In caucus with each party, the mediator gathers more information and seeks to uncover discrepancies between a person's public position and his or her actual one. By using solely the joint session, a mediator may reduce the time of meeting, gather subtle information through observing the continued interaction of the parties, and encourage the disputants to communicate directly. However, joint sessions may never allow room for disputants to moderate their positions, especially if there is substantial hostility, distrust, or a history of dispute between the parties.

Although incorporating the use of individual sessions can be time-consuming and may reinforce polarization between the parties, the disadvantages of either joint or individual sessions may be balanced by using both. Some programs as a matter of basic practice start with a brief joint session and then move immediately into separate meetings with each party, bringing the parties back together when an agreement seems at hand. Other programs prefer to remain in joint sessions as much as possible, using individual sessions only if the process bogs down or gets out of control. My preference is for the latter; I believe it reduces the likelihood of undue influence by the mediators and increases the parties' sense of involvement and ownership in the outcome. Separate caucuses involving the mediators and individual parties can be very useful at getting "unstuck," but should be used sparingly because part of the goal of most mediation sessions is to help the parties begin to communicate more effectively with each other, and this is not easily accomplished by keeping the parties separated.

Another factor to be considered in determining the structure of a session is the length of each session and the number of sessions per case. Typically relatively simple two-party disputes (those with not too many issues) can be mediated in a two- to three-hour period, with most programs initially scheduling a two-hour time block. Some programs have found that using two separate sessions gives people a chance to think about the questions raised, consult with advisers if necessary, and return with a clearer sense of the problem and a readiness to move toward agreement. Three hours appears to be an outside limit for most disputants' and mediators' concentration, focus, and stamina. Some of the more complex workplace disputes, as well as family conflicts with multiple issues and complex dynamics, and cases with large numbers of disputants may take multiple sessions. Environmental, interorganizational, and policy disputes may take months of regular meetings to work out all the issues.

## Mediator Style

As mediators become more sophisticated and as the number of mediators and the range of settings where they work increases, so has the debate about how one should mediate and what styles are most appropriate for any particular setting. In terms of format, programs can now choose (consciously or by default based on their choice of trainers) among a growing variety of mediation styles. These differing approaches are given labels that are perhaps best understood as the end points on various continuums. A mediator's style may be described as bargaining versus therapeutic, problem solving versus transformative, evaluative versus facilitative, or settlement oriented versus restorative, among other terms. A discussion of these different mediation varieties and all their subtleties is beyond the scope of this book. However, a general awareness of the different orientations is useful as programs determine their intended audience and consider what model would be most fitting.

For instance, if a mediation program is designed to serve the community as well as campus, welcoming group disputes or so-called town-gown conflicts, the program must be capable of managing multisided and often multiparty conflicts. Often the disputants in these cases have ongoing relationships; therefore, it would be important for the training to value and recognize that conflict is often set in a context of deep personal emotion that may be only tenuously related to the immediate issues. However, if a program is linked to the business school or labor relations program within a college, serving largely contractual disputes, the philosophy of the mediators might be informed by collective bargaining characteristics such as bipolarity and the need to reach a settlement that takes the form of a written agreement, requiring a training model compatible with this approach. Perhaps the program is designed to focus solely on students, building on the belief that mediation is a vehicle for personal change with an emphasis on future behavior. This too would affect the emphasis of the training. These kinds of general philosophical assumptions can influence the choice of training model that best fits a campus's needs.

The most commonly discussed style differences involve those between evaluative and facilitative mediators and between the problem-solving versus the transformative model of mediation. Evaluative mediators are characterized as more prone to narrowing the topics for discussion, pushing hard for settlement, giving the parties their opinion of what seems fair and of what a person's "case is worth," and working to narrow the settlement range in the hope that parties will agree. Facilitative mediators, on the other hand, are described as being much less controlling of the process, leaving the choice of topics and the evaluation of options clearly in the hands of the parties. Building on the increasing popularity of this kind of distinction, a mediator style survey is now available that asks mediators a series of questions to determine where they fit in terms of being evaluative broad, evaluative narrow, or facilitative broad, or facilitative narrow (Krivis and MacAdoo, 1997).

The distinction between problem-solving and transformative approaches to mediation is also commonly discussed among mediators. The introductory material from a Web site devoted to transformative mediation describes the essential differences as follows:

> The goal of problem solving mediation is generating a mutually acceptable settlement of the immediate dispute. Problem solving mediators are often highly directive in their attempts to reach this goal—they control not only the process, but also the substance of the discussion, focusing on areas of consensus and "resolvable" issues, while avoiding areas of disagreement where consensus is less likely. Although all decisions are, in theory, left in the hands of the disputants, problem solving mediators often play a large role in crafting settlement terms and obtaining the parties' agreement.
>
> The transformative approach to mediation does not seek resolution of the immediate problem, but rather, seeks the empowerment and mutual recognition of the parties involved. Empowerment, according to Bush and Folger (Bush and Folger, 1994), means enabling the parties to define their own issues and to

seek solutions on their own. Recognition means enabling the parties to see and understand the other person's point of view—to understand how they define the problem and why they seek the solution that they do. (Seeing and understanding, it should be noted, do not constitute agreement with those views.) Often, empowerment and recognition pave the way for a mutually agreeable settlement, but that is only a secondary effect. The primary goal of transformative mediation is to foster the parties' empowerment and recognition, thereby enabling them to approach their current problem, as well as later problems, with a stronger, yet more open view. This approach, according to Bush and Folger, avoids the problem of mediator directiveness which so often occurs in problem-solving mediation, putting responsibility for all outcomes squarely on the disputants [Burgess and Burgess, 1997, paragraphs 2–3].

For people interested in the transformative approach to mediation, the Web site mentioned above includes a series of questions to ask potential mediators or trainers to elicit their perspectives and determine if they would be considered to have a transformative approach.

The third (and rather similar) style distinction is between bargaining versus therapeutic approaches. Sally Merry and Susan Silbey, both professors at Wellesley College, have identified many mediation styles on a continuum between "bargaining" and "therapy" (Silbey and Merry, 1986). At the bargaining end of the continuum are mediators who have a negative view of the legal system because it is costly, slow, and inaccessible. At the same time, people who use a bargaining method feel their authority rests in their expert understanding of the law and the court system. At the other end of the continuum, mediators with a therapy style view the legal system negatively because they believe that it causes personal relationships to deteriorate. Those working in this mode see their authority as residing in their expertise in managing personal relationships. Following are characteristics of each end of the continuum as identified by Merry and Silbey:

### Bargaining

- Purpose of mediation is to reach a settlement.
- Spends more time in individual sessions.
- Assumes parties know what they want.
- Focuses on demands that can be traded off.
- Assumes conflict is caused by differences of interests.
- Assumes settlement can be reached by trading off benefits.

### Therapy

- Purpose of mediation is to help parties reach their own settlement.
- Encourages direct communication between parties.
- Assumes parties do not always know what they want.

- Helps parties to define their real issues.
- Assumes the source of conflict is a result of misunderstanding or failure of communication.
- Emphasizes resolution of conflict through rational discussion and compromise.

Clearly there is much overlap between these different categorizations of the field. As commonly portrayed, the bargaining, evaluative, and problem-solving styles are rooted in a pragmatic positional interest approach to conflict resolution, while the therapeutic, facilitative, and transformative approaches are much more personal ones that seek to discover common personal interests and the clarification of values. Within the field of practicing mediators, there are combinations of these characteristics, creating a wide range of styles. What seems most important is identifying the qualities that would best serve the needs of the program's targeted population. For example, a case between the administration and physical plant workers might be best served by a more bargaining approach to mediation, whereas a case involving formerly dating students might be better handled by a more therapeutic approach. Over time, it probably make sense to have mediators representing a variety of styles available on campus so a wide assortment of cases could be handled effectively. Of course, each mediator will contribute his or her own personal style—tone of voice, view of the world, physical conduct, and ethics—all of which will affect the shape of the process.

In addition to a host of journal articles, a number of books explore the range of mediation styles. Christopher Moore's *The Mediation Process* (1996) provides a sophisticated review of the mediation process and the techniques mediators use across a range of settings. Another important (and perhaps more controversial) book, *The Promise of Mediation* (Bush and Folger, 1994), contrasts the problem-solving and transformative approaches to mediation, advocating for the latter. Finally, *When Talk Works* (Kolb, 1994) provides detailed portraits of mediators' utilizing different styles as they carry out their work.

## A Basic Mediation Process Outline

The mediation processes used in campus programs vary, but almost all programs rely on some kind of basic structure to guide mediators as they move through the process. Transformative mediators have begun to question the wisdom of relying on overly linear models that restrict the parties' ability to discuss what is important to them, but as it stands, most mediation trainers present a basic process or mediation road map divided into stages or phases. The actual number of stages (ranging from four to seven), and how closely the mediators are encouraged to follow them, differ depending on the trainer's background and experience. The basic model I use was presented in Exhibit 1.1 as one example of how this process looks in action.

## Considerations in Selecting a Training Program

There are a number of ways to get mediators trained—for example:

- Private training consultants who specialize in higher education and provide training on campus
- Training provided by local community mediation program staff
- Training provided by neighboring colleges and universities with established programs
- National or regional training that staff travel to (training institutes)
- In-house training conducted by staff or faculty (who perhaps have gone to a training-for-trainers session elsewhere first)

The costs associated with these different approaches can vary considerably. Perhaps the most desirable method is to have a mediation specialist experienced in higher education mediation tailor his or her basic program specifically for a campus and deliver it to the group at an ideal time (perhaps a few weeks into the semester, when people's attention is relatively free, or in the summer). Given the relative scarcity of trainers focusing specifically on higher education disputes, more often the need is to locate an experienced and skillful trainer who will work to adapt his or her general format to the program needs. There are some real advantages to connecting with a local community mediation program, which can often provide ongoing consultation as the program develops, follow-up training, and perhaps even assistance with intake procedures or the provision of ongoing mediator professional development.

Some basic constraints affect the use of in-house staff to train the group. No one can learn to mediate from a book, and no one can train others to mediate effectively unless he or she is already a mediator who has experienced the process. If there are already trained and experienced mediators on campus, efforts should be made to involve them. Sending a few staff members (one is certainly not enough) to a mediation institute, perhaps combined with some training for trainers, and then having them develop a training program for the campus may work. However, this is a difficult undertaking because it puts a lot of pressure on these individuals to absorb not only the skills of mediation, but the skills of being a trainer (which are different) in a very short time. A more workable solution for developing in-house training capacity is to have a few core staff attend a mediation training early in the planning of the campus mediation effort (perhaps one offered by the local community mediation program) and then later arrange to have them work in an apprentice role with an outside trainer as they conduct the group's basic mediation training. This approach lets the would-be trainers focus on how the various training aspects of the mediation training are managed, getting coaching and support from an experienced trainer, instead of having also to learn the basics of mediation.

## Mediator Certification

A common question that is raised in relation to training involves the certification of mediators or trainers, and it is one with no easy answer. At this stage in the development of campus mediation efforts, there is no agreed-on standard and no national body providing certification. Preliminary discussions have just begun in this area. Currently basic campus trainings range from fifteen to forty hours in length, depending on the scope and complexity of cases the programs expect to handle.

There may be state requirements for mediators who are handling court-referred cases (there are, for example, in Florida, New York, Michigan, and California), and the community mediation association in the state or a local community mediation program may have set standards of their own for community mediators. Over the years, national groups such as the Association of Family and Conciliation Courts and Academy of Family Mediators have devised standards for their specialized practice areas. Program developers may want to look into the currently applicable standards in their state, because it is sometimes possible to have campus training conform to state standards, thus enabling mediators to practice in other local settings that require such training as well. Often, however, this is a complex process that requires including material that may be of marginal relevance to a particular program or may require using a select group of trainers approved by the state or association in order to qualify.

We will address the currently available codes of conduct in a later chapter, but for now it is safe to say that the question of mediator certification is still open and under considerable debate. Certificates of completion given to trainees at the close of training often testify only that the participants attended the training, not that they are in fact considered ready to mediate. These certificates, barring the development of national standards, have value only insofar as the training organization that provided them has developed credibility and respect within the field.

## Locating a Trainer or Training Program

Finding an appropriate trainer can require some investigative skills, because the number of trainers specializing in higher education is relatively small. One useful approach is to contact other campus mediation programs using the links found at the Campus Mediation Resources Web page or other means, and ask the program coordinator for referrals to potential trainers. Information on training that is offered elsewhere is found in national publications that provide calendars of upcoming conferences and trainings, most notably at mediate.com or *Conflict Resolution Notes,* published by the Conflict Resolution Center International. Program developers may also wish to check the services available from a local community mediation program or state association of mediators. They can find some training information at the growing number of Web sites dedicated to mediation and alternative dispute resolution. Also, in the Appendix to *Mending the Cracks in the Ivory Tower,* Gillian Krajewski (1998) presents the results of her survey of conflict management trainings affiliated with academic institutions. Although this list is focused on trainings for administrators and includes degree-granting programs and generic conflict resolution training in addition to mediation training, it does provide a relatively recent and broad look at what is available.

## What to Look For from the Trainers

The National Association for Community Mediation has described the qualities and responsibilities of good trainers from the point of view of the association (Brodrick, Carroll, and Hart, 1996). These ideas are relevant to campus programs as well.

> The process of helping people improve their interpersonal and facilitative skills as mediators requires a training participant to demonstrate a willingness to take risks, perform publicly, and receive critical coaching and an effective mediation trainer to be sensitive to each participant's needs and individual learning style and pace. The community mediation trainer will generally have extensive experience as a mediator in order to be accepted as a credible teacher and role model. Thorough knowledge of the mediation

process and a mediator's techniques and strategic choices is also essential. Teaching skills that a community mediation program requires of its trainers include flexibility concerning approach, effective presentation skills, an ability to promote positive group dynamics among learners, a sense of the developmental nature of skills acquisition, and a lively stage presence (Brodrick, Carroll, and Hart, 1996, paragraph 11).

Following are some specific qualities to look for in a trainer:

- The ability to adapt training to the needs of the planning and development group, particularly within a specific institutional context.

- Commitment to consult with the group prior to the actual training, so that the training program can be jointly developed.

- A willingness to help the group begin to anticipate the kinds of cases the program may have so that the role-playing component of the training mirrors potential cases.

- Shared philosophical and political values with the hiring institution.

- Concrete ties between the institution and trainers; for example, if a program is part of a state institution, it might make sense to hire trainers who are connected to a state program, or if a program is linked to the university's business school, consultants who already have expertise in this particular field may be available.

- Explicit statement of outcomes: exactly what knowledge, awareness, and skills participants will acquire by the end of the training.

- Technical assistance while the program is being implemented.

- Availability for future advanced training.

## What to Look For from the Training

Generic campus mediation trainings are typically about fifteen to thirty hours, although longer is better. Basic mediation skills training courses emphasize interactive participation, encouraging learning by doing in a constructive and supportive atmosphere. Training includes a mixture of theory and practice that strengthens the performance of trainees and provides a variety of learning techniques that reflect a sensitivity to individual learning styles. Role-play exercises are designed to reflect specific dispute types handled by the mediation program. Exhibit 4.2 provides a sample agenda for a medium-length training program.

FRIDAY 1:00–6:00; 7:00–9:00

Overview of Training Program
Campus Mediation Programs: History, Different Philosophies
Examples of Campus Conflict (video clips and discussion)
Review of Basic Conflict Management Options
Mock Mediation Demonstration by Trainer (or video demonstration)
    Break
Basic Communication Skills for Mediation: Rapport Building, Reflective Listening
    for Content and Feelings
Mediation Skills I: Teamwork Preparation, Setting the Stage, Introductory remarks
Questions, Evaluation of Day 1

SATURDAY 9:00–6:00

Warm-up Exercises
Review of Stages of Mediation
Role Play 1 (focus on opening statements, preliminary storytelling)
    Break
Using the Language of Diplomacy (avoiding trigger words, indications of bias)
Mediation Skills II: Directing Discussion, Handling Interruptions, Focusing the Issues
    Lunch Break
Goals of the Different Phases of Mediation
Role Play 2 (focus is on getting clear summary of parties' issues)
Using the Caucus (why and how)
    Break
Mediation Skills III: Generating Alternatives and Problem Solving
Role Play 3 (focus on option generation, use of caucus as appropriate)
Evaluation and Wrap-up of Day 2

SUNDAY 9:00–5:00

Warm-up Exercises
Mediation Skills IV: Techniques for Exploring Possible Agreement
Crafting a Good Agreement
    Break
Role Play 4
Review and Discussion of Any Agreements Reached
    Lunch Break
The Influence of Culture, Ethnicity, and Power
Special Program Issues: Co-mediation, Confidentiality, Volunteer Ethics
    Break
Practice Role Play 5
Review of Videotape Clips of Participants in Action (if possible)
Questions, Open Discussion
Completion of Self-evaluation Forms
Wrap-up, Evaluation/Closing

Exhibit 4.2.  Sample Agenda for a Medium-Length Basic Mediation Training Program

A good training program assumes that a broad spectrum of people are capable of being mediators and offers a multidimensional approach that is intellectually sound, experiential, relevant in content, and challenging. It has the following goals:

- Raises consciousness about the role of conflict in individual lives and within the culture
- Prepares participants for future learning by deepening their capacity for self-evaluation
- Sharpens volunteers' motivation to help people while teaching them detachment from the outcome
- Meets the program's substantive needs of structure, style, skills, techniques, and case development

## Evaluating the Mediators

The mediation approach and training program chosen will determine to a large measure what skills, knowledge, and awareness mediators must be prepared to use. It should provide a curriculum tailored to the needs and focus of a program and include a listing of training outcomes. That is, the trainers working with the program should provide a description of the skills, knowledge, and awareness that each trainee should have acquired by the end of the training period.

The nature of objectives to be achieved by the end of a training program depend on the length and type of training. Objectives for an eight-hour training will be more limited than those for a forty-hour one. Too, if training involves both program and apprenticeship stages, there may be two sets of objectives: intermediate and final ones. The important point is that the evaluation of potential mediators must be based on the skills, knowledge, and awareness that form the basis of preselection (if any) and are specifically addressed through the training. It would clearly be unfair to make a judgment based on how often eye contact was made if that behavior was not a basis for preselecting or an explicit part of the training. Explicit goals tell both the program and potential mediators what is being looked for.

Once it is clear what is being looked for, how to look for it needs to be determined. Since most training programs rely heavily on simulations or apprenticeships, observation is the primary means of evaluating potential mediators. Observation can be conducted by someone who sits in the room during simulated or actual sessions, watches through a one-way glass, or reviews videotapes of the session after it is over. If observation is being used for evaluation purposes, observers should have a preset guide of what they are looking for and some easy means of recording observations. Many programs find that a standardized check-list works well if there is room to note the occurrences of important behaviors and whether the behavior was appropriate. Section F in Resources, Forms, and Documents provides an example of an observation form that might be used while watching trainees mediate mock cases. Too, the trainer may have guides tailored to the material taught in their training.

Information obtained through observation during training can be used to give people feedback that will help them refine their skills and make decisions about who will be asked to mediate cases. For feedback purposes, the sharing of observations should immediately follow the simulated or actual session. Some groups even use a stop-action approach in simulations. This allows observers to give feedback while the role play is still going on, pro-viding trainees with the opportunity to improve their technique or strategy immediately. It may seem obvious, but both trainers and trainees can lose sight of the fact that the primary value of a simu-lation comes not from doing it but from the reflection and analysis that follow. The more closely evaluation is attended to, the more likely it is that simulations and role plays will be fully used. Sec-tion G in Resources, Forms, and Documents provides an example of the kind of instructions that trainees are given as they prepare to participate in a mediation simulation.

## Deciding Who Will Mediate

There are three major approaches to making decisions about who will be asked to mediate. There are those who believe that anyone who goes through training should be used as a mediator, as long as they abide by some basic commitments to the program. This approach is common among grassroots community programs where involvement in mediation is considered an important means of community building and empowerment and that use co-media-tion to ensure that there is at least one highly skilled mediator at each session. This approach can also be based on the assumption that continued formative evaluation feedback can ultimately bring everyone to a level of satisfactory performance.

Another approach looks at changes in skills over the course of the training period. If observational records show improvement, that person is accepted as a mediator. Again, the assumption is that with continued feedback and more experience, the level of skill will increase. These two approaches require that a program main-tain a consistent formative evaluation program in order to ensure the development of a strong mediator group.

A third approach, which may stand alone or be merged with either of the other two, is to set a minimal standard of performance. If by the end of a specified service or training period that minimal performance standard is not reached, that person is not used as a mediator.

Given the substantial investment by both the trainee and the program, it makes sense to select potential mediators carefully, provide a solid, skill-based training program, offer constant and focused feedback on skills, and tell people where they stand in terms of program requirements. Withholding observational data is withholding the opportunity to learn: it is a disservice to those who have attempted to develop new skills and to the program. Telling people that they will not be asked to mediate is hard; however, the more specific and behaviorally based the observations are and the more closely related to skills taught in the training, the easier it is to provide clear, formative feedback and summative judgments to trainees. A final decision is also easier to communicate if potential mediators have received summaries of observations throughout the training. They will already have some sense of how their skills fit the desired profile. Finally, some programs have found that having an option for people to repeat the training the next time it is offered makes it easier to be honest about how people are progressing in developing the desired skills. Such an option also reflects the reality that some people need more training than others.

## Posttraining Commitments

Many programs ask volunteers to make certain commitments to the program, either prior to engaging in the training or after the training has been completed, in order to be considered active members of the mediation pool. They are often asked to sign an agreement to this effect.

## Specialized Training Resources

Role-play simulations are quite useful for ongoing professional development of the mediator pool. In an effort to provide programs with some tools for this purpose, a selection of role-play scenarios is provided in Section H of Resources, Forms, and Documents.

There is still a relative shortage of specialized materials to assist campus mediation programs, but a number of videos, role-play collections, training manuals, and an interactive CD are available that directly address the campus situation.

## Annotated List of Specialized Resources for Campus Mediation Training _____

### Training Videos

*Roommates in Conflict: Peer Mediating Student Disputes.* The North Central College Dispute Resolution Center in Naperville, Illinois, has put together this training video for campus mediators. The case involves a dispute between two female roommates in a college residence hall. The tape includes a brief introduction to some basic dispute resolution concepts, in addition to the mock mediation. It is available for sale with an accompanying manual. NCC Dispute Resolution Center, 30 Brainard Street, Naperville, Illinois 60566-7063. Phone: (708) 637-5157; e-mail: tdc@noctrl.edu.

*Trouble in the Lab: A Mediation in Higher Learning.* The Consortium on Negotiation and Conflict Resolution (CNCR), which operates out of the law school at Georgia State University, has developed this forty-five-minute training video. It is a role play based on one developed at MIT involving graduate students in conflict over, among other issues, who will get credit for a recent research breakthrough. It uses a single mediator, presenting a classic structured mediation using a problem-solving, collaborative style. Although the role play is unique to the campus environment, the video does not elaborate on the special issues surrounding dispute resolution systems in an institution of higher education. A short training manual accompanies the tape. CNCR sells the video for a nominal fee to cover costs. CNCR, Georgia State University, College of Law, P.O. Box 4037, Atlanta, Georgia 30302-4037. Phone: (404) 651-0344; fax: (404) 651-4155; e-mail: lawlbi@gsu.edu.

*The Bench by the Wall.* Mediation@mit produced this video of a mediation involving two college roommates from different cultural backgrounds who get into a dispute involving drinking and use of the room. The case is co-mediated. Contact mediation@mit for purchase. Phone: (617) 253-8720; e-mail: carolorm@mit.edu.

*Boundaries: Sexual Harassment.* This video by John Haynes depicting a mediation of a campus sexual harassment charge is available from the Academy of Family Mediators. The case involves a divorced mother of two who has returned to college to earn a graduate degree and has filed a sexual harassment charge against the professor who directs the program. The mediator helps the parties define the problem and negotiate an agreement governing the future behavior of the professor. The tape demonstrates how the mediator helps the parties to redefine an intractable problem as a solvable one. For ordering information, go to www.igc.org/afm/afmbook.html or contact Academy of Family Mediators, 5 Militia Drive, Lexington,

Massachusetts 02421. Phone: (781) 674-2663; fax: (781) 674-2690; e-mail: afmoffice@mediators.org.

*The Mediation Session.* This video, by the Center for Dispute Settlement made in conjunction with Community College of the Finger Lakes, is a mock mediation between a professor and student. Issues included grades, a "pie o gram," and a resulting injury. The tape goes through the step-by-step process. Contact Andrew Thomas, executive director, Center for Dispute Settlement, 242 Andrews Street, Suite 400, Rochester, New York 14604-1144. Phone: (716) 546-5110; fax: (716) 546-4391.

*Teleconference on Campus Mediation.* This teleconference on campus conflict management, produced in the late 1980s by West Virginia University and hosted by Janet Rifkin and Howard Gadlin, is two and a half hours long. It contains clips of four dramatized campus conflicts: one involving a resident adviser and a hall director (one black and the other white, with possible racial issues), one involving a fraternity vice president and president, one involving two roommates, and one involving two female students and a sexually harassing professor. I have used these four examples as a good starting place for discussion and as an illustration of the kinds of issues that might be faced. At press time, availability was uncertain. Further information will be posted at the Campus Mediation Resources site.

## Technical Assistance Manuals

*The Best Practices Manual: An Interdisciplinary Approach to Service-Learning and Mediation Assistance* (1997), by Philip Moses, reports on the experiences of the Albany Law School Mediation Assistance Program, funded by a grant from the Fund for the Improvement of Post-Secondary Education (FIPSE). The project involved students from six colleges and universities working together to provide mediation services to residents of the Albany Housing Authority. The project included court-certified mediation training with quasi-clinical fieldwork apprenticeships, a seminar-style ongoing meeting, and reflective learning journals. A full account of the project and the significant learnings are included. A useful appendix of sample documents and materials is included. Government Law Center, 80 New Scotland Avenue, Albany, New York 12208-3494. Phone: (518) 445-2329; fax: (518) 445-2303.

## Conflict Resolution Skills Training CD-ROM

*Allwyn Hall: Basic Conflict Skills for College Students.* This interactive CD-ROM teaches a three-stage problem-solving process that users put into practice in their role as a student assistant in a college residence hall. Users work through three typical student disputes using an interactive process by airing all parties' views, clarifying problems, and running brainstorming sessions. *Allwyn Hall* is designed for use in a variety of academic settings: orientation, resident adviser training, student mediator training, classrooms, clusters, and libraries. It is a flexible tool that can be used in presenting to large or small groups and can be integrated into existing curricula. Technical requirements are 8 MB of RAM, a color monitor, and a CD-ROM drive. *Allwyn Hall* was developed at the Center for Applied Ethics, Carnegie Mellon University, Pittsburgh, Pennsylvania 15213, under the direction of Martha Harty (e-mail: mh51+@andrew.cmu.edu), an experienced mediator and conflict skills trainer. It was funded by FIPSE. For more information, send e-mail to Allwyn@andrew.cmu.edu or go to the Web site www.caae.phil.cmu.edu/CAAE/Home/ConflictRes/ah/frames.html.

## Training Manuals and Role-Play Collections

*Training Peer Mediators in the College and University Setting: A Trainers Guide* (1997), by Richard T. Olshak, Campus Judicial Consulting. This 170-page self-published trainer's manual is designed to support already trained mediators who want to lead a basic twenty-hour campus mediation training, with an emphasis on the mediation of student disputes. It includes step-by-step presentation instructions as well as sample handouts or overheads and role-play scripts. Student workbooks are available as well, with discounts on bulk quantities. Campus Judicial Consulting, Inc., P.O. Box 423, Normal, Illinois 61761; contact olshak@aol.com.

*Rockin' Role Plays: A Collection of the Finest for Mediation Trainers* (1996), by Barbara Davis and Sarah Corley (Asheville, N.C.: Mediation Center). This spiral-bound book includes a section of very helpful strategies for arranging and making the best use of role plays, as well as a large collection of sample scripts. The role plays focus on a variety of settings, such as the community, business, day care, elementary school, middle and high school, college and university (eleven scenarios), juvenile detention center, hospital, nursing home, and family. The scripts tend to be brief on specific character details (leaving room for improvisation) but generally realistic. (See sample scripts in Section H of Resources, Forms, and Documents.) Mediation Center, 189 College Street, Asheville, North Carolina 28801-3030. Phone: (828) 251-6089; fax: (828) 232-5140; www.main.nc.us/tmc.

The process of recruiting, selecting, training, and evaluating volunteer mediators can be time-consuming, but it is also exciting and rewarding work. Mediators are at the heart of any mediation service, and watching a group develop their skills and their ability to be of service to the community can be very encouraging. Time spent in the early stages of the program developing a well-trained pool of mediators will most certainly be repaid in the future in terms of quality of work and the reputation of the program.

# CHAPTER 5

# Publicizing the Program and Creating Referral Systems

Once it establishes a group of designated mediators, a program must turn to publicizing the mediation service and developing systems of referral, intake, and quality control. A number of challenges face new programs at this stage. Attendees at an East Coast regional conference on peer mediation in higher education identified three major obstacles they encountered in implementing new programs: reaching students and getting them to see the benefits of ADR; explaining the program to administration, staff, and faculty; and integrating ADR into the system's current practices to manage conflicts (Jameson, 1996).

## Publicizing the Program

The initial efforts of doing needs assessment, securing support for the program, and recruiting mediators no doubt made some segment of the university population aware of the new mediation initiative. Now it is time to expand this base and begin promoting the program among people who will use it. Promoting the program is an essential piece of work that requires the assistance of everyone associated with it.

### Primary Goals of Outreach

Richard Cohen, in a book on peer mediation programs for grades 6 through 12 (Cohen, 1995), describes the essential goals at this stage in the life of a mediation project:

- To inform everyone in the school that the program is ready to serve them.
- To promote the concept that is fundamental to peer mediation: It is in everyone's best interest to talk out conflicts rather than fight them out. The number of referrals received—and consequently, the impact the mediation program will have upon the school—is directly related to the degree to which students and staff understand this idea.
- To remove any stigma attached with utilizing or being referred to the mediation program. Participating in mediation should be regarded as a sign of maturity, intelligence, and strength.
- To educate the school community about the kinds of cases that are appropriate for mediation.
- To publicize the way that students and staff can avail themselves of the program's services. They should know with whom to speak when conflicts arise, how they can make referrals, and when and where mediation sessions will be held.
- To establish a positive image for the mediation program. People need to see peer mediation as something that makes an essential contribution to school life.
- To remind students, teachers, and administrators continually that the program exists. When interpersonal conflicts arise, people need to think immediately "Should this be mediated?" If you do not remind them, they may very well forget [Cohen, 1995, pp. 123–124].

Although the university setting is different from secondary schools and uses different terms for its personnel, these primary goals of outreach still hold true.

## Outreach and Promotion Strategies

Program promotion is of primary importance in the early phases of a new initiative. For this reason many programs establish a special outreach committee that assists the program coordinator in getting the word out about the program. Perhaps a subset of the planning committee may be willing to take on this new responsibility. It is also a good idea to find ways to involve members of the new mediator pool. After having participated in mediator training, many in this group may be excited about mediation's possibilities and eager to have some cases to work on. Their enthusiasm can be infectious. Although the program's target audience will influence the style and tone of outreach materials and methods (for example, materials aimed at faculty will differ from those designed for undergraduates), the goal is the same: to make people aware of mediation, what it can do for them, and how they can use it.

**Use of Resolutions.** Resolutions can be used at both the national level (for example, the Association for Student Judicial Affairs passed one supporting mediation) and the local campus level to build awareness of the new service and endorse its use. Success with this approach requires being somewhat politically savvy, using awareness of the procedures and norms of various bodies such as residence hall councils, student governments, faculty senates, or staff councils to make a good case. The program coordinator can provide a sample draft of a resolution endorsing the legitimacy and value of mediation and then assist in whatever way is needed to modify and pass the resolution. Typically someone from within the designated body should introduce the resolution and answer any questions regarding it prior to the call for a vote. Sometimes the coordinator can be present to support the passage by answering questions or making a brief report. In other circumstances, it is best to let it be an internal affair. The program developers should check with individuals familiar with standard procedure in the body in question and then strive to be respectful and persuasive within the appropriate bounds. Exhibit 5.1 provides an example of a faculty senate resolution.

**Print Media.** All campuses have a variety of publications targeted to specific audiences.* The student newspaper, one of the more widely read publications on campus, is a good place for early outreach efforts. The program developers can often place ads in the paper at a reasonable price or, even better, get free coverage through feature articles or interviews on the service. Some papers have regular columns that would be happy to feature the program. In fact, the coordinator may even be able to get a column for the mediation program if there is someone in the group creative and reliable enough to produce regular and interesting copy. Perhaps the mediation program could run a conflict resolution tip of the week, or a "looking for conflict resolution?" listing in the classifieds.

The Campus Mediation Resources Web site has links to a number of stories from other campuses that can be used as a model. One example of an interesting approach is the "Dear Fran" column in the University of Waterloo newspaper, where people supposedly "write in" with their problems, and "Fran Flanders" responds with advice. A combination of ads, interviews, feature stories, and announcements will result in broad exposure over the course of the academic year.

---

*I am indebted to Tim Griffin (1993) for many of the following ideas.

MEDIATION: A RESOLUTION

by the Stephen F. Austin State University Faculty Senate

WHEREAS, mediation can create a better university community by improving the social and working climate for students, staff, faculty, and administrators; by helping to resolve conflicts and facilitate policy; by maintaining "good relationships between individuals and groups on campus and between the institution and the local community" (Warters, 1995); and by contributing to the recruitment and retention of students, staff and faculty, AND

WHEREAS, mediation offers a life-long learning experience both through involvement in the process and through awareness of its use, AND

WHEREAS, universities require flexibility and can benefit from a mediation process empowered to respond to and to resolve any conflicts that arise among the members of the university's diverse community, AND

WHEREAS, "developing and nurturing diversity and tolerance for differences is essential for campus survival" and "mediation provides a good vehicle for working through differences in a respectful manner," (Warters, 1995), AND

WHEREAS, mediation as a means of conflict resolution supports the improvement of the primary issues of concern at Stephen F. Austin State University as defined by the ACE Project on Leadership and Institutional Transformation (Ace Project, 1996) in their September 1996 update, AND

WHEREAS, mediation is increasingly used in educational, business and personal settings to effectively resolve conflicts, AND

WHEREAS, the 75th Texas State Legislature passed Senate Bill 694, in which the legislature affirmed that "it is the policy of this state that disputes before state agencies be resolved as fairly and expeditiously as possible and that each state agency support this policy by developing and using alternative dispute resolution procedures in appropriate aspects of the agency's operations and programs" (S. Bill 694, 1997), AND

WHEREAS, the same said Senate Bill 694 defines state agencies to include institutions of higher education (S. Bill 694, 1997), AND

WHEREAS, mediation is provided as one method of alternative dispute resolution, as defined by the Texas Civil Practice and Remedies Code (Mediation, 1995),

BE IT THEREFORE RESOLVED, that the Faculty Senate of Stephen F. Austin State University recommends that the goal of establishing campus mediation services and policies for all members of the university community be incorporated into the SFASU Commission of the Future Goals for 2003.

REFERENCES

Ace Project on Leadership and Institutional Transformation. (1996). September, 1996 Update [Online]. Available: http://www.tahperd.sfasu.edu/ace/update.html [1998, February 9].

Mediation, § 154.03, Civil Practice and Remedies Code (1995). Vernons's Texas Codes Annotated. St. Paul, MN: West Group.

S. Bill 694, 75th Texas State Legislature [Online]. (1997). Available: http://www.capitol.state.tx.us/: Path: View Individual Bill Information/75th Regular Session-1997/ Enter Bill Number: SB694 [1998, February 9].

Warters, B. (1995). Making the case for campus mediation [Online]. The Fourth R, 55, 13 paragraphs. Available: http://www.mtds.wayne.edu/Makecase.html [1998, February 9].

Exhibit 5.1. Sample Faculty Senate Resolution

Used with permission.

SMACK DAB IN THE MIDDLE: UGA OFFERS CONFLICT MEDIATION

By Beth Roberts

A hypothetical conflict

Lee and Gerry share an office on campus. Space is tight in their department, and they share some expensive equipment both need in their jobs. It seems an efficient, if imperfect, arrangement.

But Lee is a sociable type, who likes to chat a bit in the course of the day about recent movies and football games and computer malfunctions. Gerry, though personable and friendly in social situations, works in silence, seemingly off in some private world.

As months pass, their working relationship begins to deteriorate. Lee decides Gerry is aloof and unfriendly; Gerry finds Lee's interruptions increasingly annoying. Both begin to avoid direct dealings—which is difficult, and even risky, since they must work together on many projects.

What happens next? Poor performance evaluations are likely; someone may quit or be fired. Add gender or racial differences to this hypothetical situation and an official grievance looms.

Certainly, before this year, a positive solution to Lee and Gerry's difficulties would have been hard to imagine—barring the sudden appearance of new, more spacious quarters or the intervention of an unusually perceptive and creative supervisor.

This academic year, however, the university has begun to offer mediation as one of the tools for resolving disagreements. The pilot project has handled 14 cases so far, involving 34 different people on campus—students, faculty, staff and administrators.

Exhibit 5.2. Sample Staff Newspaper Feature Story

*Source: Columns* (University of Georgia, Athens), March 24, 1997. Used with permission.

In a similar fashion, many campuses have newsletters for faculty or staff. Usually these publications do not run ads, but instead can offer space to make announcements or place feature stories on the project. Exhibit 5.2 provides an example of the lead-in to a story in the University of Georgia staff paper, *Columns.*

Other useful forms of print media include academic course catalogues and schedule of classes booklets, which on some campuses may include brief descriptions of student services. These may be one of the few documents that all students keep a copy of. Also widely distributed and regularly updated are campus telephone directories, which frequently include, in addition to telephone listings, a section describing campus services or that carries reasonably priced advertisements.

At Syracuse University, we encountered a problem with the

campus telephone book during our first year because our telephone number was inadvertently omitted. The creative solution we worked out turned out to be great for the program. The office producing the telephone book agreed to pay for the printing of business-card-size yellow stickers promoting the service and to provide us with mailing labels for every person receiving a telephone book. Our job was to prepare and mail a letter through campus mail explaining the mishap and advising that people place the sticker on the front of their telephone book to remedy the problem. As a result, for the next two years, the Campus Mediation Center was the first thing many people saw when they reached for their telephone book.

Student handbooks, employee handbooks, and faculty handbooks also commonly offer the opportunity to list a mediation service. The listing can include a brief description of the service in sections devoted to services and resources for the respective clientele.

Eventually the mediation center may want to look into incorporating mediation into the policy language found in these handbooks. This process can take some time, but it helps to formalize and institutionalize mediation services. (Sample policies referencing mediation are available at the Campus Mediation Resources Web site.)

Some campuses have included information in all of the materials distributed by residential life or the off-campus housing office. Mediation may be a required step before requesting a room change in the residence hall. Brigham Young University (BYU) requires landlords listing their apartments with off-campus housing to include a dispute resolution clause in their standard lease, stating that when problems arise, the landlord agrees to use mediation or arbitration, another service that the off-campus housing office offers. Section I in Resources, Forms, and Documents provides the text of the BYU lease language.

**Brochures, Cards, Flyers, and Posters.** Just about every program develops a print brochure describing its services, which can be handed out at presentations and placed on brochure racks around campus available for the display of such materials. One tip is to get some professional help designing and laying out the brochure, because the degree of professionalism in its design and content reflects heavily on the program.

A program card can be distributed by referral sources and members of the program team. It can include some useful information (maybe tips for resolving conflicts or keys to successful negotiation) as well as the requisite contact and procedure information.

Flyers and posters can be posted on campus bulletin boards in classrooms, residence halls, kiosks, and academic and nonacademic building hallways and lobbies, or placed at residence hall and other office counters, or handed out in person on a campus where there is a high level of pedestrian traffic. Some campuses support placing such flyers under the windshield wipers of cars in campus lots, helping to reach the potentially difficult target markets of commuting students and part-time faculty. Flyers are also good for stuffing in campus mailboxes, in folders provided to new members of the campus community during their orientation process, and in folders provided to students when they move into residence halls. Some flyers are designed to be information rich, providing information on how the services work and how they can be accessed; others are useful because they are eye-catching and build awareness of the existence of the service.

Variations on the idea of flyers include door hangers that are distributed in residence halls and apartment complexes and table tents that can be placed on dining hall and lounge tables.

**World Wide Web Pages.** Similar to a print brochure but potentially much more interactive and content rich (and updatable) is a Web page promoting the program. Most colleges and universities provide the necessary computer space to host a Web page, which is useful for programs that are able to find someone with the skills to develop and maintain it. Given the software programs available for Web design, it is not too difficult to convert text from the print brochure into a Web page as a starting place. Many students and faculty are regular users of the Web and appreciate the ability to go quickly to the mediation site if they have questions or want to introduce the idea of mediation to someone visiting their room or office. A few programs have developed on-line forms that interested parties can fill out if they want more information or want to make an appointment. Once the site is up and running, an e-mail message can be sent to staff and faculty announcing the availability of the site and providing the appropriate address, encouraging them to bookmark it for later reference.

As part of developing their brochure, many programs get help designing an apt logo for their program. The creativity of mediation program developers in this area has been impressive, with some Web sites having animated logos that shake hands or talk or symbolically move from conflict to accord. Figure 5.1 shows a few examples of program logos from campus mediation Web sites.

Another benefit of having a Web site is that it can provide a way to connect with similar programs across the country. The Campus Mediation Resources site has links to over 130 campus mediation sites, making it easy to find and connect with others in

Logo of the Campus Mediation Program at UC Irvine

Logo of the mediation@mit program at Massachusetts Institute of Technology

Logo of Student Mediation Services at the University of Michigan, Ann Arbor

Figure 5.1.  Sample Mediation Program Logos

Used with permission.

similar circumstances. New programs can be included on the site by sending the information to Campus Mediation Resources.

**Annual Reports.**  An annual report is a way to build awareness about the program. As ombuds Griffin (1993) notes:

> An annual report should never be overlooked as a marketing tool. If developed with that goal in mind, it can serve the function of making the reader aware of the activities and services of the office in much greater detail than most other techniques. It could be sent not

only to a few administrators, but also to local media (both on and off campus), student leaders, members of representative bodies (like student governments, staff councils, and faculty senates), department (academic and non-academic) heads, and others [paragraph 16].

For programs targeting commuter students, perhaps the best approach is to do a direct mailing of a letter, brochure, or card to their homes because these students are much less likely to read materials posted or distributed on campus. Although even a bulk mailing can be expensive, campus marketing research suggests that this approach is the most effective way to reach part-time and commuter students.

**Promotional Items.** Some programs have their logo or theme printed on promotional items for distribution at various events or locations. Some of these items are serious and tastefully done, perhaps using only the program name and contact information; others have been quite creative and even funny, perhaps appealing more to students than faculty or staff. Examples include pencils, highlighters, bookmarks, refrigerator magnets ("When We Listen, People Talk"), sticky notes ("Looking for Creative Solutions? Try Mediation"), coffee cups ("People Talk, People Listen, Things Change"), match books ("Having a flare-up? Call mediation services!"), and bumper stickers ("Mediators Do It Until Everyone Is Satisfied" or "Talk It Out: Shift Happens"). Some programs use these items as part of a fundraising strategy by selling hats or T-shirts, or giving away items in a raffle.

**Broadcast Media.** The producers of campus radio stations and cable TV networks, often students, may be interested in content for their shows and will be happy to invite some members of the mediation group to speak. On one radio show at Syracuse University, we did a dramatic presentation of a conflict and then a brief mediation that got good reviews. Some radio and cable stations will also help to develop short public service announcements that are aired periodically during the program day. Some colleges have professional video production facilities or film schools with budding student producers who will work with the mediation group to develop a short video to use in presentations. If the mediation program includes a community focus, the staff also may want to look into booking an appearance on a local radio or television talk show.

**Electronic Bulletin Boards, Kiosks, and Log-on Notices.** Many campuses have electronic message boards in high-traffic areas like student union buildings that provide a steady stream of messages. A short message about the mediation center can often be included as one of the messages, usually by reservation. Some campuses have computer-based information kiosks at high-traffic locations. These kiosks often include a touchscreen that people can tap for more information. Information on the mediation program can be included there as well. A final electronic method is the log-on screen that greets many people as they log on to their campus mainframe computer account. These initial screens often include announcements of upcoming events or technical information. At Nova Southeastern University, we had success using this method, but had an unexpected surprise as well. Our note said, "Caught up in conflict? Call the Conflict Resolution Resource Service . . . " Although we did get some cases using this approach, we also received calls from people looking for help because their printer was not working or their computer kept crashing. They interpreted our note as an offer of technical support rather than mediation!

**Presentations and Personal Appearances.** Given the sensitive nature of conflict, a crucial element of concern of potential clients is the degree to which they feel the mediation service will be a comfortable, helpful, and confidential environment. These issues can be addressed best by a personal appearance or presentation by the program coordinator. No other medium allows for the answering of questions, the establishment of personal trust, and such a complete sense of the person with whom the client may interact. The coordinator and members of the outreach committee should be prepared to offer a presentation of as brief as five to ten minutes or as long as an hour that covers basic information about the service. Possible venues for an appearance are orientation sessions for new students, staff, or faculty and various student service expos or activity fairs promoting a host of campus services.

**Letters.** Personalized form letters can be sent to department chairs, student government and organization presidents, residence hall staff and student governments, and individuals across the campus charged with providing programming for the potential constituency. Examples include the women's center, centers for minority students, and directors of nonacademic departments like athletics, the counseling center, and the library. These letters can make them aware of the availability of mediation center staff as a presenter or participant at an upcoming program or meeting of their choice. Even if the letter fails to elicit a response, it has reminded an individual to whom others turn for advice about the mediation service.

Letters explaining the mediation service can be sent to targeted groups of faculty or staff, such as those charged with student advising duties. These groups have regular contacts with students, and often it is the recommendation of a respected faculty or staff member that moves some students to take action on issues that are troubling them.

**Open Houses and Receptions.** If the mediation program has its own space, one way to build awareness of it is to sponsor an open house with refreshments and perhaps even musical entertainment. A related approach is to host a reception for all the department heads, or department heads and staff in student affairs, or human resources, or whatever other division is most relevant to the program. Although these methods require some resources for food and beverages, they do give people a chance to talk to each other and become acquainted with the program relatively quickly. It is a good idea to include advisory board members in this event as well, to help build legitimacy for the initiative and increase the ability to connect with the different attendees.

**Dramatic Presentations.** A brief demonstration role play or skit can be quite effective at capturing and keeping a group's attention. One creative approach that we used at Syracuse University was to ask faculty who were teaching large introductory lectures for an invitation to present for five or ten minutes on the mediation service at the beginning of class. We would bring two "plants" from the service who would sit in the audience near each other and begin to argue about a telephone bill or some other matter in increasingly loud tones just as the main presenter was being introduced. The presenter would say something like, "Excuse me, have you two got a problem? I'm trying to make a presentation here . . . ," at which point one of the disputants would launch into a brief complaint about the other party in tones loud enough for the whole class to hear. This exchange would pave the way to a brief presentation on the mediation service and the kinds of problems it might address. The drama and surprise factor seemed to appeal to many students, and given the large size of the lecture hall, the planted disputants were not immediately obvious as outsiders. Mock mediations can be presented in classes or staff trainings as well.

**"Each One, Reach One" Campaigns.** This approach requires the active involvement of mediators and advisory board. Each person identifies five other people he or she knows who may not be familiar with mediation services. The campaign participants are then asked to seek out one of these people each day (or week) and explain the mediation service to them. If all goes well, by the end of the campaign, one hundred or more additional people will have received a personal introduction to campus mediation.

**Syllabus Boilerplate Language.** Another interesting method of spreading the word about mediation involves identifying classes that use small groups, perhaps in laboratories, or for small group projects or writing assignments. The program prepares some boilerplate language alerting students to the mediation service and encouraging them to use it if conflicts are disrupting their small groups. Faculty are then asked to consider including this language in their syllabus or in handouts explaining the small group assignments. Along these same lines, some freshman English courses require students to write daily papers. These papers frequently focus on problems and conflicts that students are experiencing. Working with the freshman English faculty and the freshman advisers to educate them about mediation and the mediation program can be helpful if the program staff and faculty can together identify ways of providing appropriate information and referrals to students who need help with conflicts.

## Developing and Maintaining Referral Systems

Perhaps more important even than publicity is the development of effective and consistent referral systems. How to accomplish this is probably the most frequently asked question by people starting a program—and the one with the least satisfactory answer. An obstacle that everyone faces is that of changing ingrained patterns of thinking about and handling conflict. Mediation requires a creative shift in thinking about traditional responses to conflict. Basic philosophical differences between formal disciplinary systems and mediation on some campuses can make it difficult to integrate and incorporate mediation into a campus governance structure and into personal views of conflict resolution.

Philosophically, mediation appears interesting and compelling for many people, but there is generally a wide gap between support for the idea of mediation and support of the practice of mediation on a campus. The integration of behavioral changes is difficult and takes conscious attention. People may have to work hard to remember to suggest mediation as a way of responding to disputes brought to their attention. It takes a long time—and this is assuming that support is fully intended and mediation principles fully accepted. One implication is that time and effort must be spent at the beginning to educate those who will later be in positions to promote or hinder referrals. This early education of high-level administrators and front-line workers in the philosophy, practice, and meaning of mediation for a campus community will be most valuable if it allows people to find the limit of their acceptance, support, and commitment. Surface support that lacks true alignment with a person's values, perspective, or expectations may seem useful at the early stages of seeking broad campus support, but it can leave the program without disputes to mediate and is more difficult to deal with than outright opposition.

## Developing an Approach for Referrals

Despite potentially fundamental resistance, campus programs have developed a variety of means to reach disputing parties who could benefit from mediation services. In the ideal situation (other than the parties' working out their problem on their own), generally one or both of the parties to the dispute contacts the service directly and voluntarily. This really begins to occur after the program becomes known widely and some trust is established in its process. The program publicity ideas are a key part of this process. Usually in the early phases of a program, referrals come indirectly from judicial program administrators, managers and supervisors, faculty members, coaches, or residence hall staff—individuals who become aware of the problem and in conversation with one of the disputing parties recommend mediation as an option.

Ideally, from the point of view of the parties and the mediators, participation in mediation should be strictly voluntary. However, given people's reluctance to address conflict face to face, sometimes some kind of firm encouragement is necessary to get the process started. The referral sources must be clear on the benefits of mediation and how it works so that they can direct appropriate conflicts to the center. Depending on the relationship between the parties and the referral source, there may also be some subtle, or not-so-subtle, pressure applied by the referral source: "Either you two work this out, or I'll have to make a decision that I'm not sure either of you would be happy with," or "You can choose to take this issue to mediation and work on finding your own solution, or you can have it be heard by the judicial board and take your chances on the outcome." Intake workers need to be aware of these kinds of methods and do what they can to support the parties in deciding for themselves whether mediation makes sense for them.

Parties must always be able to withdraw from the process without penalty if it is not working for them. There is considerable debate among community mediation programs, divorce mediation programs, and court-based programs regarding how much encouragement or actual mandating of mediation is appropriate. Many dispute systems, both on- and off-campus, require parties to attempt mediation prior to invoking other dispute-handling mechanisms but do not require parties to reach agreement, only to make a "good-faith effort." This leaves the final decision up to the parties as to whether they wish to continue mediation.

**Making the First Contact.** It is preferable for referral sources to encourage the parties to contact the mediation program themselves. However, this is not always effective, and individuals referring cases sometimes take the lead by contacting the program coordinator or intake person and informing him or her of a potential case. Programs have to decide if they are willing to do so-called cold-calls, approaching disputing parties, neither of whom has expressed interest in mediation, to seek to persuade them to try the process. I believe this kind of approach feels intrusive and promotes defensiveness on the part of the parties. I prefer instead that the referring person speak to the party he or she thinks would benefit from mediation, letting the person know that he or she has spoken with the mediation program and asked someone from the program to call and explain the process in more detail because it might be helpful in their circumstance. This at least provides a graceful start to the process.

**Referral Forms.** Some campuses have developed mediation referral forms, available at many campus offices and distributed at the beginning of the year to students and staff, whereby individuals can refer cases (involving themselves or others) to the attention of the mediation service. These forms typically include spaces for the referring party's name and role on campus (student, faculty, staff), the parties' names (if they are different), the date and time of the referral, the nature of the dispute, the degree of urgency, other methods tried already to respond to the conflict, and any other information that is available regarding the best time to contact the parties. These forms are then deposited in some agreed-on location like a locked drop box at the program office or delivered in a sealed envelope through campus mail. This method of referral can be helpful if the program coordinator is available only part time, making it more difficult for people to get in touch with him or her directly.

Some campus programs are experimenting with World Wide Web–based intake and referral forms. The interested party is given the option when submitting the referral form to request more information through the mail, a telephone call from the program coordinator, or a response by e-mail. So far these indirect methods have proved less effective than more traditional and common methods such as direct telephone contact, voice mail, or walk-ins to the program office. As the Web becomes a more integrated part of campus life, this may change.

Most referral forms require the referral source to identify himself or herself, but some allow the referring party to remain anonymous or confidential. Use of referral forms is more common in high schools. Programs in these settings have experimented with anonymous referrals and have had success at nipping growing problems in the bud and not having problems they initially worried about, such as use of the forms as a joke or a form of harassment.

North Central College in Illinois uses referral forms as part of its student dispute resolution program. The forms are widely available and confidential, as the policy statement explains:

> Any member of the college community, including individual students and student organizations, may refer matters for mediation to the Dispute Resolution Program. Unlike traditional dispute resolution methods, mediation may be requested by students, rather than being imposed on them. As a result, it is hoped that the majority of cases will be referred by students directly to the program. A brief referral form will be made available at many campus locations including the: Office of Enrollment Management and Student Affairs, Office of the Dispute Resolution Program, Office of the Leadership, Ethics, and Values Program, Office of Academic Affairs, Office of Multicultural Affairs, Office of the Director of Residence Life, Residences of all Residence Hall Directors and Advisors, and Academic Division Secretaries. The referral form and the information it contains will be treated confidentially [North Central College Dispute Resolution Center Statement of Responsibilities, p. 9].

Some programs use a request-for-mediation form, which is similar to a referral form but may include some basic mediation rules that other programs might put on their agreement-to-mediation form (addressed in more detail later). This form assumes that the parties filling out the form are the primary parties involved, and they are formally asking the mediation program to become involved with their case.

**Coordinating Services.** An important issue that arises in the process of developing referral systems is the relationship of mediation to other processes. For instance, some programs serving students are closely linked to the student judicial system, and they receive cases that were deemed appropriate by judicial affairs administrators. On other campuses, the peer mediation program is totally separate from the judicial system and may have few contacts with the judicial program staff. On many campuses, the relationship between the mediation program and the judicial boards is clear from the start. At others there is a lot of initial testing and uncertainty about how the relationship between the two services should function, what kinds of cases are appropriate, and whether agreements reached in mediation are considered binding and enforceable by the judicial office. This is to be expected and seen as a learning opportunity. In some instances, a joint case review process may help build a better relationship between hearing boards and mediation programs, exploring possible increased cooperation between mediation and judicial affairs, at the prehearing and posthearing stages.

In a similar fashion, if the mediation center is handling employee disputes, it may get cases from the equal opportunity office, managers and supervisors, the ombuds or human resource office, or individuals who have also approached these other offices. There may be significant questions about how the mediation service relates to these other grievance processes (for example, does the "clock" stop on the time frame for using other grievance processes while mediation is being explored, can people have two simultaneous proceedings going on at the same time, or can and should different agencies check with each other to avoid engaging multiple processes simultaneously?). There are no easy answers to these kind of questions. What is required is an open dialogue with the other relevant offices to work out effective, fair, and efficient procedures.

One useful strategy is to diagram the relationships among key systems and see if they make sense and are clear. Figure 5.2 provides an example of the relationship between judicial and mediation services at the University of Illinois, Chicago. Each box on the diagram is tied to particular policy language explaining that process.

The following excerpt from the policies of the Center for Dispute Resolution located in the Dean of Students Office at the University of Florida provides another example of an approach taken by a student mediation center that works closely with the student judicial office:

> Referrals to the Center for Dispute Resolution are open to any member of the University community. Typically, referrals will come from one of three sources: self-referral, referral from a faculty member or campus office, or from the Student Judicial Affairs Office.
>
> Referrals from the Student Judicial Affairs Office have judicial charges pending and have been offered the opportunity to participate in mediation as an alternative to the formal judicial process. The advantages to mediation include: participating in a win/win negotiation, the parties determine what is appropriate action, and the student does not have a formal disciplinary record with the university.
>
> Parties referred by the Student Judicial Affairs Office are not required to reach an agreement, simply to participate in the mediation. For those cases where agreement is reached, the agreement would be binding under the Student Conduct Code, and successful completion of the process and agreement would negate any judicial

**Flow Chart of the Judicial Process**

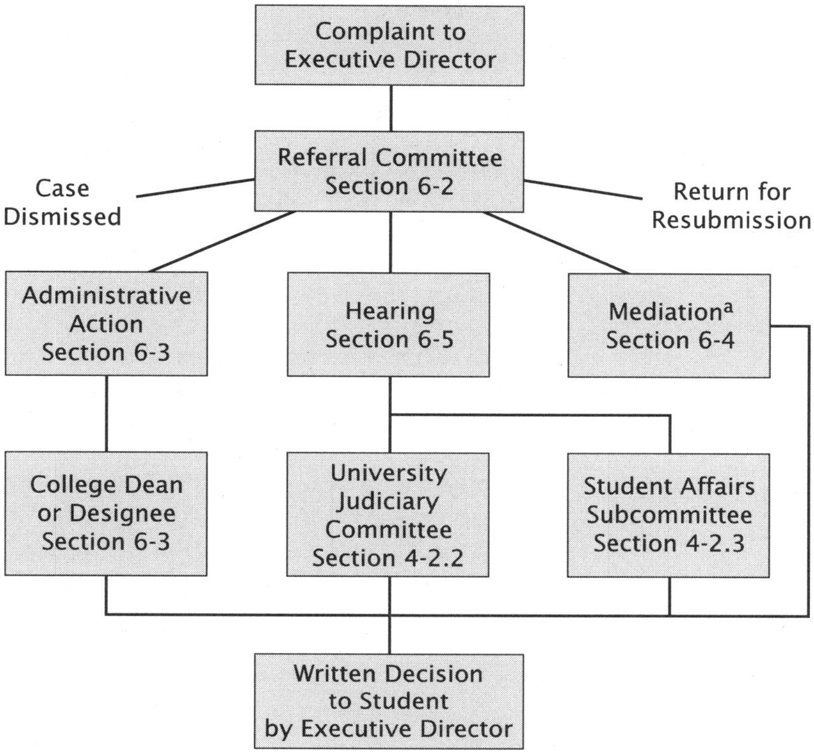

^a 6-4. Campus Mediation Center. The Campus Mediation Center cannot be utilized to adjudicate complaints involving academic dishonesty; otherwise, based solely on the complaint and, if available, the student's written response, the Referral Committee at its discretion may refer a complaint to the Coordinator of the Campus Mediation Center for action. The Coordinator of the Campus Mediation Center shall then contact the parties involved in the complaint and schedule a mediation session. The mediation session is to take place within 25 days of the referral of the complaint to the Coordinator of the Campus Mediation Center. A report outlining the settlement reached through the mediation session shall be sent to the Executive Director. If, due to the unwillingness of the parties to participate in the mediation session, or if the mediated settlement is not abided by, the Coordinator of the Campus Mediation Center shall return the complaint to the Referral Committee, noting why the mediation was unsuccessful. The Referral Committee may then refer the complaint to the Dean of the student's college or designee for administrative action, to the Student Affairs Subcommittee, or to the Senate Committee, where applicable, for a hearing. The Referral Committee may at its discretion, decide to dismiss the complaint. (From web site of Office of Student Judicial Affairs at the University of Illinois at Chicago)

**Figure 5.2. Sample Chart of the Relationship Between Mediation and Judicial Services**

*Source:* Web site of the Office of Student Judicial Affairs, University of Illinois at Chicago.

charges or record. Should agreement not be reached, the case would be referred back to the Student Judicial Affairs Office for resolution [www.oss.ufl.edu/Mediationbrochure.html, paragraphs 8–10].

Similar service coordination issues arise in programs working with staff and faculty conflicts. The planning team of the Consultation and Conciliation Service at the University of Michigan worked with the appropriate administrators to draft a policy that is now included in its book of policies. The following excerpt provides an example of an effort to articulate clearly the proper use of the service:

> Faculty and staff members may seek consultation and conciliation services directly from the Consultation and Conciliation Office. Representatives from the offices of Employee Relations, Affirmative Action and Faculty and Staff Assistance Programs will also provide consultation services wherever possible, and may refer individual faculty or staff members to the Consultation and Conciliation Office when conciliation services are requested. Such a referral may also be an appropriate course of action in cases where potential conflicts of interest exist. In addition, unit managers and administrators may refer faculty and staff members to the Consultation and Conciliation Office for assistance, or may recommend or request the services of a trained mediator to assist in resolving a dispute.
>
> With the exception of certain kinds of actions for which there exist more appropriate complaint or grievance procedures, conciliation may be sought at any time if both parties to a conflict or disagreement request or agree to it. Conciliation fails if the parties are unable to agree to a mutually acceptable outcome. Either party may choose to end conciliation efforts at any point in the process without penalty. When both parties in a formal grievance process request it, the time clock on the grievance procedure may be stopped for a time period satisfactory to both parties to allow for a good faith attempt to resolve the conflict or disagreement through conciliation [Johnson, 1996, p. 17]

This articulation of relationships can be complicated in the beginning because the various wrinkles have yet to be imagined. However, working out these kinds of programmatic relationships makes for a much less contentious existence over time. Most often a program's advisory committee can provide useful assistance in crafting initial workable arrangements that can be modified over time as need dictates. For an example of a carefully elaborated explanation of a student dispute resolution system with multiple options, readers may wish to consult the guide to *Student Conflict Resolution and Discipline at MIT*, available on the Web via Campus Mediation Resources, or directly at www.web.mit.edu/committees/conf-res/.

### Referral Guides
Another important aspect of building a referral network has to do with developing materials that make it easy for others to

understand the process and make use of it as appropriate. After the materials are developed, the task becomes getting them into the right hands. Many programs handling student cases find that one of their best sources of referrals are the residence assistants or hall directors who have day-to-day contact with students. It thus becomes important to build a relationship with these groups by presenting at their beginning-of-the-year training programs and by finding ways to meet their interests as well as the mediation program's own. Many resident assistants now have programming responsibilities that require them to schedule a certain number of events for students in their area during the course of the semester.

At Syracuse University we developed a series of short workshops that we offered to residence assistants, and many of them gladly accepted the offer to have our group present. The topics and titles of the workshops varied from year to year to keep the presentation fresh. Exhibit 5.3 provides descriptions from our workshop brochure of three of our more common offerings.

At Syracuse we developed a one- to two-hour workshop, dubbed Mediation 101, that was presented by a group of trained outreach volunteers. To get started, experienced trainers presented the workshop to interested outreach volunteers, stopping and commenting on the presentation skills as needed, to help prepare volunteers. Outreach volunteers who felt ready would then provide the workshop using a kit of overhead slides and handouts when a request was made. Section J in Resources, Forms, and Documents provides an example of the workshop outline used.

Another way we tried to connect with residence advisers was to develop a referral guide (see Section K in Resources, Forms, and Documents) that we distributed to them at staff meetings along with a stack of brochures. We also developed a similar guide using appropriately adapted examples and benefits for teaching assistants.

**Distinguishing Mediation from Other Services.** An important aspect of guiding referrals is to explain clearly what kinds of cases are appropriate for mediation and how mediation differs from other processes. In a unionized environment, or one where the most familiar mechanism for disputes has been the grievance process, many people need help understanding the differences. The staff at the Consultation and Conciliation Service addressed this question by posting a description of how mediation and grievance processes differ. This is reproduced in Exhibit 5.4. Similar guidelines can be developed in relation to student judicial affairs, sexual harassment procedures, and others.

### Making the Most of Conflict

This workshop addresses conflict as a potentially positive force, a view not commonly held in today's society. Through group participation, students' conflict styles are assessed and discussed, and an effective problem-solving model is introduced. Skills practiced in the training include reflective listening, separation of positions and interests to create "negotiation space," and strategies for conflict management.

### The ABC's of Strong Relationships

The relationships workshop is concerned primarily with interpersonal communication skills. The intent of the workshop is to provide students with a model for managing relationships that builds trust and reduces escalation of conflict. Skills addressed in the workshop include reflective listening, assertion, and conflict management.

### How to Run a Successful Meeting

This workshop introduces group facilitation skills for making meetings more effective and efficient. Topics include agenda creation, maximizing participant involvement, the role of the facilitator, sharing power, using consensus, and the technique of brainstorming. Skills gained from this workshop can be applied to meetings of student organizations, clubs, and in the workplace.

**Exhibit 5.3. Sample Student Workshops, Syracuse University Campus Mediation Center**

*Source:* Conflict Prevention Toolkit brochure, Syracuse University. Used with permission.

**Providing Feedback to Referral Sources.** An important aspect of nurturing referral systems is developing methods to provide feedback to referral sources without breaking the agreement to uphold confidentiality. The referral sources must know that the mediation center has responded appropriately, so that they can begin to develop confidence in the process. One way to accomplish this is by using a standardized feedback form that is sent to administrative referral sources after the scheduled mediation date has passed. The form provides information on whether a mediation was held and if not, why, and if an agreement (full or partial) was reached. A copy of one such form is provided in Section L in Resources, Forms, and Documents.

The process of promoting a new program requires creativity and the ability to build on preexisting relationships on campus. It also takes time, as does any other new service, before people fully understand what the program does and how it can help them.

| GRIEVANCE | CONCILIATION |
|---|---|
| Designed to allow employees to address disagreement about or alleged violation of policy or contract provisions. | Designed to address a broad range of disputes that may or may not be appropriate for the grievance process. |
| An employee entitlement. If an employee grieves, management has the obligation to respond. | A mutually voluntary process. Either party may request it, and the other party is free to accept or decline. |
| Once a grievance is filed, a response must be given within a certain time limit. | Not defined by time limits; in fact, either party may decide to withdraw from the conciliation at any point, without penalty. |
| Is formal and a matter of record. | Is informal and off the record. |
| Results in an "answer." | Results in a mutual search for a resolution, and may or may not find one. |
| At the second and third steps, asks a third party to review facts, judge the situation, and decide for or against the grievant. | Does not hear evidence, judge the situation, or provide an answer. Instead, assists parties to explore concerns, issues, and interests and look for solutions. |
| A decision is made for or against the grievant; at the third step, this is the final answer internal to the university. | Any decision will be made by the parties themselves and must be acceptable to both. Otherwise, the conciliation is stalemated, and there is no answer. |
| Is designed to review two opposing points of view. | Is designed to seek common understanding and mutual agreement. |
| Cannot be held against the employee! | Cannot be held against the employee! |

### Why Others Have Found Conciliation Helpful

- Being heard off the record, with no risk of embarrassment or retaliation
- Structured professional assistance in discussing tough issues
- Being able to explore the other party's concerns privately
- Achieving an outcome that brings "opposing sides" closer together

University of Michigan Consultation and Conciliation Service
Neutral Third-party Dispute Resolution for Faculty and Staff
All information will be kept confidential, UNLESS the concern involves threats, illegal harassment or acts of a criminal nature that pose an imminent danger to other people.

Exhibit 5.4.  Grievance and Conciliation Procedures: A Comparison

*Source:* University of Michigan Consultation and Conciliation Service. (Regents of University of Michigan, 1997.) Used with permission.

# CHAPTER 6

# Operating and Maintaining the Program

Managing the day-to-day operation of a mediation service requires a certain level of organization and consistency in order to be effective and relatively painless for all parties involved. In addition, quality control standards and procedures must be established so that the integrity of the program remains intact.

## Case Intake Procedures

Intake sessions are an integral part of the mediation process. They constitute the first step in mediation, as well as the first exposure to a program. The initial interview is the time to build the client's trust and confidence in the service and in the person handling intake. The purpose of an intake session is threefold: determining whether a case is suitable for mediation, deciding what kind of person would be the best mediator for the client, and providing the client with enough understanding of mediation so that he or she can make an educated decision as to whether mediation is the appropriate route for the resolution of their conflict.

### Determining Case Suitability

Probably the most complicated task among these three confronting the intake worker is that of deciding whether a case is suitable for mediation. Generally mediation should not be conducted with parties who are intoxicated or have major psychological disorders that seriously impair their judgment. Cases involving domestic violence are typically screened out. Also, mediation is not an appropriate substitute for therapy or counseling. When one or several of the parties to the conflict are emotionally ill or under so much stress that rational discussion would be impossible, mediation should be avoided or delayed.

There are a number of different ways to think about whether a case is suitable for mediation:

- Whether the case is likely to be solvable through mediation
- Whether anyone would be potentially hurt by using the process
- Whether there are any local practices and policies that may impinge on mediation
- Whether mediation is the best choice of processes given the parties' primary interests.

In terms of whether the issue can be solved by mediation, a number of factors come into play: whether the second party will agree to try mediation (a basic question); the complexity of the case and the number of parties involved (the more parties and issues involved, the more difficult and time-consuming the process becomes); whether the case involves values and beliefs or tangible needs (conflicts over values can be tough and may require a different approach than standard mediation); and the desire or need to determine truth or falsehood, guilt or innocence (which mediation is not set up to do).

In terms of the potential for parties to be hurt in the process of mediation, consider the following checklist of flags developed by experienced trainers from the Mennonite Conciliation Service (MCS). These issues should be seriously considered in evaluating specific cases:

1. Do the parties fully understand the process? Have they agreed with all arrangements and ground rules before the process begins?
2. Is there information indicating that any of the parties or their family members are in threat of physical danger? If so, has this been reported to the appropriate authorities?
3. Has there been physical, emotional, sexual, or other abuse of power in the relationship? Are any court actions pending involving abuse or other criminal actions between the parties?
4. Are there issues of legal competency in decision-making involving any party?
5. Is abuse of drugs or alcohol a concern? Other significant mental health problems?
6. Do extremes of power imbalance exist which would prevent legitimate negotiation?

7. Does a party express fear or intimidation from emotional dynamics?
8. Does either party appear to be totally inflexible or otherwise demonstrate bad faith or manipulation of the process?
9. Are cultural differences so significant between the parties, or between the mediator and the parties, as to challenge the appropriateness of the intervention [Price, 1995, p. 265]?

Many community and court-affiliated mediation programs have clear guidelines that require programs to screen for domestic violence or child abuse and refer these matters to other intervention services. If the program is likely to handle relationship issues, family disputes, or parent-child cases, the center coordinator should get copies of guidelines for dealing with domestic violence in mediation and prepare mediators with special training to address these topics. Sometimes these issues do not come out in the initial intake process, and mediators need to be aware of how to respond should such matters come up in a mediation session.

The politics and practices already in place on campus also have a significant bearing on what cases are appropriate for mediation. Perhaps the best way to handle the potentially problematic issues that may arise is to develop some initial guidelines for the intake person's use. Chapter Five reviewed a few examples of these kinds of policies. The planning group should already have addressed some of the broad outlines for acceptable case types and developed communication lines with other involved dispute handlers on campus so that the mediation center process can be fine-tuned over time.

Joseph Stulberg, in his book *Taking Charge/Managing Conflict* (1987), suggests a number of criteria that can be used to decide whether mediation is the best process among those available:

1. Efficiency (time and money) of the process from the participant's perspective
2. The public vs. private nature of the process
3. The degree and accuracy of fact-finding efforts necessary to support solutions
4. The precedents set by the results
5. The wisdom of the results
6. The degree of participation in the process of resolving the dispute by those who must live with the results
7. Compliance with and durability of the outcome
8. The fairness and justice of the process
9. The precedents set by using the process to resolve the particular dispute
10. The impact of using the dispute resolution process on the quality of the relationship among the disputing parties
11. The administrative costs of implementing the process [Stulberg, 1987, p. 18]

Stulberg points out that the process of mediation is strong in some of these areas and weaker in others. If parties are clear, with the coordinator's help if need be, on which of the above elements are most important to them, it can help them choose an appropriate process. For instance, mediation often takes some time in dialogue to conclude successfully, but it is often quicker than more formal remedies, like court or administrative or judicial proceedings. When compared to other methods, mediation's informal nature can greatly reduce administrative costs and direct financial costs to the parties. Because mediation requires both sides to agree to the proposed solutions to reach closure, it does not serve parties well to antagonize each other. Mediation is thus strong on maintaining or improving the quality of the relationship between parties.

Mediation has a high degree of participation by the parties, which can be important in some circumstances when people have felt left out or without a voice. The privacy of mediation promotes candid discussion and minimal hostile posturing, but it also limits the number of other people who are made aware of the problem and the number involved in its resolution. Mediation typically increases all parties' compliance with the outcome because people tend to abide by agreements achieved voluntarily, but if the agreements break down, most programs are not in a position to enforce them. The precedential value of the substantive agreement reached in mediation is limited because of the privacy of the process and because the terms reflect only the preferences and priorities of the parties present. However, the precedential value of using the mediation *process* to resolve certain disputes is high because its use acknowledges that all parties have concerns that must be addressed. Although it permits creativity in solutions, mediation does not require the parties to choose the best possible solution (whereas other problem-solving processes might). Mediation does not rely on strong factual underpinnings to justify specific terms of agreement, and mediators do not make determinations of fact. The process and outcomes of mediation may feel fair to the parties involved, but the outcomes are not subject to the kinds of fairness tests that other rights-based procedures might rely on. It should be clear by now that mediation is not the right tool for every dispute, but it is a good process for many.

## Elements of the Intake Process

The person handling intake is often also the case coordinator. The case coordinator is responsible for scheduling the session and mediators and often for being present before or during the mediation to greet the parties and provide assistance as needed. It is important to remember that the intake person can affect the way the conflict is viewed by the individual who comes to a program. Therefore, some training in both the development of a philosophical understanding of intake work and the area of specialized skills may be appropriate.

An essential aspect of intake work is the appreciation of the importance of conflict in life. Conflict is a normal part of everyday life that can be productive and of positive value. It can uncover buried issues and open them up for discussion and resolution, and it can improve the communication process between people. Therefore, it is important that intake workers honor and validate the importance of the conflict that is brought to them. This in turn allows the disputants to accept their conflict and find its significance for their lives. Since this acceptance may be the first step in changing the situation, it is crucial that the acknowledgment be made directly to the disputants.

## Goals and Characteristics of Intake Workers

The goals of the intake worker are to foster a cooperative process, establish trust, interview the disputants, and ascertain the problem. In addition to a commitment to the perspective that conflict is a normal part of life, an intake worker should possess the following skills and personal characteristics:

- Flexibility in style, since it is necessary to adopt whatever style suits the situation. It is important to frame the world in the client's terms. If a client is reluctant to discuss the dispute, the intake worker will need to take an active role in leading the conversation. Other times the client wants to direct the conversation, and the intake person responds accordingly.

- A friendly and honest manner with the ability to empathize and sympathize. This helps to build trust.

- An active and careful listener, which demonstrates interest as well as allowing for an accurate understanding of the situation.

- Comfort with eye contact, for this increases trust and encourages the parties to share information.

- Good questioning and interviewing techniques. Discovering who, what, where, and why is an important part of the work.

- The ability to be diplomatic and persuasive, especially when contacting the second party to a dispute.

Another factor to be taken into consideration when selecting intake people is their credibility with the disputants. Their visibility and reputation may determine their success. Some campuses have taken a decentralized approach to intake by designating a range of people from within the university structure acting in this capacity. At the University of Texas, San Antonio, the trained mediators and intake workers have special brass nameplates on their doors designating them as problem-solving liaisons. A decentralized group of intake workers may include affirmative action officers, student activities advisers, counseling psychologists, and graduate assistants. Initial intake interviews are thus conducted in the various offices of the interviewers. Intake people holding official positions within a college may hinder or promote perceptions of impartiality, depending on the population being served, because of their position, their reputation, or the location of their office. By contrast, at the majority of campuses, intake workers are an integral part of the mediation program staff, and their credibility rests on the credibility of the program, with interviews occurring in the project offices or on the telephone.

Regardless of what options are chosen with respect to who handles intake and where intake sessions are located, there are some basic guidelines to the formation of an intake interview:

> Intake sessions should be set up with each party individually. Many programs use telephone intake because it is convenient to arrange, but ideally the interview should be conducted in person.

> The purpose of intake is to give the client some help with his or her problem. This could mean referral or scheduling a mediation session. Thus mediation program staff need a good working knowledge (and list of telephone numbers) of resources on campus.

> The intake person should take the lead from the client as to the most appropriate interview style.

> The ideal time frame for the interview is about twenty minutes. The task is not to resolve the problem but to understand the content and issues of the dispute and explain the mediation process. Nevertheless, if the session lasts longer, that is fine. By all means, clock watching should be avoided.

> Introduce the principles of mediation immediately so as to get the disputants familiar with this approach to viewing a conflict. For example, an intake worker might ask the client to present the other person's point of view of the dispute.

Forms are important. It is critical to get the names, addresses, and telephone numbers of the people involved in the conflict, as well as a schedule of available times for mediation.

Intake workers should keep their opinions and value judgments to themselves. Their job is to provide assistance and begin to lay the foundation of mediation as a neutral process.

A sample intake form is shown in Exhibit 6.1. Although the form contains room for other pertinent information, intake workers often do not fill in this additional information until the interview is over. They feel that shifting the focus from the form to the person in front of them helps to alleviate the sense that mediation is just another bureaucratic process, a perception in clear contradiction to the goals of most mediation programs.

The precise nature of an intake session will vary due to the personality of the interviewer and client and to the interviewer's previous successful experiences. Most programs employ only a few intake people, and as a result, the workers have the opportunity to refine and polish their skills and style.

## Securing the Second Party's Participation

To secure the second party's participation, the University of Massachusetts Mediation Project (and many other similar programs) engages the first party (often referred to as Party A, or the complainant) in working with the project to get the other person to an intake interview. The complainant is asked to contact the other party to inform him of the situation and to request that he call the case coordinator for an interview. It is explained to the first party that making this contact is a strong signal to the other person that she is ready to deal with the problem and that it can be threatening and alienating to the other person to be contacted by a stranger. If the complainant refuses to make the contact, the case coordinator will handle it. He will send a letter to the second party, followed by a telephone call. If the client has agreed to contact the other party and there has been no response within a week, the case coordinator calls the first party to verify that she has made the contact and then sends the other party a letter. If the second party fails to respond to the letter, the UMass Project views it as a clear message that he is not ready for mediation or does not feel it is an appropriate form of resolution. At this point in the process, no response is accepted as the response, since mediation's success is dependent on its voluntary nature.

Campus Mediation Center
Case Information Sheet

Case Number: _____     CMC Intake Person: _____

Name of Party A:_____     Contact Date: _____

Address: _____     Phone: _____

Student:   YES   NO   If not, other university affiliation: _____ Relevant Demographic Info:

Referred to CMC by: _____

Description of Situation _____

_____

_____

_____

_____

_____

Possible times
for mediation
session

Other Party/ies Involved:

Name: _____     Name: _____

Address: _____     Address: _____

Phone: _____     Phone: _____

University Affiliation: _____     University Affiliation: _____

Relevant Demographic Info: _____     Relevant Demographic Info: _____

Date of Contacts: _____     Date of Contacts: _____

Previous interventions—legal or otherwise: _____

Possible times
for mediation
session

Other Relevant Information: _____

_____

Mediators Assigned to Case: _____

Location and Time of Session: _____

Exhibit 6.1.  Sample Intake Form

The manner in which the intake worker communicates the concerns of the first party to the second party is just as important as this initial contact between the parties. The intake person is not an advocate of one position over another or one person over another. If he is an advocate of anything, it is of the mediation process itself. His strategy is to focus on the other party's willingness to mediate and introduce the issues in a general and neutral way. A sample opening statement for a telephone contact might be: "My name is _____. I'm calling from the Campus Mediation Center, a service that helps community members resolve problems cooperatively. We were contacted by _____, who heard of our program and thought it might be a way for the two of you to settle your differences." He then briefly explains the first party's concern and interest in resolution, being clear that neither the program nor the mediator represents the first party. The intake person gives the other party a chance to explain his version by asking open-ended questions—for example: "_____ explained to me his concerns about _____. I'd like to hear your point of view. Can you tell me about this situation?" As the person responds, the intake worker must employ good reflective listening skills to begin the rapport-building process. Sometimes it is necessary to refer to a particular issue because of a glaring omission or discrepancy between the stories. Still, it should be raised in an impartial manner. This delicate balancing provides the framework for building a safe environment for the clients.

Although an intake worker and or the party may decide that a case is not suitable for mediation, the interview is still considered part of the mediation process and is bound by confidentiality. Each institution needs to make its own policies as to whether certain specific types of disclosures will be exempt from confidentiality. In most instances, they are. Moreover, depending on locality and types of cases the mediation center is handling, state or federal laws may inform this decision, in particular as relates to child abuse, spousal assault, or credible threats to harm another person. The critical point is that these philosophical and political choices are well publicized and that clients are given ample warning if the conversation veers toward this murky territory during an intake session.

Once the parties have agreed on a date, time, and location for the session, letters and a brochure are mailed out, reminding the parties of the meeting particulars, as well as informing them in more detail about the goals of the session and the mediation rules. At this stage many programs include their agreement-to-mediate form, which parties are asked to read and bring to the session for review and signing. Several sample agreement-to-mediate forms are included in Section M of Resources, Forms, and Documents. Two are from student mediation programs, and one is from a multiconstituency service. Although they vary in style and emphasis (for instance, the North Dakota program's form displays more of a transformative mediation style), these forms are all used to ensure that the parties understand the basic context for mediation and to limit the potential liability risk of the program.

Many programs, such as those handling largely roommate disputes, choose not to use agreement-to-mediate forms, arguing that they frame the situation in a way that is too formal and legalistic to make sense in the informal and low-risk settings where they work. These programs use their brochures and the mediator introductory statements to explain the mediation process and what can be expected of the service, and leave it at that. Any agreement-to-mediate form should be reviewed by the campus attorney before it is used.

Some programs include the names of the mediators assigned to the case in the package sent out ahead of time, giving the parties the opportunity to reject a particular mediator if they are concerned about other outside relationships. In this situation, the office then assigns another mediator from its roster, giving the parties a second chance to accept or reject the suggested mediator before settling on the final intervention team. Unlike in labor-management or business disputes, this process of being able to strike a certain number of mediators is not very common among campus programs. However, some variation of this approach may be particularly helpful on small campuses where there are many overlapping relationships. More typical, perhaps, is the process of asking potential mediators if they have any concerns about handling a particular case given the parties involved. This gives the mediators the opportunity to decline if it seems inappropriate or to suggest that the question be raised by telephone with the parties prior to the session to solicit their reaction to the choice of mediators. During their opening statement, the mediators clarify any significant existing relationships between the mediators and parties, providing the disputants a chance to request a new mediator if they have strong concerns.

Some programs also distribute information ahead of time specifically designed to help the parties begin to prepare for the mediation session. A sample document along these lines, prepared by Tim Hedeen, former coordinator of the Syracuse Campus Mediation Center, is presented as Section N of Resources, Forms, and Documents. Also pertinent is the "Eliciting Resistance vs. Gaining Cooperation" handout distributed by the Mediation Project at the University of Colorado (see www.Colorado.EDU/Ombuds/elicit.html).

## Choosing and Scheduling Mediators

Once the parties have agreed to try mediation, the program coordinator needs to choose and schedule mediators for the session. Programs differ as to how they manage this process, with some adopting a strict rotating roster, approaching the mediators who are next in line in the rotation first and working their way down the list. More common is some combination of objective and subjective criteria, based on the characteristics of the case, the kind of skills or knowledge that seems most appropriate for the case, the potential chemistry between the two mediators in a co-mediation team, and some effort to give all members of the mediator pool who have been deemed ready a chance to mediate. There may also be an element of self-selection, wherein mediators are able to choose in advance the kinds of cases they would like to handle or those they prefer to not be involved with.

There are both objective and subjective criteria in choosing mediators:

### Objective Criteria

- Matching of mediators with disputants in terms of age, ethnic background, sex, and other characteristics
- Teaming a new with an old mediator
- Availability
- Unfamiliarity with the parties
- Rotation

### Subjective Criteria

- Choosing mediators with complementary styles.
- Case complexity. Some mediators do well only with straightforward cases with few issues.
- Type of mediator personality or style that the case demands. Some cases demand a mediator who is strong and direct; other cases require little direction and are best suited to a more reserved and nondirective mediator.
- Matching people to cases to further ongoing training and evaluation goals. Who is in the pool of mediators, what are their strengths, and where do they need more experience?
- Pairing of a strong with a weak mediator. Perhaps it is necessary to use someone in order to match certain characteristics of the disputant, despite the fact that the case is complex and the mediator inexperienced. It might be necessary to pair that mediator with a very experienced, highly skilled one.

- Favoring of multiskilled mediators.
- Political implications. Certain cases may be appropriate for students to handle based on administrative reservations.
- Intuition. Who would disputants get along with? What is an intake worker's sense about matching a person with a particular case?

Clearly intake people must be capable of insightful and intuitive decision making. The forming of the right constellation of people is as important as the mediation process in bringing a conflict to resolution.

Regardless of the method for choosing mediators, having a regular system for keeping track of mediators' availability can save hours on the telephone and missed mediations. Depending on the caseload, two different methods are commonly used for scheduling. One approach for programs with a steady caseload—for instance, campus mediation clinics that handle cases referred from the local juvenile or small claims court—is to sign up mediators for specific time slots and then match the cases to the mediator. If there is no mediation scheduled for a mediator's time slot, that person is called (or calls the program), and the scheduled mediation time is canceled. A second approach is to schedule the mediation at a convenient time for the parties and then find mediators available at that time. In this approach, mediators fill out monthly or quarterly calendars of their availability (usually marking off times that they are not typically available on a weekly schedule) so that the program coordinator can schedule mediations at appropriate times. In either approach, the case coordinator is well advised to check with the chosen mediators to confirm their availability.

Case management practices vary considerably. A checklist of steps that need to be taken as the case progresses is useful for managing the process. A detailed script for this kind of case management approach is provided in Section O of Resources, Forms, and Documents.

At Syracuse and Nova Southeastern universities, on the day of the mediation, the mediators are provided with a packet that contains information from the intake sheet on the parties who are expected to attend, pens, a pad of blank paper, additional agreement-to-mediate forms (in case the parties did not bring theirs), a calculator (if it might be needed), an opening statement checklist (to remind mediators to cover the main points of their opening), blank agreement forms (see Section P of Resources, Forms, and Documents), a postsession report form (see Section Q), and a session evaluation form for the participants to fill out and return after the mediation.

If the parties reach an agreement in the session, the mediators work with them to draft an agreement that the parties review and then write up on a blank agreement form, which is then photocopied so that each party has a copy, as well as one for the mediation center's files. Some programs use three- or four–part preprinted blank agreement forms, keeping the top, and most legible, copy for the mediation center files. This is helpful if there is no easy access to a copier at the mediation site or the session takes place in different rooms.

After the session, the mediators are asked to discuss the case with each other, reviewing it as a learning opportunity, and then to fill out a postmediation review form (see Section Q of Resources, Forms, and Documents), which provides the center with more information about what transpired.

Shortly after the session, an evaluation form is sent to the parties inquiring about the quality of the mediation experience for them. About six months later, a follow-up evaluation is sent to see how the situation has held up. (Program evaluation issues are reviewed more fully in Chapter Seven.)

## Technology

Given the relatively small caseload of most campus programs, it is not often necessary to develop specialized computer software for case management. Nevertheless, the National Association for Community Mediation has been working on identifying a number of case intake software programs that it intends to endorse.

A programmer can also develop software for the program's particular needs. I was given a copy of an intake program that was built with FileMaker Pro that is quite nicely done. A new commercial offering, Mediation Manager, from TekData (www.tekdatainc.com) is also worth considering. One of the advantages of intake software is that it can be protected with a password, providing an additional level of confidentiality, and it is useful for preparing annual reports and summaries. Programs can also be set up to prepare correspondence.

## Protecting the Program and Participants

Just as important as promoting a program and managing its basic functions is developing ways to protect the integrity of the program and manage any risks associated with running it. As of this writing, I have no knowledge of any legal problems that have involved a campus mediation program. My thoughts here are thus largely speculative, intended to help program coordinators think broadly about the issues that might adversely affect a service. Although it is possible that a college or university could be sued for actions related to its mediation program, it is not probable if programs maintain some basic standards of practice and risk management. In fact, it may be that colleges without campus mediation services may be seen as negligent in the long run.*

## Quality Control

There is a growing awareness of the importance of quality control in mediation programs. As a good example, the National Association for Community Mediation (NAFCM) has developed a set of basic quality standards with direct relevance to campus mediation programs. High-quality practitioner development typically involves the following elements:

1. *Screening and Recruitment:* Community mediation training participants are carefully recruited to reflect the diversity of the community and screened to identify individuals whose personal skills and commitment to community service are well-suited for the role of mediator.
2. *Basic Mediation Training:* Successful completion of a basic community mediation training is mandatory for participation with a community mediation program. Preparation and role-play exercises are designed to reflect specific dispute types handled by the mediation program.
3. *Evaluation of Mediation Training Participants:* Evaluation of a community mediation training participant's mediation skills is ongoing and comprehensive.
4. *Apprenticeship:* Apprenticeship with a community mediation program follows the successful completion of a basic community mediation training and offers challenges appropriate to the general skill level of the newly trained mediator.
5. *Co-mediation Model:* Community mediation programs support the widespread use of co-mediation to provide opportunities for peer mentorship and peer review.
6. *Continuing Education:* Continuing education is either strongly recommended or often required by community mediation programs in order to retain and enhance the skills necessary to provide quality mediation services on an ongoing basis.
7. *Advanced Training:* Advanced training is required by community mediation programs that provide mediation services in substantive areas such as custody and visitation, parent-child, housing, victim-offender, commercial, special education, and public policy.

---

*I am not a lawyer and am not providing legal advice here. I strongly encourage all campus mediation programs to consider consulting their university counsel to arrange for a personalized legal risk audit or preventive checkup.

Participants in these trainings must have successfully completed a basic mediation training and must demonstrate sufficient competency in the area of advanced practice in order to provide these mediation services.

8. *Trainer Qualities and Responsibilities:* The community mediation trainer will generally have extensive experience as a mediator in order to be accepted as a credible teacher and role model. Thorough knowledge of the mediation process and a mediator's techniques and strategic choices is also essential.

9. *Trainer/Training Evaluation:* Community mediation programs solicit evaluations of the training and each trainer during and at the conclusion of each training presented. Feedback from training participants contributes to the ongoing refinement of effective training materials and styles.

10. *Standards of Practice:* Many community mediation programs, some in collaboration with their statewide association, have developed guidelines or standards of practice which govern the conduct of their community mediators. Community mediation programs believe that mediators have an obligation to the public and the profession to conduct their practice in a competent and ethical manner [Brodrick, Carroll, and Hart, 1996, on-line, paragraphs 6–15].

Campus mediation programs should strive to maintain similar quality control standards, while acknowledging that early in the program's life, opportunities for apprenticeships will be limited. As the caseload increases and the roster of mediators grows more experienced, programs should incorporate apprenticeship models. If possible, campus mediators are also encouraged to explore volunteering with their local community mediation program as a way to get more experience handling a broader range of cases.

## Standards of Practice for Campus Mediators

As the field of mediation has grown, professional groups working in different sectors of the field have begun to articulate best practices for third-party neutral intervenors. Some of these standards are now available over the World Wide Web. Following are some Web sites where they can be located:

"Due Process Protocol": www.igc.org/naarb/ (under "Protocol")

"Ethical Standards of Professional Responsibility," Society for Professionals in Dispute Resolution (SPIDR): www.spidr.org//

"Model Standards of Conduct for Mediators," American Arbitration Association/American Bar Association/SPIDR: www.adr.org (under "Codes")

"Guidelines for Voluntary Mediation Programs Instituted by Agencies Charged with Enforcing Workplace Rights": www.spidr.org//

"Quality Assurances Statement," National Association for Community Mediation (NAFCM): www.nafcm.org (under "News")

"Interim ADA Mediation Standards, "ADA Mediation Standards Work Group: www.mediate.com/articles/adaltr.cfm

The discussion of program standards specifically for campus mediation has only just begun. A working group from the Conflict Resolution in Education Network and the On-Campus ADR Committee of the Association of Judicial Affairs has begun preliminary work, but there is much to be done. There is as yet no consensus statement on best practices in campus mediation. Generally programs need to consider their responsibilities to their clients (participants in mediation), their staff and mediators, and the college and community within which they work, and develop policies and shared expectations that ensure best practice. Section R in Resources, Forms, and Documents provides two good examples of codes of conduct used by particular campus programs in their training of volunteer mediators that may be of some use in developing policies. Given the diversity of kinds of cases that campus programs handle, we may see a more careful delineation of best practices for different types of campus programs serving different populations as the field matures.

## Thinking About Liability

Given the increasing litigiousness of society in general, it is not surprising that many administrators in higher education are nervous about the legal implications of a new campus mediation program. Of course, this is true for all new services on campus. There is always an underlying concern that the university or program staff might be sued if someone is injured due to their participation in mediation.

The law of torts provides an injured person the right to sue someone else to obtain compensation. In any tort lawsuit, however, two different basic questions need to be answered. The first is whether the legal system will recognize such a lawsuit. This is a matter of public policy and is based on balancing the benefits provided to society against the rights of individuals to not be harmed. The second question is whether the lawsuit, if recognized by the courts, will ultimately succeed. This is primarily determined by the legal concept of negligence.

**Public Policy and Mediation.** Although due care is always required, a number of conditions may mitigate the potential liability of colleges or program staff providing campus mediation services. For instance, it is generally agreed that mediation (especially among peers) teaches participants a unique and important set of life skills, helping to further the educational goals of the institution. In addition, there is a growing awareness, evidenced by the relatively new campus crime statistics reporting requirements, that colleges cannot ignore the violence that sometimes occurs on campus. At the elementary and secondary levels federal, state, and local governments across the country support the establishment of peer mediation programs in educational settings. The Safe Schools Act, for instance, is federal legislation that attempts to deal with school violence. Peer mediation is specifically mentioned in this act as one creative approach to violence prevention that the law intends to encourage. We would assume that these concepts apply at the postsecondary level. We also have seen considerable federal support for the use of ADR methods in areas such as the resolution of equal opportunity disputes and access disputes related to the Americans with Disabilities Act. These kinds of public policy considerations make it reasonable to believe that college peer mediation programs may be somewhat immune to lawsuits because of their benefits. In fact, one could argue that if violence on campus escalates, liability might be imposed on colleges and universities that fail to implement violence prevention measures like mediation.

**An Internal Mechanism for Dispute Resolution.** Having a mediation program in place provides another internal dispute resolution option that people may consider prior to filing a lawsuit. This can be a benefit to the institution interested in minimizing lawsuits. Kaplin and Lee (1997), in their legal guide for student affairs professionals, point out that

> fair and accessible dispute resolution systems, besides being useful administrative tools in their own right, can also insulate institutions from lawsuits. Students who feel that their arguments or grievances will be fairly considered within the institution may forego resort to the courts. If students ignore internal mechanisms in favor of immediate judicial action, the courts may refer the students to the institution. Under the "exhaustion-of-remedies" doctrine, courts may require plaintiffs to exhaust available remedies within the institution before bringing the complaint to court [p. 327].

Adding mediation as a step in the grievance-handling process can provide a low-cost, interest-based forum for resolving the problem at hand.

**Taking Due Care.** An institution or individual has a duty or obligation, recognized by law, to conform to a certain standard of conduct for the protection of others against a foreseeable, unreasonable risk. Should a program not be immune from being sued for various public policy reasons, the program would have to show negligence in order to be found liable. In other words, it would be shown that it failed to conform to the standard required, there was a reasonably close causal connection between the failure to conform to the standard required and the resulting injury, and there was an actual loss or injury to a third party.

Generally institutions may be found negligent when they fail to abide by what lawyers refer to as the standard of reasonable conduct in the face of apparent risks. Unlike the public policy issues, the question of negligence is one that mediation programs can have some control over. Programs have a duty to protect others from foreseeable and unreasonable risks. It can be assumed that there is always some risk involved in various activities and that what a program needs to be aware of is risks that would be unreasonable to subject people to. The idea of reasonable conduct is subject to considerable interpretation, because there are no concrete rules for determining what constitutes reasonable conduct. In terms of campus mediation programs, such standards of reasonable conduct have not yet been established or tested. However, a program that follows the suggested best practices discussed in terms of case screening, program management, and mediator training should be perceived to have acted reasonably.

There are at least three potential legal duties that exist in colleges that programs should attend to in the design, implementation, and maintenance of a mediation program:

- The duty to supervise with reasonable care
- The duty to use reasonable care in selection, retention, and training
- The duty to act reasonably to prevent harm

The duty to supervise mediators properly would most likely fall on the program coordinator. The actual degree of supervision of mediators would need to meet standards of reasonable conduct in the light of the apparent risks. Fortunately, these standards are often comparable to common sense. Supervisors should consider the type of conflict being mediated, the previous history (if known) of the disputants, and the level of experience of the mediators. Most cases involving such interpersonal conflicts as noise levels, habits, return or repair of borrowed or broken items, and misunderstandings do not require a great deal of supervision. If a dispute in mediation was one in which prior violence had been an issue and the parties were thought to be volatile, the duty to supervise would increase. If mediators are very inexperienced, the need for supervision increases as well. In the case of mediation between parties who had been violent to each other in the past, it would make sense to have the coordinator present as an observer, to devise a way to engage the assistance of a nearby security guard on short notice, or to increase the size of the mediator panel. The intake worker and mediator would announce and enforce a no-weapons rule, and if face-to-face interaction seemed to escalate hostilities, caucuses would be used. The duty to supervise applies to the entire mediation process, such as during the intake process and while disputants are waiting for the session to begin. Many programs screen out cases involving violence, greatly reducing this kind of concern, and others provide special training for mediators who handle more complex cases. Various protocols for handling cases involving domestic violence are now available that provide considerations for reducing potential violence as well.

A duty to use reasonable care in the selection, retention, and training would most likely apply to the mediation program coordinator hired to manage the program. Consider the types of conflict the mediation program handles. Given the target population and the most likely kinds of cases, a particular program might decide that some advanced training for the coordinator is in order—perhaps in prejudice reduction, crisis intervention, or disability issues. The issue of selection, retention, and training might be seen to extend to the choice of mediators as well, although this is unlikely given the difficulty of defining a proper and agreed-on standard for the evaluation of mediators and the value placed on a diverse mediator pool. Nevertheless, it is wise to use reasonable care in the retention and training of mediators as well.

The duty to act reasonably to prevent harm has direct relevance to mediation programs. Whenever a program is aware of a participant's propensity to do harm, it has a duty to take reasonable steps to prevent the person from doing so. In mediation, a participant's propensity to do harm would usually be discovered in the form of threats made against oneself or others. Threats are not uncommon in mediation sessions. Thus, mediation program coordinators and mediators should become adept at determining when a threat crosses the threshold of danger that necessitates action outside the scope of mediation. When this threshold is crossed, programs may have a legal duty to warn the individuals at risk and the proper legal authorities.

A number of factors can help determine the level of danger associated with a threat: the specificity of the threat, its potential severity for harm, whether the threat is directed at an identifiable victim, whether the victim is aware of the threat, and the imminence of danger. Given the right combination of these factors, a mediation program would incur a legal duty to warn the proper people. If so, the coordinator's actions would then have to meet the standard of reasonable care. Whenever there is a concern over threats, documenting the events and the attempts to respond appropriately is important.

**Confidentiality and Its Limits.** The duty to warn is related to the issue of confidentiality, which is offered to participants in mediation. The duty to warn can conflict with the notion of confidentiality. The scope of confidentiality in mediation may be affected by the state because many states have laws that require mediators to keep certain information confidential and some states provide a privilege of confidentiality to mediators. The scope of confidentiality generally applies to premediation screening and intake interviews, the mediation session itself, postmediation discussions among mediators and supervisors, and all records associated with mediation. State and federal law also may create the duty among specified professionals, or a more general duty, to report certain crimes, such as felonies or gunshot wounds and child abuse and neglect. Because of variations in state laws and the uncertainty as to whether particular laws apply on campus as well as off, or to particular categories of professionals, I strongly suggest researching local mediation practice standards and consulting with an attorney.

**Communicating Policies.** The mediation center director should prepare well-defined and properly communicated policies that balance confidentiality issues (important to the success of mediation) and safety issues. Most mediation programs at some point—in their agreement-to-mediate forms, their brochures, or their opening statements made in mediation—clearly indicate the limits of confidentiality that apply in their program. As one example, the materials produced by the Consultation and Conciliation Service clearly state that "it is understood that s/he [the mediator] is not required to maintain confidentiality if either party is in danger of bodily harm" (Perigo, 1996, p. 19). Other programs indicate that allegations of child abuse would not be subject to confidentiality as well.

Mediation programs will always want to avoid being subpoenaed to testify about what occurred in mediation if the participating parties end up going to court over their unresolved issues. Thus, most programs include some statement in their agreement-to-mediate form indicating that mediators will not testify in these circumstances or any others and that the parties agree not to call for them to. In some states, there is now a distinct privilege for mediators, but whether this law extends to mediators on campus has not been tested. This kind of understanding is important to have internally at the university as well. It needs to be clear that no one acting as a program mediator will be ordered by a higher authority to reveal the contents of any such discussion or be disciplined for not revealing it. The only exceptions typically are if physical danger or criminal activity is present or there are other limits on confidentiality set by state law. The goal is to provide the highest level of protection for the privacy of the individuals involved.

The issue of confidentiality is a particularly salient one for ombudspersons who do some mediation but also other forms of confidential consultations, fact finding, and handling of issues like sexual harassment. Recent challenges to ombuds confidentiality have led to efforts to clarify the confidentiality privileges of campus dispute resolvers. Although this work is still in the early stages, the laws affecting ombuds may also have implications for campus mediators. Kaplin and Lee (1997) explain, "Another potential privilege of developing importance to postsecondary institutions is the 'qualified privilege' that may protect from disclosure statements of students and employees made in the context of an ombudsperson's investigation or a mediator's session. *Garstang* v. *Superior Court*, 46 Cal Rptr. 2d 84 (Court of Appeal, 2nd Dist., 1995), is illustrative"[p. 29].*

**Other Concerns.** Program coordinators should become familiar with the implications of federally mandated responsibilities that public institutions have to protect the civil rights of students and employees under Title VII (no discrimination in terms or conditions of employment based on race, religion, national origin, or sex; no sexual harassment), the Americans with Disabilities Act (access and reasonable accommodations for individuals with disabilities), and the Family Education Rights and Privacy Act (privacy of student records). In addition to reference books (Kaplin and Lee, 1997; Young and Gehring, 1973; Bickel, 1978), on-campus colleagues such as the university ombuds, legal counsel, student judicial affairs officers, sexual harassment prevention staff, and others can provide invaluable help in this crucial area of the law.

---

*\*OMBUDS: The Journal of the University and College Ombuds Association* provides more information on the issue of confidentiality of ombuds and some suggestions for maintaining records in ways that are unlikely to breach confidences (Hebein, 1996). The issue is dedicated to occasional papers on confidentiality and record keeping and is available through the University and College Ombuds Association. Editor Richard Hebein is acting faculty ombuds at Bowling Green State University.

Carefully maintaining the purity of the mediator role is a benefit with respect to reducing potential lawsuits as well. Theoretically decision makers who must decide between the interests of two or more parties are more likely to be sued by someone who is unhappy with the decision than someone who leaves the decision making in the hands of the parties where it belongs. Thus, another significant aspect of mediation that should be highlighted in program materials and maintained in practice is the lack of decision making on the part of mediators. It should also be made clear that mediators do not provide legal advice or provide therapy, and parties should not expect them to. Mediation programs should be careful not to oversell their services, promising outcomes that are not certain or implying a contract for services that it does not intend or cannot deliver.

State colleges and universities in particular should explore the applicability of state (and sometimes federal) open meetings and open records laws to their mediation programs. This is especially true if policy-related disputes are being mediated. These sunshine laws, as they are often called, recognize that most of what the government does should be subject to public review, carried out in the "sunshine" provided by open record and open meeting laws. These laws vary from state to state and thus must be checked individually.

Open records laws typically indicate that all public records are available unless they fall under a specific exemption listed by the state law. Generally a state's open meetings laws guarantees the right of the public to attend meetings of a public body in which a quorum exists and during which business will be discussed. Nongovernmental groups may also fall under an open meetings law where they are supported in whole or in part by public funds, are created by a government body, use public facilities, or perform traditionally governmental functions. The kinds of meetings that can be closed vary by state, but most laws permit the following discussions to be conducted in secret: personnel matters, litigation matters, negotiations and collective bargaining sessions, and discussions regarding the acquisition of real estate.*

## Risk Management

The major methods of liability risk management have been called risk avoidance, risk control, risk transfer, and risk retention. (A

---

*Schwing (1994) has compiled a detailed list of every state's open meetings laws, including constitution references. Useful on-line sources include the Reporters Committee for Freedom of the Press guide (http://www.rcfp.org) and the freedom of information law primer prepared by the Student Press Law Center (http://www.splc.org/resources.access.primer.html).

review of this approach in higher education generally can be found in Adams and Hall, 1976.) *Risk avoidance* is the surest way to minimize exposure to liability. This can be accomplished to some degree by appropriate case screening, but complete avoidance is not realistic. *Risk control* has a goal of reducing, rather than eliminating, the frequency or severity of potential exposure to liability by improving the physical environment or modifying hazardous behavior or activities in ways that reduce recognized risks. *Risk transfer* involves shifting the risk through the purchase of commercial insurance, or by entering "hold-harmless" agreements or employing releases or waivers. *Risk retention* involves the use of deductibles in insurance policies or other such methods, whereby the organization sets aside a certain amount of resources to handle low-level forms of liability itself.

Some campus mediation programs have begun to employ risk transfer strategies by using some version of releases and hold-harmless agreements with disputants and by purchasing special insurance from one of the carriers that insure neutrals (Complete Equity Markets insures SPIDR members, for instance), or by having the university's existing general insurance policy extended to cover the program. Nova Southeastern University was already familiar with insuring various clinical training sites and was able to include the mediation service under this existing coverage without difficulty. You may want to ask about how insurance coverage works on your campus, to see if you need to make any special application in order to be fully covered.

## Information About Legal Issues

In his article "Dealing with the Complexities of Higher Education and the Law: An Attorney's Perspective," McKee (1997) suggests three basic principles "for meeting the intricacies of the law and for staying afloat amid legalism" (p. 64): stay informed of major legal developments, consult an attorney, and "do what is right and be prepared to be sued."

A variety of resources are available with information about legal issues in higher education. The Campus Mediation Resources Web site provides links to on-line resources, including the Web sites of the National Association of College and University Attorneys, the Association for Student Judicial Affairs, and the University and College Ombuds Association. The following handbooks are useful: *A Legal Guide for Student Affairs Professionals* (Kaplin and Lee, 1997), *The College Student and the Courts* (Young and Gehring, 1973), *The College Administrator and the Courts* (Bickel, 1978), and *The Rights and Responsibilities of the Modern University* (Bickel and

Lake, 1999). Remember that the university attorney is working for the university and has it and the mediation center's best interests at heart.

Campuses are complex environments, and legal norms continue to evolve. Complete risk avoidance or prevention is an unrealistic goal, but the following points of advice are worth consideration:

- Be proactive. Rather than waiting for something bad to happen, share mediation materials with the general counsel's office, and ask for feedback on how it could be improved from a legal perspective. Think of these efforts as preventive law.

- Do good work as a mediator, stay true to the protocols, and work according to the principles that guide mediation practice. While we hope it will never happen, it is better to be sued for doing good than for doing the wrong thing.

- To prepare for a possible suit, check your college's insurance coverage, do a risk assessment of your situation and caseload, develop cooperative relationships with other campus offices, and keep your files confidential and your standards high.

# CHAPTER 7

# Implementing Strategies for Evaluation and Feedback

Research is not often a high priority for people engaged in the exciting, challenging, and often tiring work of setting up a new campus service. Nevertheless, feedback mechanisms, and in particular program evaluation research, are key to long-term program success. In addition, the field of dispute resolution in higher education as a whole is currently at a point where more research is called for. Programs that include research as a basic part of what they do are in a very good position to help move the field forward.

## The Literature on Campus Conflict Management

The literature on campus conflict management is growing in size and scope, but significant gaps remain in terms of research. In 1991 the Campus Mediation Center at Syracuse University, having recently hosted the first national campus mediation conference, prepared an annotated bibliography of work in the field (Warters and Sherman, 1991). While decidedly focused on mediation practitioners, the list contained only nineteen pertinent articles in addition to *Peaceful Persuasion*. In contrast, my 1999 bibliography, posted at the Campus Mediation Resources Web site, contains more than two hundred and fifty relevant articles, books, conference papers, and unpublished reports. Recent edited volumes (Holton, 1995, 1998) have also begun to fill the longstanding gap in terms of specialized books for the field. However, these works are primarily essays by experienced practitioners rather than reports of research or applicable theory.

In an attempt to map out the literature, Mike Elliott from the Georgia Consortium on Negotiation and Conflict Resolution reviewed 70 articles, chapters, or books on university dispute resolution. This represented a subset of the 160 written works identified for the project. Elliott (1998, p. 1) characterized the literature he reviewed as follows:

> Thirty percent applied general principles of dispute resolution (DR) to the university setting.
>
> Twenty percent focused on peer mediation among students.
>
> Twenty percent examined structural issues in higher education that feed conflict.
>
> Fifteen percent discussed specific case studies to illustrate appropriate dispute resolution.
>
> Fifteen percent studied the effectiveness and use of dispute resolution techniques in higher education.

Program effectiveness is a topic that is on the mind of many administrators and program designers, yet only a small percentage (15 percent) of the literature addresses this central question. Admittedly the reports on campus conflict management practices that do exist can be quite hard to find and gain access to. One reason is that many campus mediation projects are not freestanding but rather are incorporated into preexisting campus offices that may have many other responsibilities in addition to providing mediation. Mediation programs that do evaluate their work do not often publish the results. Most program evaluations are recorded (if anywhere) in internal annual reports that rarely reach the larger academic community.

Case studies describing campus conflicts that have been resolved by mediation are also hard to come by. When asked in confidence, mediation program directors can usually provide multiple anecdotes about conflicts that their centers have managed that without mediation may have escalated in damaging and disruptive ways. However, given the premium placed on trust and confidentiality in this work, few case studies make it into print.

Basic research on campus conflict management styles and patterns is also limited, and only a few studies have been published. A recent search of dissertation abstracts uncovered some thirty-five campus conflict-related dissertations, demonstrating great creativity among graduate student researchers. However, none of these projects appears to have made its way into mainstream journals or published manuscripts.

It appears that the newness of the topic, the sensitive nature of the issues studied, and the lack of scholarly associations, journals, or research outlets that emphasize conflict-related issues in higher education have presented considerable disincentives. A systematic analysis of the overall effectiveness of campus mediation programs and the particular utility of various forms of mediation for different types of campus conflicts has yet to be attempted. As the field matures and interest grows in the topic, more and better research undoubtedly will be conducted and published.

## Making Program Evaluation a Priority

New program coordinators may feel as if they already have a lot to attend to without adding research responsibilities. Nevertheless, it is a good idea to begin building a program evaluation plan as early as possible. There are some very practical reasons, for as accountability pressure mounts, most programs, even well-established ones, are finding that at minimum an annual report of activities is expected. In addition, many (perhaps most) outside sources of funding require a program evaluation component as a condition of support.

Given that mediation involves the well-being of others, doing evaluation research can also be considered part of the ethical responsibilities of competent mediation service providers. The jointly developed Model Standards of Conduct for Mediators (American Arbitration Association, American Bar Association, and Society for Professionals in Dispute Resolution, 1995) addresses this issue directly. One of the standards, "Obligations to the Mediation Process," indicates that "mediators have a duty to improve the practice of mediation." Clearly this implies a responsibility on the part of both individuals and programs or services to evaluate and refine the practice of dispute resolution.

A good evaluation, if planned from the program's beginning, can be a valuable management tool. Planning the evaluation as the program is being developed will sharpen everyone's thinking about the entire program: its mission, its goals, its objectives, and activities designed to meet those objectives. By organizing the evaluation, program coordinators can give their program greater structure and increase their chances of success. Ideally, program planning and evaluation should work hand in hand.

### Forms of Evaluation Research

The general field of evaluation research has experienced some shifts in emphasis since the early 1980s. The norm is no longer quantitative outcome-measurement studies driven by policymakers and funders. Shadish, Cook, and Leviton (1991) have described some of the shifts in evaluation research approaches:

> Exclusive reliance on studying outcomes yielded to inclusive concern with examining the quality of program implementation and the causal processes that mediated any program impacts. Exclusive reliance on quantitative studies yielded to including qualitative methods. Using policy makers as both the source of evaluation questions and the audience for the results yielded to consideration of multiple stakeholder groups. Concern with methodology gave way to concern with the context of evaluation practice and fitting evaluation results into highly politicized and decentralized systems [p. 32].

This movement toward more contextualized and collaboratively developed research is a positive one for campus mediation programs. Evaluation projects that address process as well as outcome and explore the interests of multiple stakeholders represent a richer opportunity for programs to learn about how they fit within their larger campus environment and are perceived by others.

There are two broad categories of evaluation research. *Formative evaluation* or *program monitoring* is used to keep track of how a program is being implemented, assess whether a project is going according to plan, document problems or new possibilities arising as the program grows, and provide useful strategic information for program developers. The other broad category of research, which may feel somewhat more threatening to program advocates, is known as *summative* or *outcome evaluation* research. This research examines the outcomes of the program to see if they meet expectations. It focuses on determining whether the program is meeting its stated objectives, whether it is worth continuing or expanding, and how effective it is.

Most programs end up doing some combination of the two, because it is preferable to gather formative information as the program develops and making adjustments as necessary, rather than going blindly forward until it becomes time to answer life-or-death questions of continued fundability.

## Potential Uses of Evaluation Research

Evaluation research can serve a number of purposes:

> *Justifying and explaining the program.* Providing credible proof to skeptics can help increase the sustainability of programs. Evaluation data are often useful for justifying, defending, or explaining a program. Sponsors may wish to know details regarding caseloads, types, and outcomes.

*Program planning and decision making.* Research can help determine how best to allocate time and resources now and in the future. Data can also be used to refine public relations or outreach strategies or to make decisions about training needs. Questions regarding duplication of services can also be explored.

*Improving services.* Research can help practitioners understand what is working and what is not and identify larger patterns that may go unnoticed day to day. For instance, systematic follow-up contacts might reveal that the compliance rate for certain kinds of agreements goes down a few months after mediation. This finding could suggest needed changes in mediation procedures.

*Addressing a specific problem area.* Having good data on areas of concern can help the mediation program respond more effectively. For instance, the director may have a concern about the limited use of the service by diverse cultural groups. Part of the monitoring might include recording the ethnicity of parties using the service.

*Assessing volunteer needs and impact.* Evaluations can be used to assess the needs, concerns, and effectiveness of mediators. Questions relating to the effectiveness of the training, ongoing mediator professional development needs, and disputant satisfaction with mediators assigned to them or the process used can be quite helpful.

Determining which of these purposes are likely to be most important to a particular effort at the start of a project increases the chances of gathering data that will be seen as credible and a good match for program needs. It also provides the opportunity to develop standardized forms and practices that will endure as the program matures.

Obviously the scope and focus of data gathering should depend on the priorities established. Goals for evaluation may depend in part on the phase of development that the project is in. In the early stages of program development, the most pressing problems confronting coordinators typically involve project implementation rather than assessments of outcomes. Translating a project plan into a working reality requires solving any number of problems that emerge in the early months of a project's existence.

Somewhat more developed programs often have a different set of organizational problems as they confront a transition to becoming institutionalized, transformed from a distinct and perhaps innovative project into a more routine campus operation. Program coordinators in these two previous instances may find that the most productive use of an evaluation is to help devise effective remedies to the specific difficulties faced in program implementation. Certainly a prerequisite for achieving satisfying results, and longer-term or less immediate outcomes, is a program that operates with at least some degree of stability. However, once programs have established some greater stability in their activities, evaluating outcomes or results becomes both more feasible and more desirable.

## Clarifying the Research Audience

An issue to address early on is identification of the evaluation's target users. Potential users include advisory board members, program administrators, staff and volunteers, senior administrators who have control over the budgeting process in this area, external funding agencies, and the evaluator. Additional consumers may include the wider campus public and local print or broadcast media. Given the need for more readily available research reports and the value that academics place on scholarly publication, the scholarly and practitioner communities are important potential audiences as well. In all instances disputants' identities must be carefully kept secure and confidential. Any case studies or reports that are generated must always remove identifying information.

Each of the potential audiences for the research will likely have an interest in different kinds of data. For example, senior administrators or funders may want to know about the volume of cases, case outcomes, client impacts, adequacy of space and resources allocated, or the development of replicable innovations. Advisory board members may be interested in how the program is doing meeting its targeted objectives, or how the program is being perceived or used by various campus constituents. Program coordinators may wonder about the amount of time spent on various aspects of the program and the return on investment, if the volunteers are being used effectively, how they might do better outreach, or where problem areas are. Volunteers may wonder what the long-term outcome of their casework is, how their skills match up, or how they fit into the big picture of the center.

The campus community may be interested in the kinds of cases the center handles, success stories, and the range of services provided. The practitioner community (people affiliated with other similar programs) may be interested in innovative responses to common problems, processes used and lessons learned during program and policy development, success stories and cautionary tales. The scholarly community may be interested in the effectiveness of particular models of mediation, patterns of conflict on campus, and the application and testing of theory in the campus mediation context. And evaluators may have interest in using the data gathered for a thesis or dissertation or for publication or presentation at a conference.

All of these different interests must be taken into account when considering the types of data to gather and the kinds of reports that will be generated and distributed. A mediation center director can always prepare a number of different reports tailored to specific readers, but only if the necessary data have been gathered. Given limited resources, some interests and agendas will receive higher priority than others as decisions are made about what questions to ask.

## Deciding Who Should Do the Evaluation

A decision must be reached whether to attempt to do the evaluation in-house or whether it makes sense to engage an outside or independent evaluator. A self-evaluation carried out by mediation program staff, volunteers, or advisory board members is usually cheaper, so if the budget for evaluation is small or even nonexistent, this may be the best available option. Other advantages are that these individuals are often quite familiar with the program's setting and history, and a relationship of trust has already been built up among the different players involved. Directly involving staff, volunteers, or board members can also help build their commitment to the success of the program as a whole. However, devoting the necessary time to conduct a useful evaluation will reduce the time that staff can spend on other program activities.

Engaging an external or independent consultant, usually more expensive, has advantages as well. External evaluators offer objectivity and a lack of vested interest that may be seen as essential in some cases. They may also have the necessary time, expertise, and computer software that staff or board members lack. External evaluators can pose particularly frank questions and elicit the kinds of feedback that might be awkward for a friend of the program to ask.

One of the real advantages of being based at a college or university is that many faculty members, graduate students, and staff are skilled in research and program evaluation techniques. With a bit of looking around, particularly in departments of public policy and public administration, public health, criminology and criminal justice, education, human ecology, psychology, and sociology, a mediation program director may be able to find a faculty member or graduate student willing to conduct the evaluation or assist in doing so. Alternatively, a faculty member may be able to arrange for undergraduate or graduate students to do the evaluation as a class project. Some campuses also have offices of institutional research that can assist, often for free.

In the end, the director may be able to combine some of the advantages of using both self and external evaluators while keeping costs down. Program staff or interns can do some of the data-gathering projects associated with program monitoring, and an experienced and somewhat more removed evaluator (perhaps a graduate student or faculty member from another part of the university) can be hired for other more summative evaluation tasks.

## Developing a Description of Program Goals, Activities, and Desired Outcomes

A clear description of the program to be evaluated needs to be developed in order to get the research process started. It will help identify the critical questions for evaluation. Sometimes a detailed description already exists. Often, however, even programs that have been around for a long time have little documentation about activities and expected outcomes. This can be remedied relatively easily by developing a program logic model. A logic model (Porteous, Sheldrick, and Stewart, 1997) is essentially a diagram illustrating five linked aspects (components, activities, target group, short-term outcomes, long-term outcomes) that together show what the program is supposed to do, with whom, and why.

There are a number of advantages to creating a logic model for the mediation program. For evaluation purposes, a logic model will do the following:

- Summarize the key elements of the program (on just a few sheets of paper).
- Explain the rationale behind program activities.
- Clarify the difference between the program activities and the intended outcomes.
- Show the cause-and-effect relationships between the activities and the outcomes—that is, which activities are expected to lead to which outcomes.
- Help identify the critical questions for evaluation.
- Provide the opportunity for program stakeholders to discuss the program and agree on its description.

Logic models are also a useful means of communicating the elements of the mediation program to policymakers, administrators, staff, external funding agencies, the media, and colleagues at other mediation projects.

The model is designed to describe what the program does

(components and activities), whom the program does it with (target group), and why (short-term and long-term outcomes). Each basic aspect is listed in a separate box, typically starting with components at the top of the page, working down to long-term outcomes and overall goals at the bottom. Working across a page is also acceptable if that seems easier. The model should have components, activities, target groups, and outcomes.

*Components* are closely related groups of activities in the program. The number of components depends on the size of the program and how it is conceptualized or administered. Campus mediation programs might have staff or volunteer development components, an outreach component, a workshop or skill-training component, a policy review and development component, and a mediation services delivery component. Each component has its own set of activities and target groups and desired outcomes.

*Activities* are the things the staff and volunteers in the program do or the services the program delivers in working toward its desired outcomes. They are thus the means by which the desired outcomes will be achieved. Pulling together all of the program documentation will help identify the activities, which are described using action verbs. The activities description may be a short paragraph describing the program's various activities, staff work plans, or program operational plans.

*Target group*s are the individuals, groups, organizations, or communities at whom the program's work and services are directed and must be specified clearly. These are the priority populations or the intended reach of the program. Target groups can be specified in terms of sociodemographic characteristics (such as age, sex, ethnicity, income, place of residence, academic status) or by university function, home department, or type of problems or behaviors.

*Outcomes* are the changes the program hopes to achieve with each target group. They are the reasons for the program's existence. Outcomes focus on what the program makes happen rather than what it does. They are the intended results of the program, not the process of achieving them. Outcomes are usually differentiated between short-term and long-term outcomes, a distinction that helps to illustrate the sequential nature of change.

Short-term outcomes are the direct results of the program on its participants. They show why the program activities will lead to the long-term outcomes. In conflict resolution skills training programs, desired short-term outcomes for participants might be increased awareness of options and choices, increased efforts to use collaborative problem-solving approaches, increased knowledge of conflict resolution services, or improvement in demonstrated skills.

Long-term outcomes reflect the consequences of the program in the broader campus community. They tend to be the ultimate goals of the program. Long-term outcomes usually take a long time to occur, but they may occasionally occur soon after a program is implemented. There will probably be only a few long-term outcomes for any given program. Long-term outcomes for a mediation program could include reduction in violence, decreased levels of bitterness or hostility, increased use of conflict as an opportunity for learning and change, reduction of administrative time spent handling disputes, improved college (or department or residence hall or school) morale, or increased sense of self-sufficiency and ability to resolve conflicts. Long-term outcomes are typically harder to measure with precision because there are so many other forces that also influence the program's target group.

There is no single way to create a logic model. The start of the work in drawing one up also depends on the developmental stage of the program. If the logic model is being developed to describe an existing program, it makes sense to start with existing activities and progress downward, taking a top-down approach. The question to ask is, "What is it that we do, and why do we think that it will create the change that we are hoping for?" For new programs or those in the planning stages, it may be easier to start at the bottom of the model, with the desired outcomes, and work up. The person creating the model might wish to revisit the mediation program mission statement or the university charge and extract a few key goals from it. The question to ask is, "What is it that we want to change, and how are we going to do it?"

## Turning Desired Outcomes into Measurable Objectives

A completed program logic model can provide useful insights into the activities and goals of a program and can be used to develop even more specific and measurable program objectives. Long-term outcomes in the logic model more or less represent the program's goals, and the short-term outcomes can be thought of as program objectives. Objectives are usually phrased in terms that can be measured (involving a specific number of participants or creating a specific percentage change in reported awareness of the program, for example) and often specify the period of time by which the objective will be achieved. This makes them well suited for use in the outcomes assessment variety of evaluation research.

## Deciding Which Research Questions to Focus On

Time and resources are always limited, and only a portion of researchable questions can be explored in a single study. It is up to the program coordinator to help guide the final selection of evaluation questions. Perhaps one of the more efficient methods is to agree on a limited number of evaluation questions at the same time that program goals and objectives are established by the planning group. If this is not possible, another strategy is to involve evaluation users by asking them to complete the statement, "We need to know _____ because we need to show/decide/account for _____." In this way evaluation users have an opportunity to participate in the design of the evaluation.

Once agreement has been reached on the range of possible questions, the final selection of evaluation questions should be based on several criteria: the benefits and costs of answering or not answering the questions (it may be that some are too costly to answer), the availability of data to answer the question, the extent to which answers to the questions will prove useful to the users, and the possibility that some of the questions may require a certain level of expertise in evaluation that is not readily available.

A number of resources are provided at the end of the chapter with information on evaluation research in general or evaluation of mediation in particular.

## Determining Measures of Effectiveness

Once key goals and objectives are established and a short list of questions for evaluation are in hand, the next step is to consider how to assess the issues. In researcher's parlance, this process is referred to as operationalizing the outcome variables. For example, many (perhaps most) mediation program evaluations explore the question of client satisfaction. The researcher who wants to explore this area must decide what kind of information will be gathered to measure the level of satisfaction. A study of mediation program evaluation strategies (O'Doherty, 1989) found that most often questions were posed to clients by telephone or on a written questionnaire. The questions most often addressed one or more of the following topics:

- General satisfaction with the process and settlement terms
- Recommendation of the process to others
- Thoughts on whether the client would use or not use the service again
- Helpfulness of the mediators or agency

These questions are thought to provide a good picture of whether a participant in mediation felt satisfied with the experience, but they are certainly not the only questions that could be posed. There are lots of other ways to come at the measurement of program effectiveness (satisfaction being but one indicator), and some appear to be more helpful or valid than others. For instance, the query, "Is it effective?" actually begs the question, "Compared to what?" Mediation may be very effective compared to, say, a physical fight, at least from the point of view of the loser or people responsible for community safety. Thus, in addition to examining whether a program is meeting the objectives that its planners set, projects may also be judged in terms of how well they fare in relation to other methods or forums for resolving conflict. In most cases, off-campus mediation projects have been compared to the courts or arbitration, using the following kinds of criteria (Tyler, 1989; McGillis, 1997):

- Satisfaction, usually of parties, but also sometimes their advocates or referral agents
- Settlement rates
- Compliance with agreements
- Time and cost (savings) to parties or system
- Perceived fairness of process and outcome
- Caseloads

These effectiveness comparison criteria, although broadly applied in the evaluation of community and court-affiliated programs, are not without their problems and critics. For one thing, true comparison requires gathering data on both mediation and whatever it is being compared to, which dramatically increases the complexity and cost of careful evaluation efforts. The utility of the criteria themselves has also been questioned. For example, questions used to measure satisfaction tend to be very general, and thus are often not very helpful in pinpointing what parts of the process are most or least pleasing to parties.

Considerably more problematic has been the heavy emphasis placed on having large caseloads and high settlement rates. Because the data on the number of cases handled and whether parties reached agreement are relatively easy to gather and calculate (and brag about), many programs and mediators use it as a prime measure of their success. Harvard Law School professor Frank Sander (1995) has called the emphasis on reaching settlement a national obsession, and an unhealthy one at that. Assuming that settlement is inherently good and should be the primary goal of mediation overlooks and diverts attention from other legitimate goals, such as empowerment, self-determination, learning from conflict, restoration of relationships, or reconciliation. Emphasizing settlement also can put unreasonable pressure on mediators and clients alike to reach agreements that may in fact be premature or ill advised and to use mediation for cases that might better be handled in another way.

A more recent criterion, perhaps even more challenging to measure, is the transformative capacity (Bush and Folger, 1994) of the dispute-handling forum. The approach sees conflict as a potential occasion for growth in two primary dimensions: through strengthening the self through deliberate reflection, choice, and action and through reaching beyond the self to relate to others. This framework suggests the need for much more careful study of the experiences and perspectives of participants in mediation.

Based on these concerns, campus mediation programs are advised to avoid measuring their program's worth primarily on the number of cases that are mediated and the number of settlements reached. Campus mediation programs help build a college or university's capacity to respond to conflicts, and this contribution must not be overlooked. The mission statement of the Mediation Center at Purdue University puts the argument succinctly. "The process of resolving conflict is educational. By establishing a forum where each party is heard, we teach listening. By creating an environment where each party can speak, we teach communication. By developing the processes that seek resolution, we teach the importance of dialogue. And, by building these processes into a method of mediating disputes we teach citizenship" (Purdue Mediation and Conciliation Center, 1999). Perhaps more unfortunate than a low caseload (which could indicate a relatively healthy community) or lower-than-average settlement rate is to have disputes arise in the community that could easily be addressed through mediation and not to have the capacity to provide it. Considering all of these issues and depending on the mediation program core goals, measuring the success or effectiveness of a campus mediation effort can involve a wide range of indicators. Some of the possibilities are listed in Exhibit 7.1, and many more could be added.

## Developing a Data Gathering and Management Plan

Once the goals and questions for the research are determined, the next step is a data gathering and management plan to define what data will be collected, from whom, and using what techniques. How the information gathered will relate to the evaluation questions must be absolutely clear so that no data are collected that will not serve an important evaluation or public relations purpose. Instruments should be as short as possible to avoid needlessly burdening respondents and squandering scarce program resources to gather and then tabulate unnecessary data.

- Number of requests for information or services
- Number of disputes conciliated
- Number of disputes mediated
- Number of successful mediations (resolution attained)
- Level of satisfaction with service reported by disputants
- Positive testimonials provided by parties
- Compliance rate of successful mediations and conciliations
- Experience, background, and number of mediators or interns who get involved with the center
- Number of referrals received and range of referral sources
- Number of walk-ins who approach the center on their own
- Number of parties returning to the dispute resolution center
- Amount and kind of training the center provides to the university community
- Number of nonmediation dispute resolution services (for example, meeting facilitations, strategic planning sessions, consultations, conciliations) provided
- Change in the perceived organizational climate on campus
- Cost savings from lawsuits and other grievances that are averted
- Amount of positive media coverage the center gets locally and nationally
- Number of former disputants who apply to be volunteers
- Number and diversity of clients served and degree to which the characteristics of the users of the service match those of the general population
- Positive change in the perceptions of disputants toward each other
- The degree to which skills learned in mediation training or at a mediation session are transferred to other settings

Exhibit 7.1. Possible Variables to Measure the Effectiveness of a Campus Dispute Resolution Center

Good evaluation designs often employ multiple methods of gathering similar or complementary information and may incorporate both qualitative and quantitative measures. If desired results converge, they can confirm in several ways that the program is moving in the right direction.

Data gathering procedures should carefully protect research subjects from any harm that might result from research, provide informed consent, limit access to identifying information, and adhere to university human subjects protocols and applicable state and federal privacy laws.

**Sources of Useful Information.** There are many potential sources of useful information. Much of the formative evaluation information comes from forms that are set up and maintained in an ongoing way by staff (often referred to as monitoring records)—for example: telephone and office contact logs, case intake forms, and public relations activity logs tracking events and number of participants involved. Organizing the data collected by a monitoring system can be accomplished in any number of ways depending on the data processing capabilities and needs. In small programs, a simple paper filing system and periodic (monthly or by semester) manual tabulation procedures might be adequate. In a larger program, data might be converted for analysis on a personal computer, perhaps using a mediation case management software package or a general statistical or graphing program. Some examples of the kinds of data that program coordinators might be interested in and related data gathering tools are listed in Exhibit 7.2.

In addition to data from monitoring records, programs may develop questionnaires, surveys, focus groups, and observation or interview guides to gather other kinds of information deemed useful for evaluation purposes. Also potentially valuable, when permissible and available, is secondary or archival data analysis of records prepared by related programs or services. For instance, it can be useful to note changes in complaint or case patterns at other programs or offices that in some way correspond to the mediation effort.

**Data Collection Instruments.** Designing data collection instruments, whether they are telephone interview guides or observation checklists, may seem relatively simple and straightforward. In fact, doing it well requires considerable experience. Data collection results can be useless or incomplete if the survey instruments are not carefully constructed. Faculty experts may be willing to assist in designing or reviewing proposed instruments. Pilot-testing each instrument with a small sample before using it is also highly recommended.

Perhaps the most common evaluation device that programs use is a simple postmediation questionnaire given to disputants, initially after a mediation and then again at some period (perhaps three months) after the session. The reasons for collecting data on more than one occasion are to determine whether the program's effects decay over time and to document trends. Despite this benefit, many programs administer only one postmediation questionnaire to ease follow-up demands on staff and disputants. An example of a typical disputant follow-up questionnaire is provided in Section S of Resources, Forms, and Documents. It includes some common questions relating to perceived mediator bias and satisfaction with the process. A longer example that was designed

| Desired Information | Possible Data Sources |
|---|---|
| Patterns of referral | Referral forms; data on referral source gathered from intake or request-for-mediation forms; case files indicating referrals made; postmediation report forms completed by mediators; interviews with referral sources |
| Information on patterns of program use by various campus constituent groups | Telephone and contact logs; demographic information gathered on intake forms; pre- or postmediation questionnaires; key informant interviews |
| Skill development of mediators | Mediator observation forms (used at training and during actual mediations); pre- and posttraining participant questionnaires; postmediation client satisfaction surveys; postmediation self or co-mediator evaluation or debriefing forms |
| Scope and extent of outreach | Public relations event log; log documenting number, kind, and location of public relations materials distributed; Web site "hit" counters; "how did you hear about center" questions at intake; media clippings file |
| Program efficiency information | Time from first contact to resolution information from intake form; length of mediation session data taken from postmediation report form; percentage of cases reaching agreement (from case files); costs per case in terms of time and money or in comparison to similar cases going through other processes |
| Information on disputants' experiences with the program | Postmediation client surveys (immediately following the session and three to six months later); follow-up telephone interviews |
| Descriptive information on cases, problem categories | Intake forms; case files; generic case summaries prepared by mediators |

Exhibit 7.2. Sample Data Gathering Methods

to be filled out electronically (developed by the Department of Energy's Mediation Office) is available on-line for review at http://www.gc.doe.gov/adr/index.html.

**Baseline Data.** Sometimes accurately measuring the impact of a program requires gathering baseline data. Program developers will not be able to determine whether their mediation program efforts have resulted in desired changes (for instance, improved climate or reduction in grievances) unless they have information on the conditions that existed before a new intervention was launched.

For programs that are interested in asking these kind of research questions, provision should be made to collect baseline data in preferably the same manner that summative evaluation data are collected. For example, if interviews with administrators and a staff survey were going to be used to measure changes in the campus climate, these same data collection approaches should also be used to collect baseline data so that the results will be comparable. For the same reason, programs should use the same basic data collection instruments for the baseline and all subsequent data collection surveys.

## Using the Evaluation Results

After the various forms of data have been collected, they need to be analyzed and prepared for presentation. Software packages for quantitative (SPSS, SAS) and qualitative (The Ethnograph, ATLASti, NUD*IST) data analysis are readily available on most campuses with large amounts of data to process. Some specialized survey programs that help streamline data analysis are also available.

Once the findings are compiled, strategies for reporting the results need to be developed that will appeal to the evaluation users. Perhaps two or three different reports must be developed to provide different kinds and amounts of information based on the intended audience. If the information will be presented to the media, a press release may be in order as well. Some readers like lots of charts and figures; others prefer text. For most audiences, evaluation reports should include implications of the findings for program operation and maintenance, expansion, redirection, and sustainability, with recommendations for future short- and long-term actions that can be taken to improve the program.

It can be quite helpful to review a draft of the results of the evaluation with core staff, advisers, and volunteers before completing the evaluation report. A meeting designed to discuss the findings can be held to get their input and interpretations. These additional perspectives can strengthen the final report and convey respect of the groups most likely to be influenced by the release of the report. An evaluation is essentially a device for program staff and volunteers to use to make adjustments and improve program services. Taken in this light, a report should not be presented as the final word on the program but rather as part of a continuous and evolving process of development and refinement.

## Examples of Campus Mediation Evaluation Designs

As you will see, in addition to evaluating a program's services, research at mediation centers can be used to explore more theoretical concerns.

**State University of New York at Albany.** One of the earliest published research studies specifically examining campus mediation was Keith Miller's article, "The Effectiveness of Mediation in Higher Education" (1987). Miller describes in detail his evaluation of the mediation program at the State University of New York at Albany (SUNY) established in 1985 and includes copies of the instruments he used. The study examined three semesters of mediation data involving eighty-five clients and twenty-seven cases. The research focused on compliance with the written agreement, client satisfaction, expediency of the resolution to the problem, deescalation of the situation, and the impartiality and confidentiality of the mediators and the center. Miller used case intake forms and an immediate follow-up questionnaire given to the parties at the close of the mediation session, followed by a long-term questionnaire that was mailed to disputants after some time had passed. The design he used is characteristic of many mediation program evaluations done in other settings. (Note that the rating scale for question 5 of the immediate follow-up questionnaire was mislabeled in the article's appendix and will need to be changed.)

**University of Michigan.** The Consultation and Conciliation Services program, at the time a new initiative at the University of Michigan, evaluated the pilot project in the following ways. As a matter of course, a monitoring record of cases was maintained that included information on employment status (faculty or staff), the university unit, how the parties were referred, nature of the concern, type of assistance given, name of consultant or mediator, time spent, and the outcome (satisfactory or no agreement). The overall pilot project evaluation incorporated information gathered on patterns of program use (that is, numbers and types of cases handled); formal client feedback (gathered by means of a postservices questionnaire); peer review (through interviews) by those involved in the start-up, including service staff, members of the planning team, mediators trained that year, and other directors in the unit the program is housed in; and cost to the university in terms of salary and program expenses.

The results of the study were compiled in a relatively short but thorough report (Johnson, 1996) that was distributed to decision makers and made available for free to interested members of the campus community. Based on the positive evaluation of the pilot project, the service was incorporated as a regular part of the university's offerings.

**Albany Law School.** The Mediation Assistance Program (MAP), a FIPSE-funded service-learning project of Albany Law School's Government Law Center, needed to conduct an evaluation of its two-year grant-funded project. (Service-learning is the process of integrating volunteer community service combined with active guided reflection into the campus curriculum to enhance and enrich student learning of course material.) The project trained undergraduate and graduate students from six area colleges and universities to serve as mediators for disputes arising among residents of the Albany Housing Authority. In order to ensure objectivity, MAP engaged the Evaluation Consortium from the nearby School of Education at the State University of Albany to conduct most of the measurement protocols and analysis. Because of the service-learning emphasis of the project, the bulk of the evaluation efforts focused on the experience of student-mediators.

Both formative and summative evaluation measures were used. Information gathered during the first semester of the program was used to make adjustments for subsequent semesters. Measurement instruments included a student self-evaluation administered before the training component and at the beginning of their service-learning experience; a participant evaluation of the mediation training; student-maintained reflective learning journals; student interviews; and a self-evaluation administered at the conclusion of the student's service-learning experience. In addition, eight students, two from each semester of the project, were interviewed as to their experiences after their involvement had concluded. Results of the evaluation were positive, and the project received an additional FIPSE grant to help replicate the service in four to five additional locations. (Full details of the project, including copies of evaluation instruments used, are reported in the *Best Practices Manual* [Moses, 1997], available from the Government Law Center.)

**Carleton University.** Catherine Borshuk, a Carleton University graduate student working on a master's degree, agreed to conduct an evaluation of the university's Mediation Centre (Borshuk, 1994). A relatively standard follow-up questionnaire was distributed to disputants after mediation to assess the effectiveness of the mediation process from disputants' point of view. However, in addition to providing a basic evaluation of the service, Borshuk and her colleagues at the Mediation Centre wanted to address some other more theoretical concerns. In particular, they wanted to explore the so-called peace virus hypothesis that suggests that an entire community benefits in second-hand fashion from formal mediation services.

To begin to get at this question, the second part of the evaluation focused on the experiences of the twenty-one volunteer mediators trained by the Mediation Centre. To test the hypothesis that mediation skills developed in training and through provision of mediation translated into the everyday lives of the mediators, a questionnaire was developed that focused on changes in the mediators' behavioral responses to conflict at home, in the classroom, and at work. In order to identify changes, a before and after test was used. Prior to participating in training, volunteers completed a questionnaire designed to measure issues such as self-esteem, coping strategies, communication confidence, and philosophies of altruism. After approximately six months of experience in the program, volunteers were asked to complete the posttest, which included a series of questions asking mediators to assess changes in the way they relate to people in their own environments and to give examples of ways in which they use their mediation skills outside the formal setting of the mediation program. The study found positive changes in mediator behavior and attitudes, with all mediators surveyed reporting use of mediation skills in their daily lives with a variety of people in many different contexts.

**Ohio State University.** An informal mediation initiative using mediation-trained resident assistants was developed and tested at Ohio State University in the early 1980s. The study (Rodgers, 1983) was conducted by Robert Rodgers, a faculty member in education and psychology whose area of expertise was college student development theories. Of particular interest was an examination of the kind of problem-solving forum that would be most developmentally appropriate (and growth promoting) for college freshmen and sophomores living in residence, and especially for those experiencing roommate conflict.

According to the theory, students tend to enter college at a level that Perry called dualism, an "absolute" stage wherein "right answers" are known by the authorities, and any divergence of opinion is simply viewed as inadequacy. A given proposition is (dualistically) either right or wrong. Students, in Perry's view, progress from dualism through stages of multiplicity, where there is no single right answer and many opinions can be equally valid, with everyone having a "right to their own opinion"; to relativism, where different answers can be correct for different contexts, and each proposition must be evaluated in terms of its particular application; to ethical commitment, where unchanging fundamental principles define the contexts for evaluating truth.

Chickering first (1969) suggested three and then (1993) seven "vectors" of growth toward individuation. He does not see definite stages and specific quantitative changes. Instead, he identifies seven areas (vectors) of growth that seem to develop somewhat independently: developing competence, managing emotions, moving toward independence, developing mature interpersonal relationships, establishing personal identity, developing purpose, and developing integrity. Developing competence in the early vectors is seen as a necessary precondition for successful competence in the later ones.

In Rodgers's baseline study, both residence assistants and a targeted group of students were assessed as to developmental levels (Perry, 1970; Chickering, 1969, 1993), and they were interviewed concerning their behavior in roommate conflicts and also how they thought they should behave in these situations.

The study found that students lacked empathy and assertiveness, typically describing a defensive style of trying to prove aggressively that they were right and the other wrong, with all of the students assessed to be reasoning in positions of dualism on the Perry scheme and still coping with Chickering's vectors one through four. Typical residence adviser responses (to tell the students to try and work it out themselves, or direct the students as to how to handle the situation) were not particularly effective and did not appear to provide an optimal opportunity for students to address their problem while not robbing students of the chance to advance their cognitive and psychosocial development.

Mediation was proposed as a more developmentally appropriate method for resolving these disputes. A subgroup of residence assistants then participated in a two-day mediation training, and residence adviser conflict interventions were tracked for a semester. Rodgers reports that control or resolution of roommate conflicts was achieved in 67 percent of the cases using mediation, compared to 25 percent for a comparison group using regular methods. Student satisfaction with mediation was significantly higher than for regular practices, and students participating in mediation showed improvement in both negotiation and assertion.

## Mediation Evaluation Resources

A number of useful research tools and guides to program evaluation are available for reference purposes. Some are tailored specifically to the mediation context, and others are more general.

## Mediation Program Evaluation Guides

Although none of the following guides focuses specifically on the higher education context, they may still be of considerable value to individuals designing evaluations of mediation programs.

*School Mediation Program Evaluation Kit,* by J. Lam. Washington, D.C.: Conflict Resolution in Education Network, 1989. This practical guide for K–12 school mediation project coordinators includes a brief introduction to program evaluation and a set of adaptable evaluation instruments: monthly report, mediation program contract, training evaluation, parental consent, and follow-up forms, as well as mediation trainee and school climate questionnaires. Each form comes with clear instructions describing the purpose of the instrument, how to administer it, and how to analyze the information gathered. Available from: http://www.crenet.org/.

*A Self-Evaluation Manual for Community-Based Mediation Projects: Tools for Monitoring and Recording Data,* by T. Roberts. Vancouver, Canada: University of Victoria Institute for Dispute Resolution, 1993. This example-filled manual comes out of an evaluation of two community-based mediation organizations in British Columbia, conducted in 1990–1991. It provides a variety of useful ideas and sample data monitoring and gathering instruments. Available from: www.dispute.resolution.uvic.ca/ or www.nicr.ca.

*Evaluating Agency Alternative Dispute Resolution Programs: A Users' Guide to Data Collection and Use,* by E. S. Rolph and E. Moller. Santa Monica, Calif.: RAND Institute for Civil Justice, 1995. The Administrative Conference of the United States asked the Institute for Civil Justice to prepare a manual and develop prototype data collection instruments to assist those with responsibility for evaluating federal agency alternative dispute resolution programs. The manual discusses issues in designing evaluations, lays out approaches to data collection, provides sample data analysis plans, and includes a number of prototype data collection instruments. Available from: http://www.rand.org/.

## World Wide Web–Based Resources

Action Evaluation Project: www.ariassociates.org/. This site provides information on a participatory assessment process known as action-evaluation. The process entails collaboratively articulating goals and objectives among the groups involved in a conflict intervention, including those funding it, those organizing and convening the intervention, and the participants themselves. The action-evaluator collects this information from the groups and summarizes it with the help of a computerized database (available over the Web browser) designed to systematize the process and organize the data. This goal articulation takes place at the outset of an intervention, allowing the action-evaluator to track how goals of various stakeholders evolve and use these goals as a basis for both designing the intervention and evaluating it along the way and at its conclusion.

Bureau of Justice Assistance Evaluation Web Site: www.bja. evaluationwebsite.org/. The BJA maintains an extensive Web site designed to provide a variety of resources for evaluating primarily criminal justice programs, but much of the information is applicable to other contexts as well. The site includes the Electronic Roadmap for Evaluation, which provides instructional materials to assist in planning, designing, and conducting evaluations of programs, and a section on evaluation resources, which includes a bibliography of evaluation materials organized by specific evaluation topics.

W. W. Kellogg Foundation Evaluation Handbook: www. wkkf.org/Publications/evalhdbk/default.htm. This downloadable handbook provides a useful step-by-step guide to program evaluation from the point of view of a major foundation.

## Useful Books on Evaluation Research

Fetterman, D. M., and others (Eds.). (1996). *Empowerment Evaluation: Knowledge and Tools for Self-Assessment and Accountability.* Thousand Oaks, Calif.: Sage.

Patton, M. Q. (1990). *Qualitative Evaluation and Research Methods.* Thousand Oaks, Calif.: Sage.

Patton, M. Q. (1996). *Utilization-Focused Evaluation.* Thousand Oaks, Calif.: Sage.

Rossi, P., and Freeman, H. (1993). *Evaluation: A Systematic Approach.* Thousand Oaks, Calif.: Sage.

Research, both evaluative and more basic, is necessary to provide programs with accurate feedback on how they are functioning. With careful planning, data gathering can become an almost seamless part of the mediation program's regular procedures, and the information gathered can be very helpful when it comes time to explain or justify or redesign the program. Research is also needed to help move the larger field of dispute resolution in higher education forward. Gaps in the literature are apparent, and it will be up to program staff and faculty and graduate students to help fill them.

# CHAPTER 8

# Expanding Conflict Management Options Beyond the Mediation Table

When the campus is treated as a community, it quickly becomes apparent that multiple functions in addition to mediation are required to regulate conflict and permit system transformation over time. Ombudsperson Mary Rowe (1991) notes that effective dispute systems should include all of the following functions:

- Expressing respect for feelings
- Giving and receiving information on a one-to-one basis
- Consultation to help people help themselves
- Shuttle diplomacy by a third party
- Mediation
- Fact finding or investigation (formal or informal)
- Decision making, arbitration, or adjudication
- Upward feedback, problem prevention, and systems change

As you will see from the numerous examples of nonmediation conflict intervention projects reviewed in this chapter, these functions (and others) are being provided in a broad range of ways. The sources and forms of campus conflict vary, so a variety of methods, both proactive and reactive, are needed. It would be foolish to assume that mediation programs in and of themselves have the capacity to serve all the dispute resolution needs of a campus. However, mediation programs are often in a good position to promote creative initiatives that will strengthen the overall campus capacity to respond respectfully and effectively to conflict.

## Group Process Intervention Strategies _____

Although most mediation programs are designed primarily to handle individual disputes, working at the level of the group is often a necessary conflict management strategy. Individual disputes may (and most often do) occur within the context of work or social groups that serve to exacerbate the dispute or moderate its effects. Campus conflicts also often involve multiple primary parties who have a stake in the issues. It can be difficult to bring these kinds of conflicts to closure unless the entire group is involved at some level. A number of different approaches can be useful for this purpose.

### Group Facilitation Services

On a growing number of campuses, for free or a small fee, a neutral trained facilitator is made available to groups that are about to engage in critical decision-making meetings, meetings on controversial topics, or problem-solving sessions where some outside support could be helpful. Outside facilitators are often accepted by a troubled group more easily than a formal mediation process might be. This may be because group facilitators do not highlight the existence of conflict unless the parties request it. The facilitator instead focuses on helping the group attend to the issues that concern them in an effective and egalitarian way. Having the assistance of someone with group process expertise and no stake in the outcome of the meeting permits all group members to focus on sharing their ideas and concerns. The facilitator takes responsibility for managing the meeting, ensuring equal opportunities for participation, and checking that any agreements made are clearly articulated and understood.

In addition to running general meetings, facilitators may offer more specialized services that meet very specific needs. For instance, strategic planning facilitators may assist a group in moving through a structured planning process, helping them reach consensus on the future directions of their unit. Some departments or divisions host annual retreats, and facilitators help develop the agenda and staff the meetings. Sessions like these provide a good opportunity to explore many conflict-generating issues.

Another special form of facilitation is known as graphic facilitation (Ball, 1998). In this process, specially trained graphic facilitators, moving beyond simple note taking on flip charts, record and organize a group's ideas using special graphics and icons on large sheets of butcher paper. Their goal is to help create rich pictures of complex situations that allow people to discuss specific issues without losing the larger context. In some circumstances, graphic facilitators work in concert with a mediator to help manage large or complex group disputes.

Programs that want to offer services like these and do not already have experienced facilitators on staff will want to get additional group facilitation training. A number of facilitation guidebooks are referenced in the Recommended Resources.

## Process Consulting Models

A method that has been particularly useful when addressing organizational or departmental conflict is commonly known as process consulting. Process consulting emerged from the organizational development field, building on the work of Edgar Schein (1975, 1987) and others. It is essentially a method of group problem solving that addresses issues and themes that are hindering the optimal functioning of the group. Rather than treating the consultant as the expert with the answers, the issues to be explored are brought to the surface using data-gathering procedures such as individual interviews or surveys that gather the thoughts and perspectives of all members of the group. The responses to the questions are then pooled (with the identifying information removed) and presented in a feedback session to the group as a series of themes or issues that the group is dealing with. The group, with the aid of a facilitator, reviews and interprets the data, formulating action plans as necessary to deal with issues of concern that have been identified. Quite often groups decide to engage in additional training in communication skills or conflict resolution methods as part of their action plans.

Some training and development, employee assistance programs, and clinical psychology programs (Wilson, 1997) have begun offering general consulting services for academic departments. Good examples of academic process consulting conducted by programs with specialized conflict resolution expertise include the Conflict Resolution Consulting Group at Syracuse University and the Conflict and Change Center at the University of Minnesota. Departments at the University of Minnesota that engage the Center's Unit Consultation Service for Conflict Management fill out the Organization Conflict Assessment Questionnaire, designed to assess the "conflict culture" of the department. An expanded version of this instrument can be obtained through *Dissertation Abstracts* (Otto, 1998).

## Generic Interventions

The generic approach, another group-level approach often used by campus ombuds, is generally called on to respond to concerns about the behavior of specific members of a unit or department, without directly confronting them or identifying the complainants who brought the concern forward. Usually this involves a presentation, film, or distribution of materials made at a regular staff or faculty meeting or perhaps at a specially called session. The session typically addresses appropriate norms or procedures (for instance, sexual harassment, humor in the workplace, or use of support staff) related to an area of concern. The suggestion for the educational presentation is often framed by the ombuds or some other appropriate administrator as a normal part of the ongoing life of the university rather than as a response to specific complaints from within the department. The general goal is to protect complainants from possible retaliation while reinforcing expectations for appropriate behavior.

## Conflict Resolution Skill Training and Coaching

Perhaps the most valuable work that campus mediation personnel do on a regular basis is to provide conflict resolution skill training. The primary work of many programs is training a diverse group of volunteer mediators from the campus community. This training can build valuable new networks and lead to increased levels of volunteer self-esteem and the regular use of these skills in volunteers' daily lives (Borshuk, 1994). In addition to training volunteers, many programs have branched out by offering training to other sectors of the campus community. Conflict resolution and mediation training has been offered to summer college preparedness programs for disadvantaged youth (Stamato, 1989), new student orientations, residential life staff trainings, student organizations, fraternities and sororities, human resource programs, peer helper programs, faculty professional development seminars, campus police, noncredit and credit short courses, teaching assistant training programs, department chair workshops, and more.

### Negotiation Skills Training

Learning how to negotiate more effectively can be an appealing concept to individuals across the university structure. People often see negotiation training as a way to increase their ability to advocate for their interests and perhaps get more of their needs met (perhaps a bigger office, more pay, or a better work schedule). Thus, offering negotiation workshops can be a successful way to begin introducing conflict resolution concepts to a motivated group.

As part of a demonstration project on the management of organizational conflict and change (which also included process consulting), the University of Minnesota's Conflict and Change Center began offering a negotiation training series aimed at supervisory-level staff and faculty. Day-long negotiation training sessions, endorsed by deans and department heads campuswide, were offered monthly at two levels of skill development. Level I negotiation training provided basic negotiation theory and an opportunity to develop negotiation skills appropriate and useful to university administrators and supervisors. Level II negotiation training offered a continuation and refinement of skill development begun at Level I. The project received considerable buy-in. By the end of two years, two hundred university faculty and staff from over one hundred academic and administrative departments had participated in Level I sessions, and employees spanning twenty-eight departments and organizations had completed Level II.

According to reports, one of the most valuable aspects of the training was the interaction and learning that took place as individuals from different parts of the campus practiced their skills together. Faculty chairs negotiated with secretaries, a member of the board of regents negotiated with an assistant director of the university laundry, and so on. A number of these participants went on to become university mediators, and others began important sources of referral to the program.

## Facilitation Skills Training

Given the importance of working effectively with groups, some campuses provide workshops on facilitation skills for group leaders. For example, on some campuses leaders of student organizations are given facilitation skills training at student leadership retreats, and university staff are invited to attend sessions on running effective meetings. Faculty members are being trained in these skills as well. As an example, the City University of New York (CUNY) Dispute Resolution Consortium, with funding from the CUNY Faculty Development Program, regularly provides workshops in facilitation skills for interested CUNY faculty systemwide. The goal of the training program is to enhance the management of difficult discussions that arise in the classroom and create a more positive, supportive environment for teaching and learning. By extension, a second goal is to enhance the management of other situations that are routinely facilitated by faculty, including committee meetings, research projects, and study groups.

## Conflict Resolution Training for Residence Hall Staff

Special conflict resolution skill training is being offered to residence assistants (RAs), who are typically on the front lines of student conflict intervention. A highly interactive CD-ROM training tool was developed by the Center for Applied Ethics at Carnegie Mellon University for this purpose. Developed under a FIPSE grant, the CD-ROM, titled *Allwyn Hall,* is built around dramatized videos of residence hall conflict situations involving five typical freshman students who encounter some common problems of rooming together, dating, and sharing resources. Trainees, playing the role of an RA, help the students in the video to work through the conflicts they encounter by listening and summarizing, clarifying the problems, and running brainstorming sessions. Also included is an on-line training coach that provides instruction in basic conflict resolution concepts and assists users who are stuck. Information on acquiring the CD-ROM can be found in the Recommended Resources section of this book or at the Campus Mediation Resources Web site.

## Conflict Coaching and Problem Solving for One

Individuals already embroiled in a conflict can also benefit from training on how to resolve their disputes effectively and nonviolently. Informal conflict resolution coaching is provided by many ombuds offices and employee assistance program services and by a growing number of campus mediation programs. This one-on-one training makes sense because in many cases, individuals involved in a dispute are not necessarily looking for a mediator; they would prefer to handle it themselves. However, they may feel uncertain as how best to approach the other party, and they appreciate help and support from a coach. Other individuals who might prefer the services of a mediator may discover that the second party in the dispute is unresponsive to invitations to mediate or agrees to mediate but does not show up at the appointed time.

To respond to this need for additional assistance, some mediation programs offer special sessions and materials for individuals who are motivated to handle conflicts on their own. Allan Tidwell's (1997) article "Problem-Solving for One" provides a detailed example of a service developed by the Macquarie University campus mediation project in Australia. The process seeks to assist the lone party in developing conflict management plans and strategies. The procedure includes a problem analysis, review of options and costs, review of communication skills needed, and the creation of a problem-solving strategy that includes plans for future action.

The Conflict Education Resource Team at Temple University also provides individual support, but in a somewhat different form. The Conflict Coaching service, based in the student counseling office, schedules sessions where individuals dealing with work-related, roommate, relational, or familial conflicts can meet with a pair of trained peer coaches to assess the dispute and their more general style of managing conflict. The coaches help the student to understand past conflict behaviors and explore potentially more effective approaches to managing conflicts in the future. The coaches also enact role-play simulations with the student to help him or her prepare for future interactions. Many of Temple's students are working commuter students who might not connect easily with a standard campus mediation program. The coaching services related to workplace disputes are promoted and perceived by many as a useful career enhancement option for individuals dealing with workplace conflict.

In addition to face-to-face coaching, many mediation programs distribute conflict-handling "tips" sheets as handouts, Web documents, and educational columns in campus newspapers or newsletters. See the Campus Mediation Resources Web site for examples.

## Conflict Prevention Activities

Another broad category of useful nonmediation activities are those designed specifically with conflict prevention in mind. Campus conflict handlers are in a good position to notice patterns of conflict over time and thus are often able to suggest methods to reduce the recurrence of similar disputes in the future.

### Preventing or Reducing Student-Faculty Conflicts

Conflicts between students and their instructors or advisers are relatively common. A growing number of initiatives have been developed addressing what is being called incivility in the classroom as well as conflicts over grading and evaluation practices, advising, interpersonal relations, and harassment. Many of these prevention and training initiatives are housed in offices of teaching and learning, teaching assistant preparation programs, or faculty professional development offices. One technique involves assisting faculty in more carefully spelling out course expectations in syllabi and verbally at the beginning of class, including such topics as a professor's absentee policy, examinations and examination makeup policies, academic integrity, extra credit, and acceptable classroom behavior. Some campuses have developed statements of student, faculty, and university shared responsibilities for classroom learning that are included in syllabi. Others have developed brief documents, distributed to teaching assistants and faculty, providing suggestions for dealing with in-class conflicts. A less common tool is student behavior consultation teams that are available for consultation when staff or faculty have concerns about a student's behavior, whether or not it violates expected codes of conduct.

**Prevention Training for Faculty.** A good example of a broadly targeted faculty conflict management and prevention training tool is the critical incidents vignettes series developed by the Learning and Teaching Centre at the University of Victoria, British Columbia. A collection of four videotapes, each containing ten dramatized vignettes, depicts a wide variety of challenges associated with teaching and learning in higher education. The tapes present a series of highly compressed case studies that pose a problem but offer no preferred solution. Each scene lasts for three or four minutes, and discussion questions follow each episode. A discussion guidebook is included.

The Center for Instructional Development at Syracuse University has also produced a set of seventeen vignettes of difficult classroom situations. These kinds of tapes are most effectively used in teaching development workshops for faculty, adjunct faculty, and teaching assistants where a facilitator is present to guide the discussion.

**Reducing Graduate Student–Adviser Conflicts.** Some student-faculty conflict prevention projects are more focused and intensive. Michigan State University's Building Mutuality/Setting Expectations Program addresses issues that can lead to conflicts between graduate students and faculty. Unresolved conflicts with their advisers can have painful consequences for graduate students, who are usually quite dependent on these advisers for financial support through assistantships, as well as more general political support as they develop and conduct their research, defend their dissertation or thesis, and request letters of reference and recommendations. The project has a number of key goals, including introducing faculty and students to the practice of interest-based negotiation skills and the process of setting expectations and resolving conflicts; raising awareness of issues of potential conflict in doctoral education; and improving graduate handbooks.

The program provides new and continuing graduate students with skill-building sessions on interest-based negotiation and conflict resolution to increase their skill level when dealing with faculty and other students. The program also engages graduate students and faculty in facilitated discussions of expectations. The discussions are triggered by viewing a few (chosen based on discipline and any presenting problems in the department) of the more than eighty available video vignettes developed by the program for this purpose. Finally, interest-based negotiation approaches are being used to establish collectively agreed-on departmental understandings of mutual expectations and responsibilities. The program is working to incorporate these understandings into departmental handbooks and the broader organizational culture.

## Reducing Student-Student Conflicts

Other prevention efforts are aimed specifically at reducing conflicts between students who live together. The work often begins before students arrive on campus, because some conflicts can be headed off through careful matching of roommates based on information provided on application forms (Lovejoy, 1995). Computers in most cases are now used to make roommate assignments on large campuses. However, some residential life programs still set aside considerable time for experienced staff who attempt to read between the lines of a student's comments in ways that a computer cannot.

Many residence life programs also promote the use of roommate agreement forms and floormate agreement forms in residence halls. The forms prompt students to discuss, often with the aid of residential assistants, a list of potentially conflicting issues with their roommates and sometimes floormates, at the start of their time living together. The forms provide a starting place for discussion and agreement building, and may be used to encourage further discussion and renegotiation if problems arise. Finally, some residential life programs have experimented with special student workshops on skills for living together (Waldo, 1989).

Another now well-developed area of prevention work is dating violence and date rape prevention workshops, offered on many campuses. These programs, often in affiliation with campus women's centers, work to build shared awareness of the problem of interpersonal violence and to prevent problems that might occur due to the lack of communication between partners or awareness of community standards. Some programs are presented to mixed groups, while others focus on same-sex groups to provide for more open discussion. The North Dakota Campus Violence Project's Web site provides a good example of a statewide campus-based effort that appeals to both men and women. As a different example, I was part of a men's group at Syracuse University, Man-to-Man, that provided workshops for men in residence halls and fraternities on sexual assault and violence prevention. We also participated in an annual coordinated national event, BrotherPeace, in which men spoke out against violence across the country. In its biggest year, fifty-four cities participated simultaneously. In Canada, the White Ribbon Campaign represents a similar ongoing annual campaign by men to eliminate men's violence against women.

Some campuses are also working to increase students' ability to function effectively within the kinds of ad hoc groups that they may encounter in laboratories and when doing group assignments for class. Some departments or individual faculty members with courses that require a significant amount of group work have developed training sessions on group skills and have built it into the curriculum. They sometimes draw on campus mediation program personnel to help develop and staff these training sessions. For instance, the Canisius College Mediation Service distributes a handout to science laboratory groups, "Group Diseases in the Science Classroom: A Reference Guide to Symptoms and Treatments" (Lyons, 1998), that provides tips on effective group work and offers mediation services should disputes arise. In a related effort, the Conflict Resolution Resource Service at Nova Southeastern University distributes a handout, "Sample Guidelines for Giving or Receiving Criticism Without Getting Hurt or Hurting Others," to student and staff groups.

Mediation programs have also worked closely with student governments. For instance, because of their perceived neutrality, mediation program volunteers have been called on to help monitor hotly contested student government elections by observing the polling sites (Volpe and Witherspoon, 1992) and serving as the first point of contact for student election–related grievances. They have also moderated candidate forums, provided recount services, and facilitated contentious budget meetings.

## Partnering on Campus Construction Efforts

Another kind of dispute prevention concept catching on at colleges and universities is called partnering; it is most commonly used to facilitate the successful completion of major campus construction projects. As an example, Carlton (1993) provides an inside view of a partnering session that California State University at Bernadino used to get a stalled $24 million health and physical education building job back on track. By using partnering, formerly opposing factions within the construction team were able to come together and work out resolutions to their problems, and avoid suing each other and the university.

Pioneered by the U.S. Army Corps of Engineers in the early 1990s, partnering has quickly become popular within the construction industry. The partnering process normally involves a one or two-day retreat attended by all stakeholders (decisions makers as well as job site supervisors) in the particular project. The retreat is usually held at a neutral location (a resort or private meeting facility) and is led by experienced facilitators who help the participants to focus on communication, negotiation, identification of mutual goals and objectives, and details of project-specific potential problems and solutions. The purpose is not to change any contractual responsibilities but rather to focus on building the working relationships among the participants. Common documents created at sessions to smooth on-site problem solving include issue escalation matrixes, detailing who has decision-making authority over what issues, and a partnering charter, which lays out general agreements in principle supported by all participants (Hunter and Hoenig, 1996).

## Labor Relations on Campus

At a recent state of the university address, Stanford University president Gerhard Casper discussed at some length a troubling trend of increased litigiousness and grievances both on his campus and nationally. He cited a recent study indicating that legal defense costs for private colleges and universities nationwide have risen 250 percent in only five years, from an average of $70,000 per claim in 1992 to an average of $175,000 per claim in 1997. He estimated that the handling of a faculty grievance at Stanford University that is complex and is appealed through the various levels takes from 350 to 500 hours of faculty and staff time. If a lawsuit is brought in such cases, it adds from 50 to several hundred hours of attorney time per side, with considerably more in some extreme cases (Casper, 1998). The overall concern of rising costs related to disputes is felt broadly, and many campuses, both public and private, are exploring ways to respond effectively. At Stanford, the president appointed a committee to explore reducing the complexity of the faculty discipline and faculty grievance procedures.

Unionized colleges and universities are also exploring ways to reduce the time and considerable costs associated with disputes that go to outside arbitrators (Julius, 1993). On some campuses this has meant increased support for and use of internal grievance mediation as a step prior to outside arbitration. Another interesting model is the one developed by four campuses within the Connecticut State University System (Pernal, 1996/1997). In this system, an arbitration-type step was built into the grievance process, but it remains within the state system rather than being sent outside. When handling faculty grievances, the system uses grievance arbitration panels with equal numbers of employees representing the administration and faculty members. These individuals, drawn from each of the three neighboring institutions, have sufficient distance from the area of dispute to guarantee some measure of detachment. Each panel comprises three members of the American Association of University Professors and three members of the administration, with the stipulation that no panel member can be from the university where the grievance originated. The grievance arbitration panel is the final step before professional arbitration is engaged. Only in the event of a tie vote can either party, if it chooses, take the issue to outside arbitration.

In order for the panels to function effectively and to bring new panelists into the process, regular training sessions are held involving human resource personnel, administrators, and faculty from all four campuses working together. This network of positive relations has proved useful as well in resolving other nongrievance disputes before they escalate.

## Interest-Based Bargaining

A number of unionized campuses are beginning to experiment with a new form of collective bargaining, known as interest-based or collaborative bargaining, in an attempt to reduce some of the negative effects of traditional contentious negotiations. Interest-based bargaining is essentially an alternative style of negotiating used to achieve positive results for both parties. The emphasis in traditional bargaining is on the relative power of the parties and their willingness to use it both in regard to specific issues as well as the overall settlement. Interest-based bargaining is instead a problem-solving and consensus approach to negotiations that focuses on the interests of the parties.

In interest-based bargaining, administration and faculty usually begin by participating in joint training provided by bargaining consultants. The workshops introduce parties to nonadversarial collective bargaining concepts, give both sides a common language, educate them as to what is involved and who is involved, and explore the steps required to develop a collaborative working relationship. The interest-based bargaining process used at the University of Montana and Eastern Washington University is well documented in a *Negotiation Journal* article on collaborative bargaining in public universities (Dennison, Drummond, and Hobgood, 1997). The United Faculty of Central, the faculty union of Central Washington University, maintains a Web site with more information on interest-based bargaining on campus. Although the process is still experimental in higher education, experience in the K–12 sector has been rather extensive, and the university setting appears poised for more work of this type in the future.

## Supporting Nonviolent Social Protest and Change _____

Although student protests today are less visible nationally than in the turbulent 1960s, they still occur with surprising regularity. A 1992–1997 study conducted by Arthur Levine and his colleague Jeanette Cureton revealed that 25 percent of today's undergraduates have participated in campus protests, up from the 1976 estimate of 19 percent. Surprising to some, the 1997 figure represents a level of activity close to the all-time high of 28 percent reported in 1968. In comparison to the late 1960s, the majority of contemporary protests are about campus-specific rather than national issues (which helps explain their relative invisibility nationally), often involve subgroups and smaller events instead of campuswide rallies, and commonly focus on issues such as multiculturalism, human rights, and college costs. While tactics have changed (including increased use of e-mail and litigation as strategies) dramatic takeovers of campus buildings still occurred on 3 percent of the campuses surveyed (Levine, 1999). It is also important to note that much current protest is directed at other groups on campus rather than at the campus administration.

Responses to campus protest have changed over time as well. At the height of the radical student protest movements in the 1960s, administrators often resorted to use of campus security or outside forces to remove protesters forcibly. The first campus ombuds programs were established in the late 1960s to provide a better response than attempting to ignore or suppress the protests and conflict. Although their focus has broadened, ombuds programs continue to provide an important opportunity for dissatisfied community members to begin addressing their concerns. With respect to protests, reports indicate that in comparison to the past, today's administrators and student protesters interact using more preplanning and notice and employ more negotiation and much less violence (Collison, 1990; Levine 1999). Because protestors and campus administrators may not have open lines of communication, campus mediation program coordinators should consider developing their capacity to respond in campus protest situations. Trustworthy campus mediation programs can greatly facilitate the negotiations required to settle many campus protests (Mikalson, 1994; Volpe and Witherspoon, 1992). However, getting all the parties to the table can be difficult and sometimes is inappropriate based on the timing, the level of organization of involved groups, or considerable power imbalances. Program coordinators may thus wish to expand their view of their role beyond that of mediator to include a larger function as a community peacemaker and networker.

The Quaker peacemaker (and mediator) Adam Curle has intervened in many complicated and extremely damaging social conflicts and has a tremendous amount of experience working informally with conflict. He reminds conflict intervenors that mediation is but one method among many and must not be treated as a panacea. "We should not always see mediation as the standard response to conflict," he says. "Instead, we should seek to establish the conditions in which mediation may be effectively practiced in conjunction with other tools for transforming violence into peaceful relationships" (Curle, 1995, p. 91).

Taking a perspective that examines the conditions in which mediation can be effective brings with it numerous larger implications. For one thing, a peacemaking perspective acknowledges that many social conflicts resulting in protest and calls for change have a developmental history often rooted in inequity and injustice. Peacemakers may have the opportunity to work with the conflict at various stages of its development, both prior to and after the emergence of public protest, attempting at all points to preserve people's dignity and minimize potential suffering. In *Making Peace* (1971) Curle suggests that a number of important aspects need to be taken into consideration as a social conflict emerges and unpeaceful relations are transformed into peaceful ones. Two key variables are the relative balance of power between the conflicting parties and the level of awareness of conflicting interests and needs. Using this framework, peacemakers face different tasks at different points in the developmental process. When awareness of an injustice or conflict is initially low, within both the negatively affected group and the larger community, peacemakers should support individual and group efforts at education. As increasing awareness of issues leads to demands for change, peacemakers should support advocacy efforts and nonviolent confrontations designed to call attention to the issues, particularly when the power imbalance is great and awareness is still increasing. Finally, when awareness of the conflict is high and the relative power of parties is more balanced due to group organizing efforts, mediation and negotiation skills training is called for.

The inclination and opportunity to take this kind of perspective on campus conflict will vary considerably depending on a program's location, staffing, and emphasis. And not all protests will fit this form. However, the ultimate goal from a peacemaking perspective is to restructure relationships (which for some is a radical notion) to produce just and peaceful relations. From this point of view, bringing up and confronting latent conflict is seen not as increasing conflict but as an intrinsic part of the larger peacemaking process.

It is important to be clear on the role one is playing in conflict situations and not to assume that the mediation office or any one person in it can provide all necessary supports. To help mediators locate their role, the late Jim Laue, a former community relations service mediator and faculty member at the Institute for Conflict Analysis and Resolution, identified a range of primary roles or functions that may be played out in community disputes: activism, advocacy, mediation, research, and rule enforcement (Laue and Cormick, 1978). Part of maintaining credibility as a mediator involves developing ways to demonstrate respect for and develop rapport with individuals playing the other equally important functions. Mediation program staff should take the opportunity to develop relationships and work cooperatively (if informally) with others on campus who serve the function of helping to research the existence or root causes of conflict, enforcing community rules and standards, advocating for needed changes, or assisting disadvantaged groups in getting organized through activism and education. Developing these kinds of relationships takes time and care, but is important to those who seek to adopt more of a peacemaking role on campus and to be respected as a mediator when the time is ripe.

A number of nonmediation innovations that have developed on campuses directly support nonviolent campus protest and expression of dissenting views. One good example is the long-standing Observer Program developed by concerned faculty at the University of California at Berkeley. The program originators felt that neutral campus staff should observe campus events where there was a possibility of a conflict. Berkeley staff volunteers are still available to act as impartial witnesses at volatile campus events, and they provide objective reports and a calming effect. Today the student services office coordinates the program. Other similar examples include peacekeeper or monitor training programs offered by some student activist groups and campus ministry offices. A typical job description for a peacekeeper is to stand on the fringe of a protest action or between two rival groups and monitor for potentially dangerous or threatening situations, moving to intervene when necessary to prevent violence. They are usually made easily identifiable through hats, T-shirts, or armbands that set them apart from the group.

Other projects work directly with current and potential student protesters, sometimes teaching the basic organizing skills necessary to educate and mobilize others to a cause. In other circumstances work involves teaching potential protestors the skills of disciplined nonviolent protest, using role plays and other training activities to prepare participants for possible challenges. Considerable information is now available on the Internet for campus activists who wish more training in nonviolent protest strategies and tactics. Two relatively well-known groups are the Center for Campus Organizing and Nonviolence International. The latter provides an extensive online bibliography of available materials on nonviolence training.

Campus mediation programs that help a university respond effectively and respectfully to campus protest are providing a valuable service by helping the campus to respond and adapt to change and by providing students with the opportunity to develop leadership skills and an awareness of their ability to make a difference.

## Responding to Conflicts over Diversity, Culture, and Values

Many campuses face conflicts involving clashes between diverse cultures, political views, and strongly held moral values. These kinds of conflicts may often involve acts of incivility or violence and can quickly become quite heated. A great deal of thinking and experimentation has occurred on how to respond best to these kinds of issues. By 1992 more than 130 American universities had enacted speech codes designed to limit the offensive language that often fuels these conflicts (Etzioni, 1993). These codes have been highly controversial because of concerns about placing limits on free speech and difficulties in determining where and how to draw the line and how to punish offenders. Given these concerns, the majority of universities and colleges have not yet developed such codes. Examples of conflict resolution–related projects that address disputes over diversity and difference are presented next. A more general source of information on campus diversity initiatives is DiversityWeb, an on-line project developed by the Association of American Colleges and Universities and the University of Maryland.

### Modified Mediation Models

In "Mediation of Race-Related Conflicts on Campus" Michel Avery (1990) describes her work at Haverford College when she was invited to develop a campus mediation project that could help respond to disputes over alleged acts of racism or prejudice (such as racist or hostile graffiti and offensive public statements). The question raised by the invitation—whether there is a role for mediation in disputes involving prejudice or incivility—is somewhat vexing. Some would argue that rather than mediation, punishment or censure of the offender is in order to send a clear signal about the inappropriateness of certain behavior. Avery and others (including me) believe that there is a role for mediative processes, but that it requires changes in the expectations for and format of the sessions.

The traditional mediation model as commonly practiced focuses on avoidance of blame, attempts to limit discussions of the past, limits participation to those directly involved in the immediate conflict, and emphasizes settlement of issues, all of which can be problematic when dealing with racism and prejudice. The model developed at Haverford was named Communication Outreach, rather than mediation, to highlight the difference in processes. The program remains distinct from the Honor Council and is designed to create a safe space where individuals who have felt victimized can speak their minds, community members can express their feelings about the incidents, and alleged offenders can have an opportunity to learn about the impact of their behaviors on others and begin to reintegrate themselves into the community. The primary goal of the process is increased understanding rather than a formal and final settlement. The model is similar in many ways to the family group conferencing and victim offender reconciliation programs that are growing in popularity in criminal justice circles.

A number of other campus mediation programs, most notably the Conflict Mediation Program at the University of California at Los Angeles and the Mediation and Negotiation Team at the University of Massachusetts at Amherst, have paid special attention to dealing with diversity disputes as they built their programs and trained their mediators. The UCLA Conflict Mediation Program (CMP) received a FIPSE grant to help develop its project and enable it to provide small stipends to participants (many of them minority students) who work with the program. In addition to composing teams of two to five persons to work with particular conflicts, CMP has initiated a series of campus forums each year on provocative topical issues with the idea of exposing students, and other members of the campus community, to constructive academic discourse and disagreement. The UCLA training program for participants consists of a series of workshops and an academic course. The course examines principles of conflict and conflict resolution with an emphasis on racial, ethnic, and other diversity-related conflicts. Workshops are directed toward the development of skills appropriate to preparing members to intervene in diversity-related disputes—for example, mediation techniques, cross-cultural communication, facilitation of group discussion, and the design of proactive dispute management programs.

Although not specifically designed to handle acts of prejudice or incivility, another valuable example of the modification of basic mediation model to handle cultural differences is the Pacific Mediation model developed by Bruce Barnes and his associates at the University of Hawaii (Barnes, 1994). The model draws on the Program on Conflict Resolution's extensive experiences working with many different cultural groups. The Pacific Mediation model, which usually involves multiple sessions, considers cultural differences in dispute-handling approaches as the sessions are designed and the intervenors are chosen. It also builds in bicultural and bilingual feedback channels that provide the intervenors with information on how the process is being perceived by the different cultural groups involved.

## Town Hall Meetings

The public convening of individuals or groups in a town meeting format to discuss controversial issues can be an effective tool for promoting respectful coexistence. During a period of considerable strain in black-white and student-administration relations at Syracuse University, I served as one of the moderators for a series of monthly town meetings held in the student center. The year-long series began with a structured session on race relations using portions of the Frontline documentary on campus racial conflict, *Racism 101,* to help frame discussion. The session was well received by students, faculty, and administrators, and the meetings were continued and expanded to cover other contentious topics on campus as they emerged.

In order to be successful, town meetings require an even-handed moderator and clear, well-publicized ground rules and procedures to prevent conflict escalation or domination of the meeting by one participant or group. The application of campus town meetings is perhaps best developed at John Jay College of Criminal Justice, part of CUNY (Volpe, 1994, 1998). What began as a short-term response to a crisis (a 1989 student takeover of the college's buildings) has become a regular part of the campus life. The monthly meetings now "serve as an ongoing proactive, preventive, and sometimes settlement mechanism for developing continuing dialogue between ethnically diverse individuals and groups" (Volpe, 1998, p. 383). The wider CUNY Dispute Resolution Consortium, with support from the Surdna Foundation, has been working to expand the use of town meetings to other CUNY campuses. In the process, it has developed a videotape and sample guidelines for town meeting facilitators.

## Dialogue Groups

Many campuses have been experimenting with the use of dialogue groups, which mediators often help to facilitate because of their training. On some campuses, groups are used during times of crisis or as a short-term experiment and on others as an ongoing part of life in their community. One of the best examples of the latter approach is the Program on Intergroup Relations, Conflict and Community (IGRCC) at the University of Michigan, Ann Arbor. The program was inaugurated in 1988 at a time of heightened racial and ethnic tensions in an effort to advance student understanding of and respect for diversity and to augment student skills in responding to intergroup conflicts.

Peer-facilitated meetings of students from different social identity groups are held each semester focusing around a particular theme or issue. Participants, numbering from ten to sixteen, meet weekly in a small group, semistructured discussion format. Readings and experientially based activities are incorporated to encourage dialogue and discussion of pertinent issues. Program facilitators define the groups by ethnicity, race, religion, gender, sexual orientation, ability, class, age, and other characteristics, depending on the chosen focus of the dialogue. IGRCC trains student peer facilitators in methods of dialogue and facilitation by means of an intensive training course. They are also enrolled in a three-credit practicum-supervision course during the semester they lead dialogues.

Conflict resolution and diversity initiatives have also been attempted on a larger scale. I was a primary trainer for a project funded by the Department of Higher Education of the State of New Jersey in 1989. The initiative provided a grant to Jersey City State College to host a statewide student leadership initiative on race relations and conflict resolution. The project, among other components, brought together teams of eight to ten students (mixed minority and majority) and staff from all fifty-four New Jersey campuses for one of three weekend workshop retreats at a conservation camp. The two-day training focused on diversity and conflict resolution skills and on strengthening relationships among the diverse team members attending from each campus.

## Creative Controversy in the Classroom

One well-developed classroom approach to developing skill dealing with diverse points of view is known as academic or creative controversy (Johnson and Johnson, 1995). The process, particularly effective when used as part of a broader cooperative learning classroom philosophy, engages students by using controversial subjects as the focal point for the development of critical thinking, complex reasoning, and problem-solving skills. The basic format requires members of a group to do the following:

- Research and prepare different positions.
- Make a persuasive presentation of their researched position.
- Refute the opposing position while rebutting attacks on their own position.
- View the issue from a variety of perspectives (reverse roles).
- Synthesize and integrate the opposing positions into one mutually agreed upon position.

In addition to providing faculty with a tool for teaching controversial subjects, research suggests that structuring controversy into lessons can result in greater motivation to learn, higher achievement, greater retention, more frequent higher-level reasoning, more creative thinking and problem solving, and more constructive social and cognitive development (Johnson and Johnson, 1995).

## Group Self-Assessment and Dialogue Tools

In addition to projects focusing on potential conflicts between groups, sometimes mediation program staff are asked to assist groups struggling with internal divisions. Although formal mediation may apply at times, especially if a small number of identifiable individuals are at the center of the controversy, many times the entire group is affected by the dispute. Group members often develop strong feelings that can lead to problems or polarization within the group if they are not dealt with. Fortunately, many exercises have been developed that trained group leaders can use to examine and address divisions within groups. These tools are designed to enable people to talk in a large or small group session when anxiety is high, with the focus being on public disclosure of information about differences within the group in a tightly structured format.

Human spectrums, one of these tools, provide a group with information about its members and its overall composition. That information can include attitudes, preferences, or positions on a topic a group is considering. The facilitator describes the opposite ends of a spectrum. The group members' task is then to arrange themselves in the appropriate order. People stand and place themselves somewhere on the spectrum. In conflict situations, one end of the imaginary line might be designated for people holding strong beliefs in support of a particular idea or position, and the other end is of people who strongly disagree with the idea or position. While standing, they are invited to share why they chose the spot they did. This process can be very revealing as people discover the range of perspectives that exist within the group and the mix of positions as different topics are raised for discussion. It also provides an opportunity for people in the middle to share how the issue is influencing them. When spectrums are properly constructed and conducted, they are totally nonjudgmental. Appropriate labels are chosen so that neither end of the spectrum nor any place on it provides a perceived advantage or benefit.

In fishbowls or Samoan circles, participants gather in two concentric circles: an inner circle with a table (optional) and four chairs and an outer circle, with ample walking and aisle space. Everyone begins in the outer circle. The issue is presented, and discussion begins. Those most interested take chairs in the inner circle, and those less interested stay in the outer circle. All are able to move in or out of the center as the discussion flows or topics change. Each speaker makes a comment or asks a question. Speakers are not restricted in what they say, but they must sit in the inner circle. Someone wishing to speak stands behind a chair, which signals those already in the circle to relinquish their chairs. No outside conversations are allowed. Comments are often recorded. Votes of opinions held by nonspeakers may be taken at the end, if desired. To close a meeting, empty seats are taken away one by one until there are no more chairs. An adaptation of this tool by Barbara Daté, sometimes referred to as the Daté Discernment Process, uses a horseshoe of chairs rather than a circle, only two speaker chairs, and the addition of a designated listener–support person chair that is occupied by a volunteer who serves as a careful reflective listener for the speaker as part of the process.

Interviews are another technique. One to three individuals from each perspective are interviewed in the presence of the entire group, followed by open discussion. In role-reversal interviews, each interviewed person is asked to pretend that he or she is a person with the opposite view.

When role-reversal presentations are used, someone from each side is asked to spend time with someone from the other side and then present their point of view to the group, allowing for corrections or additions from the interviewee.

Resources such as the Mennonite Concilation Service's *Mediation and Facilitation Manual* (MCS, 1995) and other similar group leadership materials provide information on how to apply these methods safely and effectively. Given the sensitive and sometimes volatile nature of value disputes, it pays to be well prepared before engaging in one of these kinds of activities.

## Debate Moderation

A final example in this general category of services is the provision of moderators for campus debates on controversial issues. At Syracuse University, for instance, I was asked to help moderate large public debates on the death penalty, the Gulf War, and censorship in the music industry. Although debates are often adversarial, they do provide a forum for community discussion of important issues, and they can be followed up by small group discussions that provide an opportunity for more integrative dialogue. Serving as a moderator for a public debate may also garner useful publicity for the mediation program.

## Working with Offenders

In many cases, campus conflicts involve the actions of someone who does an act that falls outside the bounds of acceptable community behavior, as spelled out in various codes of conduct or law. Another useful role that is developing on some campuses is what might loosely be referred to as postsanction services. These services are designed to work with individuals or groups who have acted inappropriately to help them learn from their behavior and reintegrate themselves into the community.

In some cases, both parties to a dispute have acted inappropriately and may receive some sanction from the campus judicial program or conduct board. For instance, in the case of a physical altercation between two or more students, multiple students may be found guilty of a violation. However, despite the sanctions, these parties still have to see each other in class or in the residence halls or on a sports team. To respond to this issue, some mediation programs facilitate postsanction sessions involving all the parties to discuss how they will relate to one another in the future. The sessions provide participants an opportunity to reestablish friendly relations if appropriate and to set basic "rules of engagement" if they do not see ever being on friendly terms.

Another useful initiative targeted for offenders are skills courses on anger management for students who have been charged with an assault or have exhibited difficulties managing their anger appropriately. In addition to providing mediation services, trained volunteers with the Campus Mediation Program at Saint Francis Xavier University in Nova Scotia facilitate short anger management seminars for referred students. Generally the dean of students mandates students to attend the session as part of a sanction, but self-referrals are also acceptable. Other campuses have developed their own workshops for men identified as being sexually or physically aggressive in dating relationships, or they take advantage of off-campus programs serving other populations.

For cases where there are very clear victim and offender, many communities (but not yet many campuses) have developed programs that bring together victims and offenders for structured interactions. The programs fit loosely under the framework known as restorative justice, going by various other names, such as victim offender mediation or reconciliation programs, family group conferencing, and circle sentencing. Most of these community models limit their services to juvenile and property offenses, but some programs have addressed more serious offenses like rape, violent assaults, and drunk-driving fatalities as well. These models are very different in their emphasis from the kind of community or civil mediation model that most people are aware of. For instance, the family group conference model involves friends and family members of both the victim and offender, who also have the opportunity to talk about their concerns. All of the models typically require more intensive preparatory meetings with the parties and focus much less on reaching an agreement and much more on dialogue, understanding, empathy, healing, and jointly discussed methods of restitution and reparation.

These programs are designed to permit victims to tell offenders how their behavior has affected them and to ask questions of offenders to learn more about why and how they acted as they did. In some cases, the victim has the opportunity to influence the kind of sanction or restitution that will be expected of the offender as a result of these meetings. Restorative justice models are valuable because they provide a setting where sanctions can be combined with an opportunity for the offender to begin to make things right again through restitution or community service. The Center for Restorative Justice and Mediation in the University of Minnesota School of Social Work and the Center for Peacemaking and Conflict Studies at Fresno Pacific University are useful sources for information and contacts.

Although there are over three hundred victim-offender community-based mediation programs in the United States, experimentation is only now beginning on college campuses. I am aware of only a small number of programs that have tried using some variation of this approach, and often the model was developed as a one-time response to a unique situation rather than as an ongoing program. Cases that have been addressed using these kinds of methods involved issues such as drunken assault, petty theft, vandalism of property, acts of prejudice (such as hostile notes or graffiti), injury from an item thrown out a residence hall window, and sexual assaults of the type commonly called date rape. Sexual assault cases are particularly controversial, and great care must be taken when considering the use of even some modified form of mediation in these kinds of circumstances. Cloke (1988) and Weddle (1992) have set forth a number of conditions that prescribe the use of structured negotiation of sexual misconduct cases on campus, and Sisson and Todd (1995) discuss their experiments using mediation in sexual assault cases at the University of Virginia.

## Fostering Positive Interaction in the Local Community

Projects that work to improve relations with and in the local community sometimes address conflicts that arise between the university and the surrounding local community. Conflicts of this sort are not uncommon. For example, a survey (London, 1991) of town-gown relations in twenty-seven college towns identified concerns over student housing and shortages of parking as top problems.

In response to these kinds of concerns, many campus programs now offer mediation services for neighborhood disputes as well as for those that occur on campus. In addition to mediation, a number of other interesting initiatives have been developed. For example, Boston College has a community assistance program (CAP) directed by the Office of the Dean for Student Development, with teams of graduate students available to respond to neighbors' complaints or concerns involving undergraduates living off-campus. The goal of the program is to resolve issues without involving other authorities. The program uses approximately eight students and a student coordinator who are on duty weekends and some holidays and may also work during special events, such as home football game days. Typically CAP responds to complaints regarding student behavior that are relayed by the college police department, but they also receive direct referrals. Over the years, as the program has become established, the number and kinds of complaints have changed, with fewer major incidents being reported. The directors of the program attribute this to the emphasis placed on using mediation and conflict resolution skills in the interventions.

Other campuses, often through the off-campus housing office, have developed good neighbor handbooks that explain community bylaws, list useful community services that may include mediation, and encourage students to introduce themselves to their neighbors. These handbooks are provided to all students who use the campus rental housing listing services to locate a place to live. Some colleges host regular "get to know your neighbors" barbecues, often in conjunction with local neighborhood associations, or provide staff who make contact with neighborhood residents and arrange informal meetings at homes within the neighborhoods. Other campuses have developed student "listening project" teams that go door to door and talk with neighbors and students alike about their concerns, and then attempt to develop policies or procedures to address these concerns.

Another valuable service offered by some colleges and universities is the use of the "good offices" of the university to help resolve local conflicts. Sometimes this involves high-ranking college officials such as the college president. This was the case, for instance, when Medgar Evers College in Brooklyn, New York, was called on to help soothe racial and religious hostilities between black and Hasidic residents of the Crown Heights section of Brooklyn. The president of the college hosted and cochaired a special community relations committee, and the college sponsored several community speakouts and hosted basketball games between black and Hasidic youths. Another relevant example at a somewhat different level was the role played by Chapman College's president when he brought Walt Disney Company executives together with officials of the city of Anaheim, California, to cement a deal that would keep the California Angels baseball team in the city. Negotiations had seriously foundered over responsibility for improvements to the stadium, and both sides had publicly declared the talks over.

## New Community Meetings

An innovative use of campus good offices, in this case to help address strong value differences dividing the community, is the New Community Meetings Initiative (NCMI), a conflict resolution model being developed and tested by the Conflict Resolution Center at the University of Oregon. The philosophy of the center is that new solutions, which benefit all community members, can arise out of collaboration between previously polarized leaders and groups. Their stated purpose is to make it possible for alienated community leaders to build community strength and cooperation in the midst of controversial issues (NCMI, 1998). The center, affiliated with the ADR program at the University of Oregon Law School and the Oregon Pacific Research Institute, works primarily with off-campus community leaders. However, the effects of their work are felt both on- and off-campus because of the broad scope of the issues they address.

The NCMI model was first applied in 1994 to the locally divisive topic of gay rights. That application produced, among other things, a six-page statement of agreements that detailed substantial common ground identified and developed by conservative Christian leaders and gay rights activists. During the summer of 1996, conservative Christians, feminists, and gay activists built on those results when concerns arose over the Promise Keepers' rental of the University of Oregon's stadium for a meeting of forty thousand followers of their conservative Christian men's organization. The Conflict Resolution Center and the university administration jointly sponsored a series of dialogues that resulted in strengthened relationships between local Promise Keepers' leaders and Eugene feminists and gay and lesbian activists. More recent work by the center focuses on issues of economic growth and sustainable development in the Eugene-Springfield area.

## Service by Academic Programs in Dispute Resolution

Another broad set of valuable community services are those provided by faculty, grant-funded staff, and students working in the growing number of academic programs in conflict studies. Because conflict studies is an applied field, most graduate-level and many undergraduate programs require students to participate in some kind of internship or practicum. The range of work being done by students and faculty is tremendously broad. A few examples are provided here, but they do not capture the true extent of the valuable work that is being done.

**Applied Practice and Theory Practice Teams.** Students in the doctoral program at the Institute for Conflict Analysis and Resolution at George Mason University participate in year-long applied practice and theory project teams (Birkhoff and Warfield, 1996) as part of their core curriculum. Students join one of three faculty-supervised teams focusing, respectively, on assessing and responding to conflicts in deeply divided societies and communities, conflicts involving governance and public institutions, or racial and ethnic conflict in schools. Students work together to assess community conflict resolution needs, design and deliver conflict resolution training sessions, organize and facilitate public meetings, coach people on new skills, mediate cases, and help design new conflict management systems. Many of the projects are ongoing from year to year, permitting work to continue as students leave the group and others join it.

**Peace and Conflict Resolution Skills Using the Public Library.** Interns from Nova Southeastern University's Department of Dispute Resolution staff a project in the Main Broward County Library called Peace Place. In addition to providing access in one section of the library to a large collection of peace and conflict materials and games, Peace Place sponsors special cooperative games for children on Saturday afternoons and skill training and resource sharing workshops for parents and teachers.

**Shop Owner-Customer Dispute Prevention.** The Center for Peace and Conflict Studies at Wayne State University has helped relieve growing tensions between Chaldean-Iraqi retail shop owners and primarily black customers in inner-city Detroit neighborhoods through the Harmony Project, now in its third phase. The first phase of the project involved a long series of negotiations between shop owners and local neighborhood associations on perceived areas of tension surrounding the stores. The result was a list of joint agreements addressing concerns of both shop owners and their customers and local neighbors that is posted in all shops and around the neighborhood. Current work involves training local community liaisons from each community who make themselves available to respond immediately to disputes arising at any of the participating stores.

Conflict intervention, transformation, and resolution projects of many forms are being developed and applied on and by college and university campuses across the country. While complementary to mediation, these efforts go well beyond it in scope. Initiatives addressing conflict prevention, training, group processes, living amid diversity, dealing with value disputes, and maintaining positive town-gown relations have all added tremendous value to the life of the campus community. As the field of dispute resolution in higher education matures, these kinds of innovative efforts are likely to spread, and campus mediation program personnel are sure to be involved.

# RESOURCES, FORMS, AND DOCUMENTS

## A: Statements of Purpose for Conflict Resolution Programs

### Purdue University

The process of resolving conflict is educational. By establishing a forum where each party is heard, we teach listening. By creating an environment where each party can speak, we teach communication. By developing the processes that seek resolution, we teach the importance of dialogue. And, by building these processes into a method of mediating disputes we teach citizenship. The Purdue Mediation and Conciliation Center is founded on the principle of Partnership and Service Learning. Embedded in its mission is the intention to support existing conflict resolution processes and procedures while conducting research on the discourse of mediation and its effectiveness. Recognizing that the mission encompasses both the process of effective mediation and the product of an informed citizen, the Center's purpose is both functional and educational [www.tech.purdue.edu/orgs/mediate/about.htm].

### Salisbury State University

The Center for Conflict Resolution at Salisbury State University endeavors to address conflict in the service of social change. Our aim is to replace adversarial and violent modes of resolving conflict with nonviolent, collaborative processes and techniques. We want to provide tangible ways for individuals and groups to communicate constructively, thoughtfully and compassionately. We seek to enhance cooperation among people in conflict so that they see their mutual involvement and responsibility. We wish to assist in meeting the needs of all people in our communities [www.inter-com.net/npo/cfcr/].

### Washington State University

*Washington State University (Pullman, Washington) Human Relations and Educational Services Mission Statement*

Washington State University's Human Relations and Educational Services' institutional mission is to support the University's mission of teaching, research, and public service/outreach by providing leadership and services that empower university constituents with the ability and processes for effective human relations and for creating an inclusive institutional climate. Guided by the institutional mission and institutional values, the program provides facilitative and educational processes for the creation of inclusive environments that enable university personnel and students to accomplish institutional, professional and personal goals. Specifically, the program provides the following to Washington State University students, employees and faculty:

> Educational opportunities and experiences for students, employees and faculty to create a cognitive, affective and behavioral foundation for interacting with cultural differences and addressing conflict;

> The development of student, employee and faculty skills and abilities to peacefully and constructively address differences;

> The development of constructive human interactions in a complex, multicultural learning and work environment;

> Conflict resolution processes and services for addressing disputes;

> And the development of collaborative partnerships with the university community and surrounding institutional communities to address issues of inclusion and climate [www.wsu.edu/~hres/mission.htm].

### Syracuse University

*Syracuse University Campus Mediation Center Organizational Structure and By-Laws 1991*

The Campus Mediation Center is a collaborative project of the students, faculty, administration, and staff at Syracuse University. Its primary purpose is to provide members of the University community direct assistance in creatively and nonviolently resolving their interpersonal disputes. The core function of the Center is to provide trained volunteer mediators who help facilitate a problem-solving process that supports the nonviolent resolution of disputes, and which still leaves the final responsibility for resolving the dispute up to the parties involved. The process of assisting parties in reaching agreement or resolving their dispute is intended to be impartial and free from any threat or any perceived threat of either student, administrative, or academic manipulation. In addition to providing mediation and meeting facilitation services, the Center offers a variety of community-building and skills-training activities. One of the Center's goals is to provide an opportunity for interaction among various aspects of the university community that have often remained separate and distant from one another due to social and organizational boundaries.

**Massachusetts Institute of Technology**

I. Purpose: Conflict is not new to a university setting where students from many diverse backgrounds come to learn and work in a tightly-knit, often competitive and pressured community. mediation@mit was therefore created to supplement the MIT's existing dispute resolution system.

II. Mission: mediation@mit has a three-fold mission:

1. To offer MIT students a forum for constructive dispute resolution, in a formal and confidential setting, that is, formal mediation

2. To train members of the MIT community in mediation and other dispute resolution techniques and encourage the use of such techniques in informal as well as formal settings

3. To educate members of the MIT community about the value of constructive dispute resolution and promote peace on campus [mediation@mit training materials, 1995].

## B: Goals and Objectives Planning Document

### Peer Mediation Center Goals and Objectives 1994–95

The purpose of Georgia State University's Peer Mediation Center is to educate students on the peaceful expression of conflict within the university community. We believe that college students are effective at resolving their own concerns. We believe that peer mediation offers students the ability to learn life skills and control their own problem solving process.

GOAL 1. Enhance the present dispute resolution system at GSU
*Objective 1.* Develop Peer Mediation Center (PMC) for GSU students

#### Action Plans

A. Establish Advisory Committee

B. Benchmark with other peer mediation programs

C. Define procedures for implementation

D. Establish and maintain linkages with Georgia Office of Dispute Resolution; Board of Regents Working Group on Dispute Resolution; Metro Atlanta mediators

E. Select peer mediators from those trainees participating in the Peer Mediation Center Training

*Objective 2.* Create student ownership of their disputes and solutions

#### Action Plans

A. Offer a private, voluntary, impartial environment in which to resolve conflict

B. Provide impartial peer mediators

C. Locate convenient space for mediation

GOAL 2. Implement mediation training for university community
*Objective 1.* Conduct biannual formal campus mediation training

#### Action Plans

A. Advertise and recruit students, staff, and faculty to participate

B. Engage professional trainers

C. Develop training materials and resources

D. Maintain a dispute resolution library

E. Teach conflict resolution skills which can be utilized at home, work, and school

F. Seek approval from the Georgia Office of Dispute Resolution

---

*Source:* © Tanya Sikes and Georgia State University. Used with permission.

*Objective 2.* Offer educational programs on conflict resolution

### Action Plans

A. Train PMC participants to facilitate workshops

B. Present advanced seminars for PMC mediators

GOAL 3. Educate GSU community on positive value of peer mediation

*Objective 1.* Design promotional materials/announcements to create awareness of PMC

### Action Plans

A. Design and distribute brochures

B. Advertise in Signal (the student paper), GSU TV and radio, posters

C. Maintain a relationship with student organizations

D. Participate in Orientation and Information days for students, faculty, and staff

*Objective 2.* Educate persons working with students on the process of mediation.

### Action Plans

A. Provide clear referral guidelines to all offices involved with students

B. Add PMC to GSU's official student support list

C. Work with new residence hall coordinators

GOAL 4. Measure the effectiveness of Peer Mediation Center

*Objective 1.* Evaluate Peer Mediation Center

### Action Plans

A. Identify variables and collect data on PMC

B. Analyze and evaluate data

C. Produce annual report to be presented to Provost/VP of Academic Affairs, VP of Student Life and Enrollment, and PMC Advisory Council

D. Identify and survey the utilization of PMC by students

*Objective 2.* Assess Peer Mediation Center Training

### Action Plans

A. Assess skills and effectiveness of mediators

B. Evaluate trainers and materials

## C: Job Descriptions for Program Personnel

**Program Coordinator Job Description, Syracuse University**
The Program Coordinator will be a Graduate Assistant who is supervised by a faculty member associated with the Maxwell School's Program on the Analysis and Resolution of Conflicts or the Program in Nonviolent Conflict and Change.

Responsibilities: The Program Coordinator is expected to:

- Conduct case screening, intake, and follow-up
- Organize record keeping and prepare statistical reports
- Manage the day-to-day administration of the mediation center
- Conduct direct conflict conciliation
- Identify and arrange outreach/education to referral sources
- Schedule mediations and mediators
- Prepare/direct publicity and marketing programs
- Coordinate the selection and training of volunteer mediators and assist in mediator training as appropriate
- Implement policies as determined by the Supervisory Board
- Serve as ex-officio member of Executive Committee and Supervisory Board

Qualifications: Candidates must be matriculated graduate students in good standing at Syracuse University. Strong verbal and organizational skills are required. Experience as a mediator and/or formal education in methods of nonviolent conflict resolution preferred. Remuneration: the time commitment will be 20 hours/week during the academic year. A cash stipend equal to the Maxwell School Graduate Assistant rate and tuition remission (12 credits) will be provided. If summer work is necessary and desired, additional remuneration will be provided.

**Faculty Supervisor Job Description, Syracuse University**
The Faculty Supervisor will be a Syracuse University faculty member associated with the Maxwell School's Program on the Analysis and Resolution of Conflicts and/or the Program in Nonviolent Conflict and Change.

Responsibilities: The Faculty Supervisor is expected to:

- Provide technical expertise to the CMC Coordinator, staff, and volunteer mediators

*Source:* Syracuse University (1991). Used with permission.

- Provide direction and advice to the CMC and staff
- Regularly review intake procedures with Coordinator
- Regularly review process and content of mediation sessions with Coordinator
- Provide leadership for ongoing skill development of volunteer mediators
- Provide accountability for budgetary decisions
- Provide liaison functions for the Center's interaction with other Syracuse University administrators and faculty
- Provide ongoing additional instruction in mediation and conflict resolution

Qualifications: Candidates should be Syracuse University faculty members who possess considerable expertise in the theory and practice of mediation and conflict resolution.

Remuneration: The Campus Mediation Center budget has been designed to provide approximately 10 percent of the Faculty Supervisor's annual salary so that sufficient time and attention will be allocated to the ongoing operation of the Center.

### 1987 Pilot Project Job Description, University of Oregon

This position was jointly funded by Associated Students University of Oregon [ASUO] and Student Affairs

*Title:* Mediation Specialist

*Rank:* Instructor

*Qualifications:* Bachelor's required. Experience must include counseling, legal advocacy, and communication facilitation in complex organizations. Strong oral and written communication skills are necessary.

*General:* The mediation specialist reports directly to the Dean of Students, Division of Student Affairs. The person in this position will work closely with the ASUO Office of Student Advocacy, the Conduct Coordinator, the Office of Academic Advising and Student Services and faculty/staff grievance committees as appropriate. The person in this position will provide direct mediation services appropriate to the needs of the University community. The mediation specialist will act as liaison to students, student groups, faculty and appropriate committees in the execution of duties. The mediation position is jointly sponsored and funded by the Associated Students of the University of Oregon (ASUO) and the Division of Student Affairs.

*Responsibilities:* The mediation specialist is responsible for the development and coordination of mediation services and programs for the University. Areas of specific responsibility include:

*Administration:* Assess and prioritize areas within the university community for:

1. Program development needs and direct services
2. Re-evaluation of undergraduate grievance procedures
3. Conflict resolution training

Establish a mechanism (advisory board) to design, implement and evaluate programs.

*Program Development:* (a) Provide interpretation and clarification to students, staff, faculty and organizations in matters of overlapping jurisdiction and procedure; (b) Develop a mediation policies library, including policies, procedures and records relating to mediation, student advocacy and grievances; (c) Develop written resources, guidelines and procedures for distribution to individuals, groups, and office staff involved in conflicts; (d) Determine policies on liability, confidentiality of records and make recommendations for change; (e) Consult with student affairs and ASUO staff to design evaluation processes relating to individual case resolution and position viability.

*Service:* (a) Provide facilitation in the resolution of two-party conflicts (student-student, student-faculty, student group-student group); (b) Facilitate clarification of role, policy or procedure in multi-party disputes

---

*Source:* Hale (1987). Used with permission.

### D: Trainee Nomination Form

Dear Residence Hall Staff Member,

The Community Relations Committee (CRC) is sponsoring a free Mediation Skills Training Workshop as part of its community skills development program. The 20-hour training will be held _____, beginning Friday evening, and running all-day Saturday and Sunday. In addition to current Community Relations Committee members, we will be able to provide this valuable training to ten additional student volunteer mediators from the College. We would like your help in identifying students whom you think might be good mediators for our community. We want to assemble a diverse group of students who represent all academic levels, racial and ethnic backgrounds, cliques, and so on. Qualities that nominees might possess include respect of their peers, good communication skills, a sense of fairness, confidence, empathy, responsibility and commitment. Students who successfully complete the training will serve their peers by mediating interpersonal conflicts.

Nominees will be invited to submit applications indicating their interest in participating, and a lottery system will be used to choose the final participants from among the submitted applications. We hope to inform chosen participants by _____. If you are yourself a student and are interested in participating in the training, please fill out the attached application form and submit it to the box in the housing office. Thanks in advance for your assistance. Sincerely,

Community Relations

- - - - - - - - - - - - - - - CLIP HERE - - - - - - - - - - - - - - - -

---

**Community Relations Mediator Nomination**

I would like to nominate the following students to be mediators because I would respect and trust them to help resolve a conflict:

1. _____ Hall of Residence _____

2. _____ Hall of Residence _____

3. _____ Hall of Residence _____

Signature _____ Date _____

After you've filled out the form, please fold it up, staple or tape it shut and deliver it to _____ **by Friday,  /  / .**

## E: Volunteer Mediator Application Form

Name: _____

Permanent home address: _____

Home phone: (____)_____  Campus phone: _____

Campus address: _____

E-mail address: _____

**Please specify:**

___ Undergraduate student        ___ Graduate student

   Major: _____  Program/Discipline: _____

   Graduation date: _____  Completion date: _____

___ Nonexempt staff  ___ Exempt staff      ___ Faculty

   Staff department/                        Department:

   Position: _____      _____

Are you proficient in any languages other than English?

   ___ Yes  ___ No   If yes, which one(s)? _____

What other kinds of volunteer experience (past/present) have you had? (Include length of service.)

Do you have any areas of specialization or special training? (Examples include: substance abuse counseling, legal training, working with youth, domestic violence prevention, consumer issues, marital counseling, labor/management negotiations)

**Mediation-related experience:**

Have you received any formal training in mediation?

___ Yes  ___ No    If yes, where, when, and what sort of training have you had?

Have you ever done formal mediations (that is, for a program)?

___ Yes  ___ No    If yes, how long have you been doing formal mediations? Since _____

Any related training experiences and/or academic course work? (Please list)

On the back of this sheet, please describe what interests you about becoming a mediator for the Campus Mediation Center. What strengths do you bring with you?

If available, please include a copy of your resumé with this form.
    Resumé included?    ___ Yes  ___ No

If selected as a volunteer mediator, I agree to the following terms:

___ To complete all required training sessions [dates here]

___ To serve as a mediator as often as once per month as scheduled

___ To uphold the necessary ethics and confidentiality standards

Signature _____

## F: Mediator Performance Evaluation Sheet

Mediator:_____     Role Play _____

Observer: _____

Party A: _____     Party B: _____

Stage of mediation completed prior to evaluation (check one):

____ Signed agreement          ____ Verbal agreement

____ Evaluated options         ____ Identified options

____ Identified issues         ____ Storytelling completed

### PERFORMANCE EVALUATION SCALE

1 = Unsatisfactory; needs substantial improvement
2 = Somewhat unsatisfactory; needs some improvement
3 = Satisfactory; effective
4 = Very effective
5 = Outstanding

1. How do you rate the mediator's performance?

   a. Clarity in explaining the mediation process     1  2  3  4  5

   b. Posture as neutral/impartial                    1  2  3  4  5

   c. Sensitivity to confidentiality                  1  2  3  4  5

   d. Ability to elicit information and clarify issues  1  2  3  4  5

   e. Ability to facilitate communication between
      the parties                                     1  2  3  4  5

   f. Ability to establish shared ground rules        1  2  3  4  5

   g. Ability to control and conduct the session
      without domination                             1  2  3  4  5

   h. Ability to generate movement toward
      agreement                                      1  2  3  4  5

   i. Ability to create options without imposing
      on parties                                     1  2  3  4  5

   j. Ability to empower one or both disputants
      (if applicable)                                1  2  3  4  5

   k. Ability to help draft the agreement
      (if applicable)                                1  2  3  4  5

   1.  Ability to work effectively with co-mediator
       (if applicable)                                      1  2  3  4  5

2.  If attempted, was caucus appropriately used?

3.  Please describe the mediator's image as projected by his or her
    body language:

Additional comments, notes, and suggestions:

## G: Role-Play Practice Guidelines

### Why Role Play?

We are using role playing in this training because it provides you an opportunity to experience the ideas presented and integrate them as skills and behaviors. In addition, you will likely gain insight into common disputant feelings and behavior in mediation.

### Guidelines for Mock Disputants

Carefully read your case description, and ask the trainer for clarification if something is not clear. Most role-play instructions suggest behaviors and tendencies, and improvisation is okay as long as you don't add details that substantively change the nature of the dispute. Those playing the disputant role should not be hard in their roles, but at the same time should not be soft. Try to stay in character until time is called unless the trainer or coach requests a time-out, specifically asks you for feedback, or suggests a change in the direction of your character's role. Try to incorporate the typical give-and-take mentality, and be as realistic as possible. That does not mean you should act really nasty or extremely stubborn, because you should know that each trainee will get to play the roles of mediator and disputant. And as no one has to tell you, what comes around, goes around.

### Processing the Role Play

At the end of each role play, we will talk about the experience in both small and large groups. Generally feedback will follow these basic guidelines:

1. The mediators will process their thoughts and feelings from the role play.

2. The disputants will be invited to process their feelings as they experienced them in the roles.

3. The coaches and observers will provide specific observations.

4. The group may ask specific questions about strategies, feelings, and so on. These questions are not judgments but consultations.

5. The group may discuss other possible mediator moves.

*Source:* Adapted from Syracuse University (1991). Used with permission.

**External Role-Play Observer Guidelines**

Your role as external observer is to provide direct and accurate (factual) feedback to group members regarding technique and behavior. Your primary focus should be on the mediator and secondary focus on the "disputants." Be prepared to jot down quotes, responses, and observations of body language. BE SPECIFIC! It really helps.

Feedback should be presented in the following sample formats:

1. "When you said [quote], I felt [emotion], because _____."

   "When you said [quote], I observed 'disputant A' [behavior or response]."

   "At _____ point in the mediation, I noticed you [behavior].

2. Praise or otherwise highlight excellent responses or ideas.

3. Note process or procedural errors directly.

4. Discuss other possible approaches the mediators could have tried.

Feedback to the mediators can be followed up by questions to solicit group opinions:

1. "[Disputant's name], how did you feel when [mediator] said/asked _____?"

2. "[Ask disputant], would it have made a difference if the mediator had said [done] _____? In what way [etc.]?"

## H: Scripts for Role-Play Practice

### JOAN AND DAVID: Faculty-Student Dispute

#### General Information for Mediators

It's hard to believe that this kind of situation would have ever happened at Antioch. A faculty member and a student in a shoving match. And all over a request for a five-day extension on a paper.

David, a senior, is a student in Joan's seminar. Joan is an expert in Latin American history and politics. Both have reputations for being outspoken. Since the beginning of the term, there have been repeated clashes in class as Joan and David engaged in frequent, extensive, and often heated discussions on the nature of U.S. influence in Central and South America.

The problem that brings them to mediation occurred within the past week and involved some physical contact. Both have agreed to participate in the mediation, though neither is pleased at having to do it. David's friends and advisor have strongly advised him to mediate rather than face possible disciplinary action based on Joan's complaint. Joan's faculty chair encouraged her to mediate rather than requiring administrative action on David's complaint.

#### Confidential information for Joan, a faculty member

At first you were interested in having David in class. He is very bright, engages in class discussions, and has a reputation for being an aggressive debater. As a campus leader, David has made important contributions to the community. As a student, he is widely viewed by the faculty as having a brilliant mind and strong analytical skills. Too often students in your seminars have offered only superficial polemic in place of thoughtful analysis and debate. You hoped that with David in the class, other students would be encouraged to participate actively in class discussions. And yet when you engaged him in debates, the situation seemed to take on a decidedly hostile tone. Instead of being a catalyst that energized others in the class, David became a provocateur, challenging your ideas and engaging you in arguments that distracted the class from what you had planned to teach. You've had students who've played "devil's advocate" before, but with David, the game had another dimension—a hidden agenda.

When he approached you last week about an extension for the final paper, he acted as though he were entitled to the extension and he was asking only as a matter of form. When you questioned

---

*Source:* Role play by Michael Lang © 1996. Used with permission.

the need for an extension, he became angry, and accused you of being out to get him since the beginning of the quarter. You replied that he was out of line. He started to come around the desk and you got up to meet him, putting your hands lightly on his chest to stop his progress and saying, "Just back down, David." He pushed your hands away, saying, "Get your fucking hands off me." Staggering backwards, you shouted at him, "Get out, now!"

A promising opportunity has gone more sour than you could have imagined. Initially you thought David would be a candidate for a prestigious graduate fellowship in international politics at Oxford (a fellowship you once received). You were prepared to sponsor him, endorse his application, and help him with the process. Now, all that you had hoped for him vanished, and in its place are feelings of anger, disappointment, and frustration.

### Confidential information for David, a student

As a major in international studies, you took Joan's seminar because you have a deep interest in international politics, and Joan is a highly regarded teacher and expert in the field. She only came to campus a year ago, and until now you hadn't been able to study with her.

You felt that Joan has been out to make an example of you in front of the other students. From the first class she had called on you frequently to address an issue under discussion. And then she engaged you in debates, challenging every assumption and argument you offered. You've felt frustrated, and angry. And so you decided that if she wanted to argue, you'd give her things to argue about, and you deliberately took provocative stances just to piss her off.

Then, near the end of the quarter you went to her office to ask for an extension of five days on the research paper she assigned. You had a good reason: the opportunity to attend an important four-day student conference in Baltimore. As a student leader at Antioch, you've been involved in other meetings and conferences on student leadership. Because of that involvement, you'd been asked to attend this meeting. When you went to her office to ask her for the extension, she didn't want to hear your reasons, and said that you'd better have it in on the deadline. You began to argue with her and tell her that her treatment of you the whole quarter has been unfair. You did raise your voice, and began to move around the desk to talk with her more directly. She came around the desk, and met you. Putting her hands on your chest, she told you to get back, or something like that. She had no right to touch you, and so you pushed her arms away and told her to "Leave me alone." She then told you to leave her office and you did.

What a lousy way to end your college career. You had high hopes that Joan would become a mentor this year, help you with decisions about graduate schools, and perhaps even support your application for the fellowship in international studies which she once held at Oxford. Now, instead you've got to deal with this stupid complaint, and any hope of her support has gone up in smoke.

### THE BENCH BY THE WALL: Student-Roommate Dispute

### Information for Mediators

This is a roommate dispute, between Bob and Ali (or Bobbie and Alia). It takes place in March. Ali does not speak English well.

### General Instructions

Bob and Ali, both freshmen, decided to room together last fall (it is now March) because they thought that they had a lot in common. Both are immigrants and their families now live in New York City. Ali was born in Egypt, came to the U.S. two years ago, and speaks Arabic at home. He speaks English passably but with some trouble. Bob was born in St. Moritz, Switzerland, and speaks Italian at home. His English is fluent including American slang, and he also speaks French and German. He has lived in the U.S. for five years. Ali was raised as a Muslim and Bob was raised as a Roman Catholic.

At MIT, Bob immediately made lots of friends, and at first invited Ali to join in their activities. Ali always refused and Bob has quit inviting him. At first they did a lot together but now Bob mostly does things with his other friends. Now Bob rarely even comes in their room alone except to sleep. Bob and Ali rarely speak. Ali does not like most of Bob's other friends.

Bob's friends come over to the room a couple of times a month. Very often they drink and their voices get loud. Ali complains and says he can't study. Ali also objects to alcohol on religious grounds. He told them, "The Koran says, 'Drinking will be your ruin.'" Bob and his friends just laugh, but it does make Bob feel uncomfortable when Ali refers to his religion.

Last week Bob and his friends were chugalugging in the room, and tried very hard to get Ali to join in. The more he resisted, the nastier the comments became, until finally one of the friends insulted Ali's mother (by implying she had slept with one of them). (If the roles are played by two women, the insult is that

*Source:* ©mediation@mit 1996. Used by permission. A videotape of this role play is available for purchase. For information, contact mediation@mit. Phone: (617) 253–8720; e-mail: carolorm@mit.edu.

Alia's mother slept around, and Alia doesn't know who her real father is.) Ali was so upset that he left his room. Ali and Bob have reached a hurtful stalemate.

Ali's TA called Bob to discuss mediation. Bob agreed to mediate but acts as though he does not take mediation seriously. Ali made the initial call to request mediation.

### Bob's Confidential Instructions

Bob comes from a family which does not have much money but is very close, and family is important to him. He's proud of the speed in which he learned American ways, and feels he is now indistinguishable from any other lapsed Catholic in the U.S.

People are important to Bob. It's obvious to him that "becoming American" is best done through group activities, which often happen to include alcohol. Bob doesn't party with his friends every night, and they just have "a few beers." He is furious at Ali's objections to his drinking, especially because that makes him sound just like his (Bob's) mother. He doesn't see alcohol as a religious issue. Deep down he is worried about his own drinking because his father is alcoholic.

Bob used to like Ali a lot and is really upset with him now for withdrawing and becoming so critical. But he does want to patch things up and be friends, if possible.

When Ali's TA called, Bob was flabbergasted to learn that Ali had been so affected by the incident with his friends that his grades suffered. Bob also became very concerned when the TA categorized his behavior as harassment. He agreed to mediation to avoid a possible harassment charge.

### Ali's Confidential Instructions

Ali's family lives in a Muslim community and he does not want to assimilate. Maintaining his religious beliefs and practices is especially important to him. His close ties with his family are important to him. His family is wealthy. He will only be considered successful in his family if he is a financial and academic success.

This conflict with his roommate is a real source of distress for Ali. He hates conflict. Also Bob is his only friend at MIT, and he feels lonely now that he is cut off from him. After the incident with Bob's friends, he spent the night on a bench by the wall in the main lobby. He knows he cannot go on like that. He also cares about Bob and is worried that Bob drinks to excess. (Bob parties every weekend and even sometimes during the week, but doesn't always get drunk.) Ali's concern for Bob is based primarily on his perception that Bob is or could be hurting himself by abusing alcohol, not on religious grounds.

Ali is very uncomfortable being around people who drink because in his family the Muslim prohibition against alcohol is particularly strongly upheld.

The day after this incident Ali flunked a quiz. Afterwards his TA asked him about the sharp deterioration in his work this term, and Ali confided in him about his trouble with his roommate. Ali begged the TA not to do anything about it because that would only make matters worse. The TA convinced him to look into mediation, and Ali agreed that the TA could call Bob to sound him out.

Ali is desperate to keep this situation from his parents or from any public scrutiny to avoid embarrassment. But it has to stop because his grades are suffering, so on his TA's advice, and after the TA got Bob to agree, he requested mediation.

(Do not try to fake an accent or broken English. Let the mediators know of your trouble with English by occasionally mentioning that you have trouble understanding or making yourself understood.)

## CLASSMATES IN CONFLICT: Classmates Paul and Ringo

### Paul's Point of View

Paul is currently enrolled in several upper level business courses. As a junior, he has been doing fairly well in his academic coursework but has been having some trouble with his group in one of his classes. At the start of the semester, Paul was assigned to a group with three other students by the professor of the course. Paul was chosen as the leader of the group and given the task of evaluating his group members throughout the semester based on participation in group activities and quality of finished assignments. Ever since the start of the term, Paul has noticed that John and George (two of the group members) show up to class on a regular basis and hand in their assignments on time. Ringo, on the other hand, is usually late to class if he makes it at all and sometimes doesn't have his part of the group assignment ready by the due date. This forces Paul, John, and George to finish Ringo's share of the assignment in order for the group to receive a good grade.

Paul has just handed in his mid-term evaluation of his group members and given John and George perfect scores while Ringo has received a lower-than-average rating. Ringo, having been called to the professor's office and told of his poor performance, has come to Paul to find out why he received such a poor evaluation. Paul

*Source:* ©Dispute Resolution Services University of Central Florida, mediate@pegasus.cc.ucf.edu. Used with permission.

tries to explain to Ringo the reason for the poor evaluation, but it quickly turns into a shouting match. Paul tells Ringo that if he can't work with the group, then he should withdraw from the course.

News of this meeting finds its way back to the professor and the professor calls Paul and Ringo into his office. The professor makes it clear that this situation is something that they may experience while working in the business community and that they must learn to resolve their differences. The professor also makes it clear that, per the syllabus, each of the four group members will receive half of their final grade based on their group's performance and that it would be beneficial to each of the group members to resolve this quickly. The professor recommends mediation.

### Paul's Position

Paul wants to make an A in this course in order to keep up his good overall average. He plans on pursuing his MBA at an Ivy League college and needs a really high GPA in order to be competitive. Paul enjoys working with John and George but doesn't understand why Ringo can't participate in the group work and complete his assignments on time like the others. Paul wants Ringo to start coming to class on time and completing his share of the group work.

### Ringo's Point of View

Ringo is currently enrolled in several upper level business courses. As a junior, he has been doing fairly well in his academic coursework but has been having some trouble with his group in one of his classes. At the start of the semester, Ringo was assigned to a group with three other students by the professor of the course. The other students are Paul, John, and George and they all seem fairly nice. Paul was chosen as the leader of the group and given the task of evaluating his group members throughout the semester based on participation in group activities and quality of finished assignments. Ever since the start of the term, Ringo has noticed that Paul gives John and George the easiest parts of the group assignment and splits the remaining parts between the two of them.

Ringo has had to work several part-time jobs in order to cover the cost of living and divides his time between school and work. Ringo has also had to keep up his overall grades in order to keep his scholarship. He is sometimes late to class but tries his best to make it there every time. He has also had some trouble finishing his part of the group assignments on time because of the late hours spent at work. Ringo feels bad about putting additional pressure on Paul, John, and George but needs to keep working in order to make it through school.

Paul has just handed in his mid-term evaluation of his group members and given John and George perfect scores while Ringo has received a lower-than-average rating. Ringo, having been called to the professor's office and told of his poor performance, has come to Paul to find out why he received such a poor evaluation. Ringo tries to reason with Paul and tells him that he needs a good evaluation in order to keep his scholarship, but it quickly turns into a shouting match. Paul tells Ringo that if he can't work with the group, then he should withdraw from the course.

News of this meeting finds its way back to the professor and the professor calls Ringo and Paul into his office. The professor makes it clear that this situation is something that they may experience while working in the business community and that they must learn to resolve their differences. The professor also makes it clear that, per the syllabus, each of the four group members will receive half of their final grade based on their group's performance and that it would be beneficial to each of the group members to resolve this quickly. The professor recommends mediation.

### Ringo's Position

Ringo wants to continue working with the other group members, but wants the assignments split evenly. He needs to make a good grade in this course in order to keep his scholarship and at the same time, needs to keep working at his part-time jobs in order to pay for living expenses. He feels like the other group members don't understand his situation and are no longer interested in working with him. Ringo wants Paul to divide the assignments equally and be a little more flexible with the assignment due dates.

### UNREQUITED LOVE: Student-Student Dispute

### General Information for Mediators

The disputants, both graduate students, are a former couple. Mary has filed a complaint of harassment with the Campus Judicial Program, claiming that Joe has been following her around on campus, harassing her, and calling her at home late in the evening. Joe claims that Mary has possession of some of his property and she has been unfairly avoiding him. They were referred to mediation.

### Mary's Confidential Information

You have filed a complaint of harassment against Joe with the campus judicial office. You and Joe grew up together in Pittsburgh and

*Source:* ©Bill Warters 1994. Used with permission.

had a relationship during high school. You went your separate ways for undergraduate school. You were reunited when you both ended up attending graduate school here at Penn State about two years ago. After dating for a few months when you were both new to campus, you lived together for a spell, with Joe moving into your apartment. After about six months you decided you needed to break off the relationship, and you made Joe move out. The arguing and Joe's drinking was just too much to deal with. That was almost nine months ago. You *really* want to be left alone by Joe and want Joe to stop talking about you, your five-year-old child Erica (who you had raised on your own during your undergraduate days), and your new fiancé (Dave) to all your mutual friends. Joe has been following you around on campus and calling you at home late into the evening, trying to reestablish the relationship. He even came over drunk one night and knocked on your bedroom window, wanting "to talk." You want no further contact with him. Joe also keeps mentioning the TV. You feel the TV rightfully belongs to you because when Joe bought it you were supporting the both of them and living in your apartment. Although you are very skeptical of this whole mediation process, you're willing to give the agreement a try if one is reached.

### Joe's Confidential Information

You and Mary grew up together in Pittsburgh and had a relationship during high school. You went your separate ways during undergraduate school. You were reunited when you both ended up attending graduate school here at Penn State about two years ago. After dating a few months, you lived with Mary and her five-year-old daughter Erica in her off-campus apartment for about six months. (She still won't tell you who Erica's father is, saying it's none of your business.) Mary broke off the relationship after six months, claiming that you guys argued too much, and that your drinking was a problem. Even though it's been nine months since you moved out, you still feel that you love her and you still discuss her with your mutual friends, hoping to keep the flame alive.

You were referred to the Campus Judicial System for harassing and threatening Mary. You can't believe it, because you've always been very nice to Mary when you see her, giving her flowers, or writing poems for her, nothing rude or "harassing." You think Mary's new beau, Dave, is just out to get you, and is pushing Mary into pressing charges. You would very much like to renew your romantic relationship with Mary and have the charges against you dropped. You admit that you have been approaching Mary on campus and trying to talk to her as well as calling her at home in the evening, but what's wrong with that? Besides, Mary still has the TV you bought when you lived together, as well as some CDs and you think you should get them back, since it was your money that paid for them. You're excited to try mediation, because it will give you a chance to talk with Mary one-on-one, and perhaps persuade her to take you back, or at least to drop those silly charges against you.

## SEXUAL HARASSMENT? Student-Faculty Dispute

### Ken Brown's (Student) Confidential Information

You are a junior vocal performance major at Naperville University. You are there on a music scholarship that pays three-quarters of your tuition; it is because of this scholarship that you are able to afford and stay enrolled at NU. Your grade point average must stay at a cumulative 3.0 average in order to renew your scholarship for your senior, and final, year. The school is very strict about scholarship renewal policies. You also know that a 3.0 cumulative average depends directly upon a successful 4.0 performance in all of your classes this semester. You are receiving "A's" in all of your classes, except for Advanced Music Theory, in which you are currently receiving a "C."

Dr. Mary Smith is the instructor of this class, and she is also your academic advisor. She has been giving you private lessons and spending a lot of extra time with you as compared with other students. You know that she has put in far more personal time towards helping you than is expected of her. You have been feeling very confused about her personal interest in you and very uncomfortable with the recent interactions you've had with her.

While you've felt that you and she have a more open and personable relationship than most students/teachers have, lately you think it's gone too far. She has had far too much physical contact with you than you feel is normal and comfortable. Frequent touching of you has occurred in most of your recent private lessons. She has also commented repeatedly about how you're sure to succeed in the vocal performance industry because of your good looks. You are disturbed by these advances and comments because you feel she doesn't take your hard work seriously, and that she thinks your success is related to your physical appearance and not your talent.

Finally, last week during a private lesson she asked you to retrieve some aspirin from the top drawer of her desk. You complied, but became very uncomfortable when you had to dig around past an opened box of condoms to find it. You feel like she intentionally wanted you to look in that drawer.

*Source:* ©Tom Cavenagh, North Central College, Naperville, Illinois. Used with permission.

The final straw was last week when she asked you out for a drink after your private lesson which finished around 10 P.M. You definitely felt that she implied that if you dated her, your grade would improve to an "A." Now you feel it's gone too far, and you filed a sexual harassment report with the school. They recommended mediation, and you agreed because you are embarrassed about the incidents and want to keep the matter private. You also have to continue working with Dr. Smith through your senior year because she is the music department chair.

### Dr. Mary Smith's Confidential Information

You are a music professor and the Music Department Chair at Naperville University. You've been Ken Brown's advisor for the nearly three years that he's been at NU (he is about to finish his junior year). Early in his studies with NU's music department, you noticed his great potential as a vocalist, and you played an influential part in his decision to declare a vocal performance major. You have grown very fond of Ken during his time at NU and enjoy working with such a promising vocalist.

This semester Ken has, to your surprise, been doing below average work in your Advanced Music Theory class. This class is the capstone for any type of music major. You are concerned about his performance because it is essential for a music major to do well in this particular class, and more importantly, because you know he may lose his music scholarship if his grade doesn't improve. You also know that he won't be able to afford to continue his college education at NU if he doesn't have the scholarship funding.

You've been putting in late hours devoted to providing him private vocal lessons. You have wanted to do anything possible to encourage him to keep working hard, and you've also offered to assist him with his theory homework. You've really tried to help him along, from putting in extra time for lessons, to helping with his homework, to even offering to buy him a drink one night to help him loosen up, as you've noticed how stressed he seems lately.

You know that Ken has a lot going for him given his musical talent, especially because he is a very attractive young man. You've told him on a number of occasions how you are sure he has the potential to succeed in the competitive music industry; his good looks coupled with his vocal talent should give him an edge over others in the field.

Ken is one of your favorite students. You've always felt that the two of you have an open, personable relationship. You are hopeful that your relationship with Ken will continue even after he graduates. You've been trying to let Ken know how much you care about him by giving him extra help with his theory.

You were a profoundly surprised and troubled to learn that

Ken filed a sexual harassment report naming you with the University. Now that you think back to your recent interactions with Ken, you are beginning to think that maybe he feels uncomfortable with the physical closeness and contact that the two of you have had during the private voice lessons. For instance, you share a piano bench while sitting at the piano and you may have occasionally touched his diaphragm to feel for his breathing patterns. However, this happens during the normal delivery of any voice music lesson. The school recommended mediation, and you readily accepted because you are anxious to keep the whole thing quiet.

### COLLEGE FLEXTIME: Staff-Supervisor Dispute

#### General Information for Mediators
A support person in the Admissions Office (Chris) asked for mediation with the director of admissions (Robin). The director reluctantly agreed, provided it was not too time consuming.

#### Chris's Confidential Information
You are a support person in the Admissions Office. You have been there almost two years. In your last job you had a lot of input into decision making. When you try to offer suggestions here, the director, Robin, doesn't listen or seem to care. You're used to having flexibility in your job description and in your hours. Recently you offered to work late on Mondays and Tuesdays in order to come in late on Thursdays. You proposed this because:

1. You want to take a special class on Thursday mornings.
2. Monday and Tuesday are the busiest days.
3. Students might appreciate having extended business hours.

However, you didn't have a chance to give your reasons. Robin was very short with you, immediately saying that it wouldn't be possible, and you've been reluctant to bring it up again. You were talking with friends about this problem, and they suggested mediation. You thought it was a great idea. You like the work and the other staff here. You don't know Robin well, but are willing to be open minded.

#### Robin's Confidential Information
You are Director of the Admissions Office. You have been there 12 years and are responsible for supervising a staff of ten people.

---

*Source:* Reprinted with permission from Rockin' Role Plays. ©The Mediation Center, Asheville, North Carolina, 1996.

Chris is relatively new (1½ years), kind of flaky, and often comes up with off-the-wall suggestions. The latest one involved Chris working late sometimes and coming in late sometimes.

You run a tight ship. You think staff should be able to express their opinions, but then they need to accept your decisions. You're not opposed to change, as long as it's well thought out and well reasoned.

You have been under a lot of stress lately because it's been really busy, you have a lot of paperwork to complete, decisions to make and endless meetings to attend.

You admit that sometimes you are short-tempered with people. When Chris suggested mediation, you agreed, if it wouldn't take too long. You are somewhat skeptical about mediation (afraid it could undermine your power).

## TEACHING LOAD: Faculty-Faculty Dispute

### General Information for Mediators
Associate Professor Newbury and Department Head Wilson are in conflict over assigned courses. Associate Professor suggested mediation, and Department Head agreed.

### Associate Professor Newbury's Confidential Information
You were assigned to only introductory classes, *again*, for the second time. You feel like you have done your share of this kind of grunt work and deserve a more interesting and convenient class load. You think you are being taken advantage of because you have low status in the department. If you had a more interesting teaching load, you might get re-inspired to work on a research project that has been on hold for some time, and then you would have more status. You requested a mediation with Department Head Wilson.

### Department Head Wilson's Confidential Information
You assigned Associate Professor Newbury to introductory classes for a second term because you knew that s/he did a great job with the schedule last term. You didn't think s/he would mind the schedule—it actually involves fewer teaching hours, and you thought Associate Professor Newbury would appreciate that, because it gives him/her a chance to focus on a research and publication project s/he has been working on for almost two years.

---

*Source:* Reprinted with permission from Rockin' Role Plays. ©The Mediation Center, Asheville, North Carolina, 1996.

## I: Resolution Agreement for a Rental Dispute

*Dispute Settlement:* All controversies between the landlord and a BYU [Brigham Young University] student tenant with respect to the rental facilities or to their agreement(s) shall be submitted to the BYU Off-Campus Housing Office for mediation if either party to the controversy so requests by serving written notice to the BYU Off-Campus Housing Office. Both parties agree to make a good-faith effort to settle such controversy through mediation and to be governed by the BYU Housing Mediation Rules unless the BYU Off-Campus Housing Office declines to mediate the controversy. If mediation fails to resolve the problem, either party may request arbitration by the BYU Housing Arbitration Board (hereinafter "board"). If either party requests arbitration, both parties agree to submit to the jurisdiction of the board and be bound by its decisions as rendered in accordance with its rules and regulations. Any BYU student who fails to comply with board decision(s) may have a hold placed on his or her university records and a stop and discontinuance on registration. Landlords who fail to comply with such decision(s) will lose university approval of their facilities. If civil court action or arbitration are pursued to enforce the terms of this agreement, the nonprevailing party agrees to pay all costs in connection therewith, including a reasonable attorney's fee.

*Source:* Brigham Young University Student-Landlord Rental Agreement, article 9. Used with permission.

## J: Workshop Outline for Introductory Mediation Training

This is a very basic one- to two-hour orientation workshop. Adapt pace to the time available.

1. Introductions—why here, with enthusiasm
2. Agenda Review (overhead 1):
    a. Briefly present workshop agenda
    b. Check in with participants to find out:
        (1) If they agree on the agenda
        (2) What you can emphasize or skim over
3. Conflict Overview
    a. Arm wrestling exercise (instructions on overhead 2); socialized to compete and think win-lose even when it benefits us to cooperate or collaborate
    b. Brainstorm on meaning of word conflict (post on blank newsprint sheet)
        (1) Sum up what heard
    c. Conflict unavoidable; occurs because we are interdependent
    d. Review positives: new information, fuel change, relieve tension, help inform creative action (post on blank newsprint)
4. How do people typically deal with conflict?
    a. Brainstorm—punish, retaliate, avoid, escalate, stuff it
    b. Techniques we've learned often not healthy or productive
    c. Our skills can leave us when immersed in conflict
    d. Conflict escalation spiral or staircase
        (1) Tell story as example of conflict escalation
5. What is mediation ?
    a. Antidote for spiral of lost trust, built resentments, stress and tension
    b. What it is not: Judge Wapner, Dr. Ruth, Kissinger, Perry Mason, etc.
    c. Definition
       (overhead 3)

---

*Source:* Developed by Syracuse University Campus Mediation Center Training Committee, circa 1990.

    (1) Voluntary process

    (2) Assisted by a neutral trained facilitator (aware of biases, experts of the process)

    (3) Discuss and resolve their dispute (parties are the experts of the conflict)

6. Mediation on a continuum of other interventions (overhead 4)

    ◄──── controlled by self ────── controlled by others ──►

    bargain negotiate, conciliate, mediate, arbitrate, adjudicate

   a. Example of conflict—where it fits

7. Kinds of cases CMC [Campus Mediation Center] has handled (flesh out examples): friends, roommates, coworkers, landlords-tenants, student-faculty, group conflicts

8. Core qualities and skills of a mediator that make the process work

   a. Reflective listening

    (1) Content/feelings; emotions must be dealt with first (overhead 5)

    (2) Exercise: divide up in pairs, give one party private written instructions to listen poorly (squirm, no eye contact, etc.) while other talks; switch roles and repeat with different poor listening instructions given to second listener

    (3) After explaining reflective listening, give quick demonstration of effective listening in action

   b. Problem solving (7 steps) (overhead 6)

    (1) Quick summary; start with a how-to statement

    (2) Brainstorming versus evaluation

    (3) Reality check

    (4) When to use

   c. Basic process skills of mediator: (establish trust, facilitate communication, clarify issues and common interests, minimize power imbalances) (overhead 7)

9. Flow of mediation (overhead 8 and handout)

   a. Weave in specific case or scenario, emphasize future focus

   b. Emphasize movement from past to present to future

10. A mock dispute using audience volunteers reading set script or role play using CMC volunteers (get role play from CMC) (3 sets of scripts)

11. The benefits of using mediation at Syracuse University (overhead 9)

    a. Review benefits

    b. Contrast mediation with litigation (overhead 10)

       (1) Use role-play example and come up with what would have happened in small claims court: 80 percent versus 30 percent effectiveness

12. Questions and answers

## K: A Mediation Referral Guide for Residential Assistants

### Making a Referral to Campus Mediation: Guidelines for Residential Assistants

Campus Mediation Services will provide students or staff who are in conflict with a pair of neutral co-mediators, chosen from a pool of trained volunteers. Together they facilitate a problem-solving process in which the parties themselves define the issues and work toward the creation of a mutually agreeable resolution. If the parties reach an agreement, it is usually formalized and put into written form. The process typically takes 1–2 hours, but will vary depending on the case. Sessions can be scheduled during the day, evening, or weekend to meet the particular needs of the people involved. The process is private and confidential and does not result in a student record or file that might return to haunt students or staff in the future.

### What kinds of cases does the Campus Mediation Program handle?

The Campus Mediation Program is designed to handle interpersonal disputes between two or more people in an interdependent living or working situation. Examples include conflicts between roommates, hallmates, boyfriends and girlfriends (both current and ex), members of councils or working committees, residence staff members, and others. The content of the disputes will vary, although some common concerns will be noise levels, study habits, phone and utility bills, borrowed or broken items, relationship problems and misunderstandings, work-related conflicts, name calling, and minor forms of harassment.

### What are some advantages of using mediation?

- Mediation settles disputes privately and confidentially, out of the public eye. Disputants can modify their positions without fear of losing face in front of their friends or coworkers. Also, no student file or record results from using the process.

- It's fast and convenient. Mediations can usually be held within seven days of first contact, before things escalate and get worse or more complicated.

- By bringing in neutral mediators from outside, the process takes the RA out of the center of the conflict and can thus help them maintain credibility and neutrality in the eyes of the other members of the floor or hall.

---

*Source:* Written by Bill Warters.

- It focuses on problem solving rather than placing blame, and thus gets away from an unproductive battle to prove who's right or wrong.

- It's flexible and creative. Because the solutions are tailor made for the particular situation, there is a high likelihood that they will be lived up to and will last.

- The process of mutual resolution gives people a place to start for future interactions.

- It's educational. The participants learn communication skills and methods to avoid future conflict, so that your job as an RA may be easier in the long run.

- There is little risk. Agreements are voluntary. In the case of an impasse, all appropriate legal and procedural options, such as the judicial system, are still available.

**When should I use the Campus Mediation Program?**
You will have to use your own good judgment about when it makes sense to make a referral to campus mediation. However, mediation may be particularly appropriate and helpful in situations where you feel as though you have hit an impasse and have been spending a lot of time on particular individuals with little visible behavioral improvement. You may feel like you are becoming biased or that people perceive that you are taking sides in a conflict and it's polarizing the floor. You may feel that the uncontrolled conflict is putting you at risk of losing credibility with residents or with other staff. You may just be fed up with the situation. The Mediation Program provides a professional way to handle disputes before they escalate, and a way to deal with them constructively if they have gotten out of hand. Mediation can be particularly useful for handling those difficult relationship issues that do not involve violations of university policy but which may still disrupt life on the floor.

Also, if you happen to be in conflict with another RA, mediation can provide a confidential and private setting to work out your differences without the necessity of bringing in your supervisors or involving other staff. In addition to conflicts between individuals, the Mediation Program can often assist in resolving group conflicts. You should call the program coordinator if you are involved in a group conflict that you think could benefit from mediation. These types of cases will be considered on a case-by-case basis. In general, mediation is not a replacement for the important day-to-day work that RAs perform to maintain the quality of life on their floor. However, it does represent an additional valuable tool that can help make the work of RAs easier and more effective.

### How do I make a referral?

In order for the process to work, you have to have at least one party to the conflict who is willing to initiate contact with the Mediation program. This can be accomplished by talking with one or both parties about the mediation process, and encouraging them to call the coordinator to find out more about the service. You don't have to go to the hall director in order to make a referral, and the Program will not involve them in the process if that is your preference. However, if your rapport is good with your hall director, it makes sense to consult with them about all the options before choosing one. If a hall director is involved, she or he can strongly recommend mediation to the parties, perhaps as an alternative to a judicial hearing board if things have reached that stage. You may want to call the mediation service yourself and discuss the case with the coordinator before recommending it to the parties involved. The Program staff can help you think about whether the case is appropriate for mediation, and of ways to approach the parties that might increase the likelihood that they would be willing to try it.

Once at least one of the parties has called the Mediation Program, an intake worker will talk with them about their conflict, and describe how the service operates and assess whether or not mediation makes sense. If the first party is interested in trying mediation, a brief intake questionnaire will be filled out over the phone or in person, and then the second party will be contacted, either by letter and then phone, or directly by phone if they are already expecting the call. If the second party is willing to try mediation after they have heard a description of what it is and how it works, a mediation session will be scheduled as soon as is possible. At the session, the parties will meet together with the mediator team and go through a problem-solving process designed to assist disputants in coming up with a solution to their conflict that is satisfactory to all parties.

### What happens afterward?

Although the session itself is confidential, upon completion of the case, a form will be sent to the person or office that made the referral, informing them of whether the parties actually showed up for mediation, if an agreement was reached, and if any other referrals were made. The particular content of the agreement remains confidential, and it will be up to the parties if they want to share it with others or not. After approximately three to four weeks, the Mediation Program will follow up with both parties to see how the agreement is holding up, and to offer further assistance as required.

## L: Case Referral Follow-up Form

To:                                              Date:

The Conflict Resolution Service has responded to a referral for mediation that you sent to us. In order to keep you informed of the status of the referral, a follow-up of the case is presented below. As you know, the specific details of the case and any terms and conditions of the proposed solution must remain confidential.

CASE INFORMATION

Disputants:    _____    _____

              _____    _____

              _____    _____

Nature of Dispute: _____

_____

CASE RESOLUTION

___ Full Agreement Reached      ___ Partial Agreement Reached

___ No Agreement                ___ No Mediation held (below)

IF NO MEDIATION HELD

___ Disputant refused mediation   (Who: _____)

___ Disputant failed to appear    (Who: _____)

___ Disputant withdrew complaint  (Who: _____)

NOTES/COMMENTS:

Thank you very much for your support and referrals. If you have any questions, suggestions or comments, please feel free to call us at (xxx) xxx-xxxx.

_____

*Source:* Conflict Resolution Resource Service, Nova Southeastern University.

## M: Agreement-to-Mediate Forms

### Texas A&M University Student Conflict Resolution Services

AGREEMENT TO MEDIATION

Case Name: _____ SCRS# _____

Parties Involved: _____

The undersigned parties hereby agree to have mediation services provided by the Student Conflict Resolution Services (hereafter referred to as SCRS) for their dispute concerning:

Name: _____

1. MEDIATION RULES: SCRS will administer the mediation in accordance with its Mediation Rules. All parties recognize that mediation is a voluntary settlement negotiation and that the mediator is not a judge and has no authority to force a settlement on the parties. A settlement or agreement shall be reached in this dispute only if the parties to this dispute agree in writing that this settlement or agreement is fair and in their best interest and voluntarily entered into.

2. MEDIATOR: The parties agree the SCRS will select a mediator in accordance with SCRS's rules. The parties recognize that the mediator may or may not be an employee of Texas A&M University or the SCRS.

3. FEE: There is no fee for students of Texas A&M University.

4. CONSULTING WITH ATTORNEYS: The parties recognize that the mediator is not giving legal counsel or analyzing anyone's legal rights.

5. PRIVATE SESSIONS (CAUCUSES): The mediator may hold brief sessions with only one party. These "private sessions" are intended to improve the mediator's understanding of the participant's position. Information gained in a private session is confidential unless the participant agrees to have it brought up in joint session.

6. CONFIDENTIAL: The parties recognize that the mediation is confidential and that settlement negotiations and any other part of this mediation process are inadmissible in any litigation or arbitration of their dispute, to the maximum extent allowed by law. The parties specifically agree they will not subpoena, depose, or otherwise attempt to require the mediator to testify or produce records, notes, or work product in any future proceedings.

_____

*Source:* Texas A&M University Student Conflict Resolution Services. Used with permission.

7. PARTIAL INVALIDITY: In the event that any provision of this Agreement is invalid, the parties agree that all remaining provisions shall be deemed to be in full force and effect.

_____

Party

_____

Date _____ 19__     Mediator

## North Central College Dispute Resolution Program

AGREEMENT TO MEDIATE

1. We agree that _____ shall operate as our mediator for and through the North Central College Dispute Resolution Program.

2. We agree that the role of the mediator is to assist us in reaching a mutually acceptable settlement agreement. The mediator is neither a judge nor jury, and will not render a decision, nor give legal advice. Furthermore, in the absence of an agreement, the mediator may not discipline a student for conduct which gave rise to the mediation. We understand that to be informed of our rights regarding this dispute resolution procedure, we must consult the North Central College Student Handbook. We accept full responsibility for any agreement that we reach and understand that it is binding, and if violated may lead to disciplinary consequences.

3. We agree to keep all statements and communications made in the course of the mediation absolutely confidential, both on campus and off; the mediator makes the same promise. Should an agreement not be reached, and further disciplinary action be taken, the mediator shall not disclose that a mediation took place, nor reveal any information provided during the mediation. We shall not subpoena the mediator to testify in litigation on any matter, nor will we request the production of any records or documentation in the possession of the mediator for any purpose.

4. We agree that mediation is a voluntary process and that any party may terminate the mediation at any time. While in mediation we shall speak truthfully and participate in good faith.

Name (Printed): _____

Name (Signed): _____

Date: _____

_____

_Source:_ Thomas D. Cavenagh for the Legal Issues in Higher Education Conference, University of Vermont, October 3, 1994. Used with permission.

### University of North Dakota Conflict Resolution Center

A Guide to Participants in Mediation

Mediation is a process in which a neutral mediator assists individuals in conflict to discuss issues of concern to them, and in so doing develop a better understanding of their concerns and the perspectives of other participants. This leads to making voluntary and informed decisions.

There are some important principles that are a part of mediation and it is important that participants are aware of them. These principles include:

1. *Mediation is voluntary.* Participants should not feel forced in making decisions during mediation and always have the option to discontinue participation.

2. *Mediation involves informed decision making.* This means that full disclosure of relevant information is expected. It also implies that participants may wish to consult attorneys or other experts. Mediators may choose to terminate the mediation if they believe participants are not able to make informed decisions, such as when participants withhold or misrepresent information.

3. *Participants themselves make decisions in mediation.* There are two aspects to this. First, participants are solely responsible for making decisions. Second, there are many types of decisions that participants may make, including whether or not to pursue mediation, who should be involved in the discussion, how to explore additional information, what options are preferable, whether or not decisions are written, and so on.

4. *Mediators are neutral.* Mediators will not make decisions for the participants nor make any judgements of who is right or wrong. Mediators have no stake in any particular outcome and treat all participants in a fair and balanced way. The main goal of the mediator is to help create an environment for the parties to make voluntary and informed decisions.

5. *Mediation is a confidential process.* Mediators will not reveal anything that happens or is said during mediation to any other person, outside of the Conflict Resolution Center, except as permitted by law. Allegations of child abuse or threats of future harm to any person shall not be held confidential and may be revealed as appropriate by the mediator. Likewise, participants themselves are asked to keep confidential everything that is communicated during mediation, except as they agree otherwise or as permitted by law. Any documents that are produced as a result of the mediation,

---

*Source:* University of North Dakota Conflict Resolution Center (1998).

such as a summary of decisions reached, may be used by participants in subsequent relevant proceedings.

I have read, understand and agree to follow the principles related to mediation as described in the Guide for Participants in Mediation.

I agree to make full disclosure of all relevant information.

I understand the limits of confidentiality as described.

I agree to keep confidential everything that is communicated during mediation except as agreed to by the participants or as permitted by law.

_____      _____

Signature of Participant                                           Date

_____      _____

Signature of Participant                                           Date

## N: Information Sheet for Parties Preparing for Mediation

### Preparing for Your Mediation

This sheet was developed by the Campus Mediation Center to aid you in preparing for your mediation. It contains useful information to help you understand the process as well as your own role in mediation. Please read this sheet prior to your mediation.

### What Is Mediation?

Mediation is an effective means for people in conflict to work through their issues and arrive at a solution everyone can live with. Mediation involves impartial mediators helping you and the others in your dispute. At the mediation, each party will identify their needs and interests, as well as solutions for the future.

Our mediation services are free and confidential, and are scheduled to accommodate all parties. Mediation is not about right and wrong. It is about working out past problems and looking at future possibilities.

### What Will Happen at the Mediation?

The mediation process starts with each party having an opportunity to share their view of the conflict, with no interruptions. You should be prepared to discuss what has brought you to mediation and what your needs and interests are in this conflict. This is an opportunity to lay out your concerns, not to "make your case." Mediation is not about proving anything; it's about resolving differences and finding a workable solution.

The mediators will then help you to shift gears to problem solving. Problem solving involves all parties looking at possible ways to resolve the issues at hand. As there is usually more than one issue to work on, this part of mediation demands creativity and flexibility on the part of you and the other parties. Your mediators will help you to arrive at an appropriate solution that all parties can agree to.

When you reach a solution that meets everyone's needs, the mediators will write up an agreement for all parties to sign. Everyone who signs will receive a copy of the agreement. This agreement is a contract, and all those who sign it are expected to live up to its terms.

### Your Role in the Mediation

Mediation will be only as successful as you make it. Your responsibilities in mediation are to:

---

*Source:* Handout prepared by Tim Hedeen, 1994, for Campus Mediation Center at Syracuse University. Used with permission.

1. Decide what the issues are for you in this conflict.
2. Look for solutions.
3. Work with the other parties to determine which solution is most appropriate.

Remember: you construct the agreement; the mediators run the mediation. You should come to the mediation ready to work toward a resolution of the problems involved in your dispute.

### Confidentiality Is Important in Mediation

Confidentiality allows people to be comfortable working on tough issues. Mediation creates an environment where you can honestly and openly address the issues of the conflict.

Confidentiality is important because it allows people to work out issues and problems that they might not wish to share with others. Only those people present at the mediation know the content of the session, and the mediators are bound not to share any information relating to the content of the session outside of the mediation.

### If You Have Any Questions or Concerns:

Please call the Campus Mediation Center staff at 443-3870. We are committed to making your mediation a successful one.

## O: Procedural Summary of the Case Management Process

### I. Initial Intake Procedures

A. Party One Calls

*Ask them if they are familiar with how the center works

1. Brief description of the program

   a. Been here x years, funded by…

   b. Free service (one person connected to University in conflict)

   c. Place where people in conflict can come together in a safe environment to work out a common agreement

   d. You would meet with two neutral trained mediators, not judges or juries, to help you both come up with a solution you both can live with

   e. Voluntary and confidential process

   f. Other options remain open (court, counseling, judicial, doing nothing); either party can withdraw or choose not to settle at session

2. Brief description of process (if they ask)

   a. Come together with two neutral co-mediators

   b. Each person has a chance to tell their story

   c. Process of clarifying issues

   d. Generate possible solutions

   e. Work towards a written agreement

3. Have them tell you about their situation (write this on form)

   a. Use your fantastic listening skills, note positives as well as negatives about other person or situation (can help when addressing other party)

   b. Also get a sense of how long this conflict has been going on

   c. Q: Are there other issues you feel you want to resolve?

   d. Q: Do you know if _____ is interested in doing mediation?

4. If case is questionable, discuss whether issue seems conducive to mediation

---

*Source:* Developed by Joy Meeker and staff, Syracuse University Campus Mediation Center.

5. Fill out information on intake form

   a. Any previous action on this? (like legal action, small claims, campus judicial, RA, security, unionized case)

   b. Times they can meet for 2 hours (helpful to know times that they are generally not available)

6. Explain the CMC process from this point:

   a. Who will contact the other party?

     (1) They can arrange it with the other party first, but need to contact CMC ASAP afterwards to confirm, and CMC will at that point call Party 2 for confirmation and clarifications.

     (2) CMC can contact the other party, first by letter and then phone call. (Collect name, address, suggested best times to try and reach second party.)

*IF at this point mediation is agreed upon:*

   b. Meetings are usually arranged within 2–3 days

   c. CMC will send you info on the center when mediation is agreed upon

   d. CMC will contact you by phone on the day before the mediation

   e. Encourage them to call if they have any questions or concerns prior to the session

   THANK THEM FOR CALLING!!

B. Contacting the Other Party

(If first party is going to discuss doing mediation with the other, Party 1 should call CMC with the information, and CMC will call Party 2 to confirm)

1. Send Party 2 a form about receiving a request for mediation

2. After they have received the letter, call them saying you are responding to a call from _____ about the conflict the two parties have with each other

   a. Ask them if they received the letter

   b. State that it is a voluntary process that we think they may be interested in

   *Stress the positives that the first party mentioned

   Example: "She said she was hoping that it could be worked out"; "He mentioned that he wanted to avoid it from escalating"

    c. Ask if you can tell them briefly about the center and the process (see A.1 and A.2)

    d. Let them know you are interested in hearing from them about their concerns, issues, perception of the situation

3. If they are hesitant here are some strategies that you may want to be aware of:

    a. They may be hesitant for good reasons—and not ready (and not all cases work for mediation)

    b. In our experience those who go through mediation have found it very helpful (over 80 percent come up with an agreement)

    c. Focus is on how people can move on with their lives

    d. Ask them what they would like to see happen

        *Reality check (if they want it to go away)

        Q: What would avoiding this problem do for you?

        Q: How could you see this being resolved in court?

        *May want to remind them of cost, time, and loss of control in court

    e. Remind them of the advantages (free, quick, at their convenience, confidential and the parties themselves control the agreement)

    f. Ask again, "Would you be willing to give it a try?" or "Would you like to think about it? I'll be back in touch in a few days."

4. WHEN Parties Have Agreed to Mediate

    a. Arrange a common time and a good location for the mediation session

    b. Clarify who will be attending session (i.e., any additional parties beyond primary?)

    c. Send "agreement to mediate" to both parties with date and time of mediation and brochure

    d. Arrange two mediators to case

        (1) Conscious of parties' needs (gender, ethnic diversity, age)

        (2) Ask first mediator if they want to be matched up with someone who is more experienced, or if wants to help less experienced mediator, or if they want some review before the mediation

        (3) Secure second mediator

(4) Send both mediators a short thank-you note for accepting the invitation together with a confirmation of the date, time, and location of the mediation session

5. If second party declines to participate, contact first party, inform him/her of the decision and try to assist him/her in considering other options for resolving the situation. Close file.

## II. Before the Mediation

A. The day before the mediation confirm with both parties via telephone

B. If it has been awhile since the mediation was set up with the mediators, call them to remind them of the time/place

## III. Mediation Day

A. Make sure that a mediator packet is ready

1. Opening Statement Checklist
2. Several CMC Agreement forms
3. Blank sheets of paper and pens
4. Mediator's report form
5. Stages of mediation handout
6. Calculator
7. Additional Agreement-to-Mediate forms

B. Make sure that the intake information is with the file

C. Remind mediators to mention that an evaluation form will be sent to them in about a week (after the mediation)

D. After the mediation ask mediators:

1. To process mediation with each other
2. To fill out postmediation form
3. Please write one paragraph on the conflict and mediation in terms which respect confidentiality for future use in evaluation

## IV. Postmediation Follow-up

A. Type up the paragraph description on mediation submitted by mediators, update case file.

B. If the case was an official referral, send the Case Referral Follow-up form to the person who referred Party 1. Keep details of session confidential.

C. After a few days send out the evaluations to parties (with self-addressed envelope)

D. After another week check to see if parties responded; send a reminder and mention they could call for a second form if they want

E. Highlight any written evaluations that would be helpful to use in evaluation report—including those written by mediators—and indicate if the parties would be good people to write up a "testimony" on the value of the center.

## P: Blank Mediation Agreement Form

### Mediation Agreement

We, the undersigned, understand and voluntarily agree that the following constitutes a mutually acceptable solution for our dispute and all parties shall abide, in good faith, by the following terms and conditions:

Signatures: _____ Date _____

_____ Date _____

Witnesses: I/We, the undersigned mediator(s), having been designated by the Campus Mediation Center (CMC), witness the above agreement.

Signatures: _____ Date _____

_____ Date _____

_____

*Source:* Syracuse University Campus Mediation Center.

## Q: Postmediation Report Form

Following a mediation session, the mediators complete a report to inform the staff of important facts about the case. These include referrals, length of session, and concerns.

Postmediation Report

Date of Mediation: _____     Location: _____

Mediator(s): _____ and _____

Case (as appears on case file): _____

Starting time: _____ Ending time: _____ Elapsed time: _____

PARTICIPANTS

| Name | Role (complaint, respondent, observer, attorney, etc.) |
|------|--------------------------------------------------------|
| _____ | _____ |
| _____ | _____ |
| _____ | _____ |
| _____ | _____ |

Please write a one-paragraph description of the dispute and the mediation in terms that respect the confidentiality of the participants.

_____

_____

_____

_____

_____

_____

Amount of money (if any) agreed to be exchanged: _____

If made, referrals to other campus services: _____

_____

_____

Any special follow-up required/recommended? _____

_____

_____

Postmediation reminders:
1. Place folder in secured place for CMC staff to recover
2. Process/debrief mediation with co-mediator and/or observer(s)

Thank you very much for your service to the campus community.

_____

*Source:* Adapted from a form by the Syracuse University Campus Mediation Center.

## R: Standards of Practice for Campus Mediators

### Syracuse University Campus Mediator Guidelines

These guidelines represent the obligations the mediator has toward the campus community and toward the Parties. The items listed are to be considered as morally binding obligations, not merely a list of "rules of the game."

### Ethical Concerns: The Mediator and Mediation Center/Community

1. To keep an open mind, an intellectual impartiality. To clearly formulate issues, not conclusions.

2. To give a full, best effort to each case: good faith.

3. To make a principled decision to decline or withdraw from a case if you know the parties and/or if you feel you cannot mediate it in good faith. There is further responsibility to look for any reasonable probability of bias or other interference occurring due to the nature of the case.

4. To represent the Campus Mediation Center and the process competently and professionally.

   a. Become and remain proficient in the skills of mediation.

   b. Accept and follow through efficiently on all assigned cases.

   c. Maintain loyalty to the process.

   d. Maintain the spirit as well as the appearance of confidentiality and honesty.

5. To provide the mediation service as a volunteer, not amenable to payoffs, outside entrepreneurship, etc.

6. To represent the Center in a professional manner when talking to individuals or the press, and to direct members of the press to the program coordinator if they intend to print a story about the program.

### Ethical Concerns: The Mediator and the Parties

1. To encourage but not manipulate or coerce settlement. Agreement is up to the parties.

2. To give each party a fair hearing.

   a. Facilitating, supporting communication.

   b. Maintaining and defending the rights of each party to be heard.

   c. Listening: There is frequently real virtue in not speaking.

---

*Source:* Ready-Set-Go Program Development Packet by Bill Warters.

3. To keep confidences unless a party gives permission to share the information or the law demands a nonconfidential response.

   a. Being candid, sincere in responses.

   b. Not exposing unnecessarily weaknesses or factors extraneous to the negotiation.

4. To respect parties' rights to disagree and to work out their own result or their right not to work out a result.

5. To refuse to mediate a case if it becomes apparent that there has been a pattern of repeated domestic violence or intimidation in an interpersonal relationship, and to suspend mediation if it becomes apparent in the course of the mediation session itself.

### North Central College (Naperville, Illinois) Volunteer Mediator Policy

POLICY FOR STUDENT MEDIATORS

Mediators have one of the most important roles on campus: assisting others in resolving the disputes that prevent peaceful coexistence. They are often entrusted with confidential and highly sensitive information. Therefore, they must be carefully selected, trained and evaluated, and held to the highest standards of honesty, good faith and sound judgment. The following policies address many crucial concerns:

CONFIDENTIALITY

All matters handled by, or referred to, the North Central College Dispute Resolution Center are confidential. All information regarding people who use, request the use of, or are referred to the program must be treated as absolutely private and highly sensitive. Mediators may not divulge any such information to anyone outside the program in any way. This policy applies to all current and former mediators and should be enforced rigorously. Violation of this policy should result in immediate dismissal from the program, and should lead to formal disciplinary action.

CONFLICTS OF INTEREST

In order to ensure the fairest possible dispute resolution system, mediators are required to excuse themselves from cases assigned to them when a conflict of interest is present, or when the appearance of a conflict is present. It is impossible to describe every possible

*Source:* Thomas D. Cavenagh, North Central College Dispute Resolution Center. (708) 420–6918; e-mail: tdc@noctrl.edu. Used with permission.

conflict of interest, so mediators are advised to request a replacement if they have any doubt about the actual or apparent impartiality of their work. Several examples of cases in which a conflict of interest exists include: a case involving a roommate of the mediator, a case involving a boyfriend or girlfriend of the mediator, a case involving a lab partner of the mediator, or a case involving an athletic, forensic or model United Nations teammate of the mediator.

The single most important source of mediation case referrals is the student body. Student mediators have the crucial responsibility of providing guidance to students involved in disputes who could make use of the Center. Naturally, a mediator who assists a student in self-referral of a case could not mediate that case. However, the mediator may assist the student in preparing the case for mediation by recommending the process to the student, explaining the process to the student and helping to prepare the mediation referral form.

## COMPLIANCE WITH COLLEGE POLICIES AND RESPONSIBILITIES

Mediators are expected to maintain the highest standards of conduct and reputation. Mediators who fail to comply with expectations of the community will be removed from the roster of mediators. Because the position of mediator is one of great trust, the Center director has broad latitude in determining whether the conduct of a mediator disqualifies that mediator from continued service.

## SELF-EVALUATION

In all cases, the mediator must complete a brief self-assessment form. These forms will be used by the Center director to plan further training and to assist mediators in developing important skills. All forms will be treated as confidential.

## ASSIGNMENT OF CASE

The assignment of a case to a mediator will be done by the Director on a case by case basis. In assigning a case to a mediator, the director will consider many things including the complexity of the case, the time-frame within which a mediation conference must be scheduled, and the need to provide a mediator who is absolutely impartial. The director will attempt, as well, to provide a mediator who is best able to provide the disputants with a conference setting which is conducive to productive settlement discussions. Finally, where appropriate, the Director may assign co-mediators to a case.

## APPEAL

In very rare circumstances parties may appeal the outcome of the mediation process. Because the process is voluntary, the mediator makes no decision, and the outcome was crafted by the parties, the only real grounds for such an appeal is mediator misconduct.

UNSUITABLE CASES
When should solutions to conflict NOT be negotiated?

- Harmful future conduct
- Strong due process considerations
- Preservation of legal rights
- Lack of capacity
- Repeated conduct
- Non-negotiable outcomes, i.e., alcohol

## S: Mediation Follow-up Form

Please take a few moments to complete the following brief questionnaire. Your assistance will help us evaluate the service provided by the Mediation Center. All information you give will be completely anonymous, and you can refuse to answer any of the questions.

1. How satisfied were you with mediation as a way of settling your dispute? (Please circle one)
   a. Completely satisfied
   b. Somewhat satisfied
   c. Neither satisfied nor dissatisfied
   d. Somewhat dissatisfied
   e. Completely dissatisfied

2. Would you return to the Mediation Center with a similar problem? (Please circle one.)
   a. Definitely
   b. Probably
   c. Maybe
   d. Probably not
   e. Definitely not

3. Would you recommend mediation to others having similar problems?
   a. Definitely
   b. Probably
   c. Maybe
   d. Probably not
   e. Definitely not

4. Have you ever recommended or suggested mediation to others?
   a. Yes
   b. No

5. Who initiated the mediation session (i.e., who first contacted the Mediation Center?)
   a. I did.
   b. The other party did.
   c. Other (explain) _____

*Source:* Based on a form developed by Catherine Borshuk for the Carleton University Campus Mediation Centre. Used with permission.

6. From your experience with mediation, do you feel you've learned any conflict resolution tactics that you could use in other disputes?

    a. Definitely yes

    b. Probably yes

    c. Maybe

    d. Probably not

    e. Definitely not

7. Going into the mediation session, were you expecting to reach a written agreement with the other party?

    a. Yes

    b. No

8. Did you reach a written agreement with the other person/party through mediation?

    a. Yes

    b. No

9. How satisfied were you with the written agreement or outcome?

    a. Completely satisfied

    b. Somewhat satisfied

    c. Neither satisfied nor dissatisfied

    d. Somewhat dissatisfied

    e. Completely dissatisfied

10. Is your agreement still being upheld?

    a. Yes

    b. No

    c. No longer applicable

    d. Terms of agreement have been completed/satisfied

11. Approximately how long ago was your dispute mediated?

    _____ Years  _____ Months  _____ Weeks

12. Do you feel you were treated fairly by the mediators?

    a. Yes

    b. No

13. Were your concerns given as much attention by the mediators as those of the other person/party?

    a. Yes

    b. No

14. Do you feel the mediators took a neutral stance in mediating your dispute?

    a. Yes

    b. No

15. Is there anything that you think should be done to improve the mediation program?

    a. Yes

    b. No

    Please provide any comments:

16. Are you:

    a. Male

    b. Female

17. What is your age in years? _____

Thank you for taking the time to complete this questionnaire.

Please return it in the enclosed self-addressed envelope as soon as possible.

# RECOMMENDED RESOURCES

## Campus Conflict Resolution–Related Resources

Association for Student Judicial Affairs Alternative Dispute
Resolution Committee
William Fischer, Chair
5 Quad Way, Hitchcock Hall
University of New Hampshire
Durham, New Hampshire 03824
Phone: (603) 862-3377
Fax: (603) 862-4787
E-mail: wfischer@cisunix.unh.edu
http://asja.tamu.edu/default.htm

Campus Mediation Resources Web Site
www.mtds.wayne.edu/campus.htm
c/o Bill Warters
College of Urban, Labor, and Metropolitan Affairs
Wayne State University
3248 Faculty/Administration Building
656 West Kirby
Detroit, Michigan 48202
Phone: (313) 993-7482
Fax: (313) 577-8800
E-mail: w.warters@wayne.edu

Consortium on Peace Research, Education and Development
c/o Institute for Conflict Analysis and Resolution
George Mason University
Fairfax, Virginia 22030-4444

Phone: (703) 993-2405
Fax: (703) 993-3070
E-mail: copred@gmu.edu
www.gmu.edu/departments/ICAR/copred/
(Publisher of *The Global Directory of Peace Studies Programs*
*[1995–1996]*)

Dispute Resolution Resources (Links and Listings)
Nova Southeastern University Department of Dispute Resolution
School of Social and Systemic Studies
3301 College Avenue
Fort Lauderdale, Florida 33314
Phone: (954) 262-3000
Fax: (954) 262-3968
E-mail: ssss@ssss.nova.edu
www.nova.edu/ssss/DR/resources.html
Includes list of conflict resolution programs in higher education

DiversityWeb
E-mail: diversity-web@umail.umd.edu
www.inform.umd.edu/EdRes/Topic/Diversity/Response/Web/
Extensive on-line information source for campus diversity work.

National Association of College and University Attorneys
One Dupont Circle, Suite 620
Washington, D.C. 20036
Phone: (202) 833-8390
Fax: (202) 296-8379
E-mail: nacua@nacua.org
www.nacua.org/sections/ladr.html
See the association's section on Litigation and Alternative Dispute
Resolution

University and College Ombuds Association
c/o Tom Sebok, UCOA Secretary
Ombuds Office, CB 112
University of Colorado at Boulder
Boulder, Colorado 80309-0112
Phone: (303)-492-5077
Fax: (303) 492-2110
E-mail: sebok@spot.colorado.edu
www.colorado.edu/Ombuds/UCOA/index.html
For copies of the special journal issue on confidentiality concerns,
contact editor Richard Hebein, (419) 372-2015, rhebein@bgnet.bgsu.edu

See also the on-line editions of the *Journal of the California Caucus
of College and University Ombudsman*: www.ombuds.uci.edu/
JOURNALS/

## On-line Discussion List

The CCRNet (Campus Conflict Resolution Network) e-mail discussion list is a moderated listserv that currently includes some four hundred dispute resolvers interested in conflict resolution on campus. Subscribers receive copies of all mail sent to the list by members, and the subscriber's messages go out to everyone as well. To join this group send the command:

*subscribe ccrnet your name*

to the subscription address,

*listproc@pulsar.acast.nova.edu*

Where it says "your name," use your actual name, such as Jane Doe or John Smith, not an e-mail name. Thus if I were subscribing, I would type "subscribe ccrnet Bill Warters" in my message, and address it to the listproc address. Place nothing in the subject line or anything else in the body of the message (like an automatic signature, for instance) because this is processed by a rather picky computer instead of a person. If you are successful, you should receive a welcome message explaining more about the listserv discussion list. Questions or concerns about the listserv should be directed to the moderator (currently a person named Cody) at ccrmod@pulsar.acast.nova.edu. You may leave the list at any time by sending an "unsubscribe CCRNET" command to the listproc@pulsar.acast.nova.edu address.

## Specialized Written Resources on Campus Conflict

Holton, S. (1995). *Conflict Management on Campus.* New Directions for Higher Education, No. 92. San Francisco: Jossey-Bass. This special issue focuses specifically on conflict management in higher education. It is a well-rounded collection of twelve chapters and an appendix that should be of interest to people working in higher education domains. For ordering information, contact the publisher, Jossey-Bass.

Holton, S. (Ed.). (1998). *Mending the Cracks in the Ivory Tower: Strategies for Conflict Management in Higher Education.* Bolton, MA: Anker Publishing Company. With a particular focus on department chairs and deans, this edited book helps analyze the many kinds of personal and institutional conflicts most commonly faced in higher education and provides suggested methods for conflict management and resolution. Contributors share their expertise with case studies, questions, examples, and strategies, inviting readers to use this practical guide to "mend the cracks in your own towers."

Symposium on Conflict Resolution in Higher Education. A conference entitled "Reflective Practice in Institutionalizing Conflict Resolution in Higher Education" was hosted by the Consortium on Negotiation and Conflict Resolution at Georgia State University in May 1998. A series of working papers were prepared by participants and are available through the consortium: Georgia State University College of Law, P.O. Box 4037, Atlanta, Georgia 30302-4037. Phone: (404) 651-1588; fax: (404) 651-4155; e-mail: cncr@gsu.edu or visit the Web site at law.gsu.edu/CNCR/

*The Ombuds Handbook: A Practical Guide to Establishing and Operating an Ombuds Office on a College or University Campus* (1999) is available from the University and College Ombuds Association (see address above) for people who are developing new ombuds services.

## National Dispute Resolution Organizations

Academy of Family Mediators
5 Militia Drive
Lexington, Massachusetts 02421
Telephone: (781) 674-2663
Facsimile: (781) 674-2690
E-mail: afmoffice@mediators.org
www.igc.apc.org/afm/

American Bar Association
Section of Dispute Resolution
740 Fifteenth St. N.W.
Washington, D.C. 20005-1009
Phone: (202) 662-1680
Fax: (202) 662-1683
E-mail: dispute@abanet.org
www.abanet.org/dispute

Conflict Resolution Education Network (CREnet)
1527 New Hampshire Avenue, N.W., Fourth Floor
Washington, D.C. 20036
Phone: (202) 667-9700
Fax: (202) 667-8629
E-mail: nidr@crenet.org
www.crenet.org
Has a Committee on Higher Education

National Association for Community Mediation
1527 New Hampshire Avenue, N.W., Fourth Floor

Washington, D.C. 20036
Phone: (202) 667-9700
Fax: (202) 667-8629
E-mail: nafcm@nafcm.org
www.igc.org/nafcm
Publisher of a good general conflict resolution skills curriculum
used with Americorps volunteers

National Conference on Peacemaking and Conflict Resolution
(NCPCR)
c/o Institute for Conflict Analysis and Resolution
George Mason University
4400 University Drive
Fairfax, Virginia 22030-444
Phone: (703) 993-2440
E-mail: ncpcr@gmu.edu
www.gmu.edu/departments/NCPCR/
Sponsors of a major biannual national conference

The Network: Interaction for Conflict Resolution
(Canadian National Conflict Resolution Association)
c/o Institute of Peace and Conflict Studies
Conrad Grebel College
University of Waterloo
Waterloo, Ontario N2L 3G6, Canada
Phone: (519) 885-0880
Fax: (519) 885-0806
E-mail: nicr@nicr.ca
www.nicr.ca/

Ombudsman Association
Executive Office
5521 Greenville Avenue, Suite 104-265
Dallas, Texas 75206
Phone: (214) 553-0043 (9 A.M.–4 P.M. Central Standard Time)
Fax: (214) 348-6621 (9 A.M.–4 P.M. Central Standard Time)
E-mail: 73772.1763@CompuServe.com
web.mit.edu/negotiation/toa/

Society for Professionals in Dispute Resolution
1527 New Hampshire Avenue, N.W., Third Floor
Washington, D.C. 20036
Phone: (202) 667-9700
Fax: (202) 265-1968
E-mail: spidr@spidr.org
www.spidr.org

Victim Offender Mediation Association
c/o William T. Preston, Administrator
4624 Van Kleeck Drive
New Smyrna Beach, Florida 32169
(904) 424-1591
(904) 423-8099 Fax
E-mail: voma@voma.org
www.voma.org

## Additional Useful On-line Resources and Organizations _____

Alternatives to Violence Project USA
National Office
P.O. Box 300431
Houston Texas 77230-0431
Phone: (713) 747-9999
Fax: (713) 747-9999
E-mail: AVPUSA@AOL.com
www.avpusa.org
Great conflict resolution training manuals

Center for Information Technology and Dispute Resolution
Online Ombuds Office
221 Hampshire House
University of Massachusetts
Amherst, Massachusetts 01003
Phone: (413) 545-5879
Fax: (413) 545-1640
E-mail: ombuds@legal.umass.edu
www.ombuds.org

Conflict Research Consortium Web Site
Guy Burgess or Heidi Burgess, Co-Directors
University of Colorado
Campus Box 327
Boulder, Colorado 80309-0327
Phone: (303) 492-1635
Fax: (303) 492-2154
E-mail: burgess@colorado.edu
www.Colorado.EDU/conflict
The most extensive on-line conflict resolution resource

Conflict Resolution Center International
204 Thirty-seventh Street
Pittsburgh, Pennsylvania 15201-1859
Phone: (412) 687 6210

Fax: (412) 687 6232
E-mail: crcii@conflictnet.org
www.conflictres.org/
Maintains an international directory of intervenors

Mediation Information and Resource Center Web Site
P.O. Box 51090
Eugene, OR 97405
Phone: (541) 302-6254
www.mediate.com
Extensive on-line resource for mediators

Nonviolence International WWW site
P.O. Box 39127
Friendship Station, N.W.
Washington, D.C. 20016
Phone: (202) 244-0951
Fax: (202) 244-6396
E-mail: nonviolence@igc.apc.org
www.igc.apc.org/nonviolence
Includes an annotated bibliography of nonviolent action training

Nonviolence Web
P.O. Box 30947
Philadelphia, Pennsylvania 19104
Phone: (215) 724-4633.
E-mail: nvweb@nonviolence.org
www.nonviolence.org

Program on Negotiation Clearinghouse at Harvard Law School
1563 Massachusetts Avenue
518 Pound Hall
Cambridge, Massachusetts 02138
Contact: The Clearinghouse
Phone: (617) 495-1684
Fax: (617) 495-7818
E-mail: srankin@hulaw1.harvard.edu
Publishers of tools for negotiation training

Victim-Offender Reconciliation Program (VORP)
Information and Resource Center
19813 N.E. Thirteenth Street
Camas, Washington 98607
Phone: (360) 260-1551
Fax: (360) 260-1563
E-mail: martyprice@vorp.com
www.vorp.com

## Mediation Resources _____

Beer, J., with Stief, E. (1997). *The mediator's handbook* (Rev. and exp. 3rd ed.). Gabriola Island, B.C.: New Society Publishers. Good basic mediation manual.

Bush, R.A.B., & Folger, J. (1994). *The promise of mediation: Responding to conflict through empowerment and recognition.* San Francisco: Jossey-Bass.

Goldberg, S. B., Sander, F., & Rodgers, N. (1992). *Dispute resolution: Negotiation, mediation, and other processes* (2nd ed.). Aspen: Aspen Publishers.

Kolb, D., & Others. (1994). *When talk works: Profiles of mediators.* San Francisco: Jossey-Bass.

McGillis, D. (1997). *Community mediation programs: Developments and challenges* (NCJ 165698). Washington, D.C.: National Institute of Justice.

Mediation Information Resource Center. www.mediate.com.

Mennonite Conciliation Service. (1995). *Mediation and facilitation manual: Foundations and skills for constructive conflict transformation* (3rd ed.). Akron, PA: Mennonite Conciliation Service. Extensive mediation and facilitation manual, from a Christian perspective.

Merry, S. E., & Milner, N. (Eds.). (1993). *The possibility of popular justice: A case study of community mediation in the United States.* Ann Arbor, MI: University of Michigan Press. Good review of community mediation theory and practice in the United States.

Moore, C. (1996). *The mediation process: Practical strategies for resolving conflict* (2nd ed.). San Francisco: Jossey-Bass. The most widely used scholarly and practical book on mediation.

National Institute for Dispute Resolution Task Force. (1991). *Community dispute resolution manual: Insights and guidance from two decades of practice.* Washington, D.C.: National Institute for Dispute Resolution. Very helpful tips on managing programs.

## Dispute Systems Design _____

Costantino, C. A., & Merchant, C. S. (1996). *Designing conflict management systems: A guide to creating productive and healthy organizations.* San Francisco: Jossey-Bass.

Department of Veterans Affairs ADR and Mediation Resources Web site: www.va.gov/adr/index.htm. This site, although focused on federal government agency ADR initiatives, provides useful sample documents and guidelines.

Slaikeu, K., & Hasson, R. (1998). *Controlling the costs of conflict: How to design a system for your organization.* San Francisco: Jossey-Bass.

Society for Professionals in Dispute Resolution, Organizational Conflict Management Sector, www.spidr.org/ocm/, c/o John Conbere, jconbere@ix.netcom.com

Ury, W. L., Brett, J. M., & Goldberg, B. (1988). *Getting disputes resolved: Designing systems to cut the cost of conflict.* San Francisco: Jossey-Bass.

Various Authors. (1989). Symposium on Dispute Systems Design. *Negotiation Journal, 5,* 357–407. Includes seven articles on dispute systems design.

## Group Facilitation

Auvine, B., & Others. (1977). *A manual for group facilitators.* Madison, WI: Center for Conflict Resolution.

Avery, M., & Others. (1981). *Building united judgement: A handbook for consensus decision making.* Madison, WI: Center for Conflict Resolution.

Ball, G. (1989). *Using graphics with groups.* Los Altos, CA: Geoff Ball & Associates.

Facilitator Central Web site: hsb.baylor.edu/html/fuller/fac/. An excellent starting point for on-line information relating to facilitation in all its aspects.

Fisher, R. J. (1997). *Interactive conflict resolution.* Syracuse, NY: Syracuse University Press.

Kaner, S. (1996). *Facilitator's guide to participatory decision-making.* Gabriola Island, BC: New Society Publishers.

Schwarz, R. M. (1994). *The skilled facilitator: Practical wisdom for developing effective groups.* San Francisco: Jossey-Bass.

# REFERENCES

Academe Today. (1998, July 13). Business officers honor 5 universities for cutting costs. *Academe Today: A News Service of the Chronicle of Higher Education.*

Adams, J., & Hall, J. (1976). Legal liabilities in higher education: Their scope and management (Part II). *Journal of College and University Law, 3*(335), 360–369.

American Arbitration Association, American Bar Association, and Society for Professionals in Dispute Resolution. (1995). *Model standards of conduct for mediators.* Washington, D.C.: Author

Auerbach, J. S. (1983). *Justice without law? Resolving disputes without lawyers.* New York: Oxford University Press.

Ausubel, J. (1998). *The university as a system and the system of universities.* New York: Sloan Foundation. Available from: w3.scale.uiuc.edu/economics/university.html.

Auvine, B., & Others. (1977). *A manual for group facilitators.* Madison, WI: Center for Conflict Resolution.

Avery, M. (1990). Mediation of race-related conflicts on campus. *Conciliation Quarterly, 9*(3), 5–7.

Avery, M., & Others. (1981). *Building united judgment: A handbook for consensus decision making.* Madison, WI: Center for Conflict Resolution.

Baldridge, J. V. (1971). *Power and conflict in the university: Research in the sociology of complex organizations.* New York: Wiley.

Baldridge, J. V., Curtis, D. V., Ecker, G. P., & Riley, G. L. (1978). *Policy making and effective leadership.* San Francisco: Jossey-Bass.

Ball, G. (1989). *Using graphics with groups.* Los Altos, CA: Geoff Ball & Associates.

Ball, G. (1998, April). Beyond flip charts: Graphic facilitation focuses a group's thoughts. *CONSENSUS: A Quarterly Publication of the MIT-Harvard Public Disputes Program.*

Barnes, B. (1994). Conflict resolution across cultures: A Hawaii perspective and a Pacific mediation model. *Mediation Quarterly, 12*(2), 117–133.

Barnes, B. (1998). *Designing a conflict resolution system for the University of Hawaii system: Economic considerations and the unionized campus.* Paper presented at Reflective Practice in Institutionalizing Conflict Resolution in Higher Education Conference, Georgia State University, Atlanta.

Beeler, K. D. (1986). Campus mediation: A promising complement to student judicial processes. *Southern Association for College Student Affairs Journal, 7*(1), 38–45.

Beer, J., & Stief, E. (1997). *The mediator's handbook.* (Rev. and exp. 3rd ed.). Gabriola Island, B.C.: New Society Publishers.

Bergquist, W. (1992). *The four cultures of the academy.* San Francisco: Jossey-Bass.

Bickel, R. D. (1978). *The college administrator and the courts.* Asheville, NC: College Administration Publications.

Bickel, R. D., and Lake, P. (1999). *The rights and responsibilities of the modern university: Who assumes the risks of university life?* Durham, NC: Carolina Academic Press.

Birkhoff, J., & Warfield, W. (1996). The development of pedagogy and practicum. *Mediation Quarterly, 14*(2), 93–110.

Birnbaum, R. (1988). *How colleges work: The cybernetics of academic organization and leadership.* San Francisco: Jossey-Bass.

Blau, P. (1973). *The organization of academic work.* New York: Wiley.

Boice, R. (1996). Classroom incivilities. *Research in Higher Education, 37*(4), 453–487.

Bolding, J. T., & Van Patten, J. J. (1982). Creating a healthy organizational climate. *Administrator's Update: American Association of University Administrators, 3*(3), 1–9.

Borshuk, C. (1994). Benefits of a peer mediation service: An evaluation. *Interaction, 6*(1), 3–6.

Boyer, E. (1990). *Campus life: In search of community.* Princeton, NJ: Princeton University Press.

Brett, J., Barsness, Z., & Goldberg, S. (1996). The effectiveness of mediation: An independent analysis of cases handled by four major service providers. *Negotiation Journal, 12*(3), 259–269.

Brodrick, M., Carroll, B., & Hart, B. (1996). *Quality assurance and qualifications.* Washington, DC: National Association for Community Mediation. Available from: ⟨http://www.igc.org/nafcm/news4.html⟩.

Burgess, G., & Burgess, H. (1997). *Transformative mediation website.* Boulder, CO: Conflict Research Consortium. Available from: www.Colorado.EDU/conflict/transform/tmall.htm.

Bush, R.A.B., & Folger, J. (1994). *The promise of mediation: Responding to conflict through empowerment and recognition.* San Francisco: Jossey-Bass.

Carlton, J. (1993). Working it out. *Successful Meetings, 42*(12), 102–107. Casper, G. (1998, October 29, 1998). State of university address. *Stanford Report Online Update.*

Casper, G. (1998, Oct. 29). State of university address. *Stanford Report Online Update.* www.stanford.edu/dept/news/report.

Chickering, A. W. (1969). *Education and identity.* San Francisco: Jossey-Bass.

Chickering, A. W. (1993). *Education and identity* (2nd ed.). San Francisco: Jossey-Bass.

Clark, B. (1970). The new university. In C. E. Kruytbosch & S. L. Messinger (Eds.), *The state of the university* (pp. 17–26). Thousand Oaks, CA: Sage.

Clark, B. R. (1963). Faculty organization and authority. In T. E. Lunsford (Ed.), *The study of academic administration* (pp. 37–51). Boulder, CO: Western Interstate Commission for Higher Education.

Cleveland, D. (1995). *Conflict Resolution Resource Survey.* Unpublished manuscript. Broward Community College.

Cloke, K. (1988). Date rape and the limits of mediation. *Mediation Quarterly, 21,* 77–83.

Cohen, M. D., & March, J. G. (1974). *Leadership and ambiguity: The American college president.* New York: McGraw-Hill.

Cohen, M. D., March, J. G., & Olsen, J. P. (1972). A garbage can model of organizational choice. *Administrative Science Quarterly, 17*(1), 1–25.

Cohen, R. (1995). *Peer mediation in schools: Students resolving conflicts.* Glenview, IL: Scott Foresman.

Collision, M. (1990, May 2). Negotiation, not violence, is the rule today when students clash with administrators. *Chronicle of Higher Education,* pp. 30–32, 44.

Costantino, C. A., & Merchant, C. S. (1996). *Designing conflict management systems: A guide to creating productive and healthy organizations.* San Francisco: Jossey-Bass.

Cunningham, P. J. (1984, Summer). Taking the conflict out of grievance handling. *Journal of the College and University Personnel Association, 35,* 8–11.

Curle, A. (1971). *Making peace.* New York: Barnes and Noble.

Curle, A. (1995). *Another way: Positive response to contemporary violence.* Oxford: Jon Carpenter Publishing.

Dana, D. (1984, Fall). The costs of organizational conflict. *Organizational Development Journal,* 5–6.

Davis, B., & Corley, S. (1996). *Rockin' role plays: A collection of the finest for mediation trainers.* Asheville, NC: Mediation Center.

Dennison, G. M., Drummond, M. E., & Hobgood, W. P. (1997). Collaborative bargaining in public universities. *Negotiation Journal, 13*(1), 61–81.

d'Errico, P., Katsch, E., & Rifkin, J. (1980). Legal studies and mediation: An academic/public model of conflict resolution. In J. McCarthy (Ed.), *Resolving conflicts in higher education* (pp. 48–55). New Directions in Education, Vol. 32. San Francisco: Jossey-Bass.

Duryea, E. D. (1986). Evolution of university organization. In M. W. Peterson (Ed.), *ASHE reader on organization and governance in higher education* (pp. 165–182). Lexington, MA: Ginn Press.

Elliott, M. (1998, May 8–9). *Review of the literature on conflict resolution in higher education.* Paper presented at the Reflective Practice in Institutionalizing Conflict Resolution in Higher Education Conference, Georgia State University, Atlanta.

Engram, B. (1985). Mediation and conflict resolution (for resident assistants). In G. Bliming (Ed.), *The experienced resident assistant* (pp. 159–166). Dubuque, IA: Kendall/Hunt Publishing.

Etzioni, A. (1993). *The spirit of community: The reinvention of American society.* New York: Simon & Schuster.

Fetterman, D. M., Kaftarian, S. J., & Wandersman, A. (Eds.). (1996). *Empowerment evaluation: Knowledge and tools for self-assessment and accountability.* Thousand Oaks, CA: Sage.

Fisher, R. J. (1997). *Interactive conflict resolution.* Syracuse, NY: Syracuse University Press.

Folger, J., & Schubert, J. (1985). *Resolving student initiated grievances in higher education: Dispute resolution procedures in a non-adversarial setting* (Research Report 3). Washington, DC: National Institute for Dispute Resolution.

Force, N. T. (1991). *Community dispute resolution manual: Insights and guidance from two decades of practice.* Washington, D.C.: National Institute for Dispute Resolution.

Gadlin, H. (1991). Careful maneuvers: Mediating sexual harassment. *Neotiation Journal, 7*(2), 139–152.

Gadlin, H., & Paludi, M. (1990). *The use and abuse of mediation for sexual harassment cases.* Paper presented at the First National Conference on Campus Mediation, Syracuse University.

Girard, K., Rifkin, J., & Townley, A. (1985). *Peaceful persuasion: A guide to creating mediation dispute resolution programs for college campuses.* Amherst, MA: Mediation Project.

Gmelch, W. H. (1995). Department chairs under siege: Resolving the web of conflict. In S. Holton (Ed.), *Conflict management in higher education*. New Directions for Higher Education, no. 92. San Francisco: Jossey-Bass.

Gmelch, W. H., Carroll, J. B., Seedorf, R., & Wentz, D. (1990). *Center for the Study of the Department Chair: 1990 Survey*. Pullman: Washington State University.

Goldberg, S. B., Sander, F., & Rogers, N. (1992). *Dispute resolution: Negotiation, mediation, and other processes* (2nd ed.). Aspen, CO: Aspen Publishers.

Gose, B. (1994, August 17). Lawsuit "feeding frenzy": Some university lawyers say claims against campuses are out of hand. *Chronicle of Higher Education*, p. A27.

Griffin, T. (1993). Techniques for marketing the college and university ombuds office to faculty, staff, and students. In *The Journal 1993: California Caucus of College and University Ombudsmen*. Available at: http://www.ombuds.uci.edu/Journals/1993/marketing.html.

Hale, S. J. (1987). *A mediation program model for the University of Oregon*. Unpublished master's thesis, University of Oregon.

Harman, K. M. (1989). Culture and conflict in academic organization: Symbolic aspects of university worlds. *Journal of Educational Administration, 27*(3), 30–54.

Hartzog, C. (1995). Intervention in L.A.: Conflict prevention and mediation program at UCLA. *Educational Record, 76*(1), 44–52.

Hebein, R. (Ed.). (1996, Spring). *Occasional papers on confidentiality and record keeping* (Vol. 2). Boulder, CO: University and College Ombuds Association.

Hobbs, W. C. (1974). The "defective pressure-cooker" syndrome: Dispute process in the university. *Journal of Higher Education, 45*(8), 569–581.

Holton, S. (Ed.). (1995). *Conflict management in higher education*. San Francisco: Jossey-Bass.

Holton, S. (1996). *Conflict management programs in higher education*. Bridgewater, MA: Bridgewater State College.

Holton, S. (Ed.). (1998). *Mending the cracks in the ivory tower*. Bolton, MA: Anker Publishing Company.

Holton, S., & Warters, W. C. (1995). Conflict management programs in the United States and Canada (Appendix). In S. Holton (Ed.), *Conflict management in higher education*. New Directions in Higher Education, no. 92. San Francisco: Jossey-Bass.

Hunter, K., & Hoenig, J. (1996). *Partnering: A promising process is now a proven tool*. Honolulu, HI: Dispute Prevention and Resolution. Available at: http://www.lava.net/DPR4ADR/serpart.html.

Jameson, J. K. (1996). *Diffusion of a campus innovation: Integration of a new student dispute resolution center into a university culture*. Paper presented at the Conflict Studies: A New Generation of Ideas, University of Massachusetts, Boston.

Johnson, D., & Johnson, R. (1995). *Creative controversy: Intellectual challenge in the classroom* (3rd ed.). Edina, MN: Interaction Book Company.

Johnson, S. (1996). *Shared interests: Conciliation/mediation for faculty and staff at the University of Michigan (report and evaluation of the pilot period)* (Pilot Project Report). Ann Arbor: University of Michigan.

Julius, D. J. (Ed.). (1993). *Managing the industrial labor relations process in higher education*. Washington, D.C.: College and University Personnel Association.

Kaner, S. (1996). *Facilitator's guide to participatory decision-making*. Gabriola Island, B.C.: New Society Publishers.

Kaplin, W. A., & Lee, B. A. (1997). *A legal guide for student affairs professionals* (3rd ed.). San Francisco: Jossey-Bass.

Katz, N. (1995). What's in a name: Capturing the essence of campus mediation. *Fourth R, 55,* 7, 15, 26.

Knechel, S., Moore, E., & Moore, H. (1984, January). A mediation workshop for residential staff. *Journal of College Student Personnel Association,* pp. 86–88.

Kolb, D., & Others. (1994). *When talk works: Profiles of mediators.* San Francisco: Jossey-Bass Publishers.

Krajewski, G. (1998). Conflict management programs for administrators. In S. Holton (Ed.), *Mending the cracks in the ivory tower* (pp. 239–252). Bolton, MA: Anker Publishing Co.

Krivis, J., & McAdoo, B. (1997, December). A style index for mediators. *Alternatives.*

Lam, J. (1989). *School mediation program evaluation kit.* Washington, DC: Conflict Resolution in Education Network.

Laue, J. H., & Cormick, G. (1978). The ethics of intervention in community disputes. In G. Bermant, H. Kelman, & D. Warwick (Eds.), *Ethics of social intervention.* New York: Halsted Press.

Leal, R. (1995). From collegiality to confrontation: Faculty-to-faculty conflicts. In S. Holton (Ed.), *Conflict management in higher education* (Vol. 92, pp. 19–25). San Francisco: Jossey-Bass.

Levine, A. (1999, February 26). A new generation of student protesters arises. *Chronicle of Higher Education,* A52.

London, D. (1991, April 3). Top problems in college towns: Parking and housing. *Chronicle of Higher Education,* A21.

Lovejoy, C. (1995). Predicting fall semester breakups in college roommates: A replication using the Social Satisfaction Questionnaire. *Journal of College Student Development, 36*(6), 594–602.

Lyons, B. (1998). *Group diseases in the science classroom: A reference guide to symptoms and treatments.* Canisius, NY: Canisius College Mediation Service. Available from: (http://www.canisius.edu/~morriss/bio201/groups.html).

Marske, C. E., & Vago, S. (1980). Law and dispute processing in the academic community. *Judicature, 64*(4), 165–175.

McCarthy, J. (1980). Conflict and mediation in the academy. In J. McCarthy (Ed.), *Resolving conflicts in higher education.* New Directions for Higher Education, no. 32.

McDonald, C. B. (1994). *ADR clinic directory (law schools).* Malibu, CA: Pepperdine University.

McGillis, D. (1997). *Community mediation programs: Developments and challenges* Washington D.C.: National Institute of Justice.

McKee, P. (1997). Dealing with the complexities of higher education and the law: An attorney's perspective. In L. Jones (Ed.), *Preventing lawsuits: The role of institutional research.* New Directions for Institutional Research, no. 96. San Francisco: Jossey-Bass.

Mennonite Conciliation Service Staff (MCS). (1995). *Mediation and facilitation manual: Foundations and skills for constructive conflict transformation* (3rd ed.). Akron, PA: Mennonite Conciliation Service.

Merry, S. E., & Milner, N. (Eds.). (1993). *The possibility of popular justice: A case study of community mediation in the United States.* Ann Arbor: University of Michigan Press.

Mikalson, J. (1994). Campus conflict resolution in Connecticut. *Fourth R, 49,* 33.

Miller, K. (1987). The effectiveness of mediation in higher education. *Journal on Dispute Resolution, 3*(1), 187–217.

Millet, J. D. (1962). *The academic community: An essay in organization.* New York: McGraw-Hill.

Millet, J. D. (1978). *New structures of campus power: Success and failures of emerging forms of institutional governance.* San Francisco: Jossey-Bass.

Moore, C. (1996). *The mediation process: Practical strategies for resolving conflict* (2nd ed.). San Francisco: Jossey-Bass.

Moses, P. S. (1997). *Best practices manual: An interdisciplinary approach to service-learning and mediation assistance.* Albany, NY: Government Law Center of Albany Law School.

New Community Meetings Initiative. (1998). *Homepage of Conflict Resolution Center.* Eugene: University of Oregon Conflict Resolution Center. Available from: http://gladstone.uoregon.edu/~stvhnchk/crc/.

Nerad, M., & Miller, D. S. (1996). Increasing student retention in graduate and professional programs. In J. G. Haworth (Ed.), *Assessing graduate and professional education.* New Directions for Institutional Research, no. 92. San Francisco: Jossey-Bass.

O'Doherty, H. (1989). Mediation evaluation: Status report and challenges for the future. *Evaluation Practice, 10*(4), 8–19.

Otto, A. L. (1998). *Resolving workplace disputes: The role of organizational culture in organizational change.* Unpublished doctoral dissertation, University of Minnesota, Minnesota.

Patton, M. Q. (1990). *Qualitative evaluation and research methods* (2nd ed.).Thousand Oaks, CA: Sage.

Patton, M. Q. (1996). *Utilization-focused evaluation* (3rd ed.). Thousand Oaks, CA: Sage.

Pence, S. (1996). *The University of Michigan Student Dispute Resolution Program, Winter, 1996 Program Report.* Ann Arbor: University of Michigan.

Perigo, D. (1996). *Shared interests: Conciliation/mediation for faculty and staff at the University of Michigan.* (Pilot project report), University of Michigan.

Pernal, M. (1996/1997). A collaborative approach to grievance-arbitration resolution at higher education institutions. *CUPA Journal, 47,* 27–29.

Perry, W. (1970). *Intellectual and ethical development in the college years.* New York: Holt, Rinehart, & Wilson.

Peterson, M., & Spencer, M. G. (1990). Understanding academic culture and climate. In W. Tierney (Ed.), *Assessing academic climate and culture.* New Directions for Institutional Research, no. 68. San Francisco: Jossey-Bass.

Porteous, N. L., Sheldrick, B. J., & Stewart, P. J. (1997). *Program evaluation tool kit.* Ottawa, Canada: Ottawa-Carleton Health Department.

Price, A. (1995). Questions of appropriateness. In J. Stutzman & C. Schrock-Shenk (Eds.), *Mediation and facilitation training manual: Foundations and skills for constructive conflict transformation* (3rd ed., p. 265). Akron, PA: Mennonite Conciliation Service.

Purdue Mediation and Conciliation Center. (1999). *Mission statement of Purdue Mediation and Conciliation Center.* West Lafayette, IN: Purdue University. Available from: http://www.tech.purdue.edu/orgs/mediate/about.htm.

Reuben, R. (1996, August). The lawyer turns peacemaker. *ABA Journal,* 55–62.

Roberts, B. (1997, March 24). Smack dab in the middle: UGA offers conflict mediation. *Columns.*

Roberts, T. (1993). *A self-evaluation manual for community-based mediation projects: Tools for monitoring and recording data.* Vancouver, Canada: University of Victoria Institute for Dispute Resolution.

Rodgers, R. F. (1983). Using theory in practice. In T. K. Miller, R. B. Winston, & W. R. Mendenhall (Eds.), *Administration and leadership in student affairs* (pp. 111–144). Muncie, IN: Accelerated Development.

Rolph, E. S., & Moller, E. (1995). *Evaluating agency alternative dispute resolution programs: A users' guide to data collection and use* (MR–534–ACUS/ICJ). Santa Monica, CA: RAND Institute for Civil Justice.

Rossi, P., & Freeman, H. (1993). *Evaluation: A systematic approach* (5th ed.). Thousand Oaks, CA: Sage.

Rowe, M. (1990, April). People who feel harassed need a complaint system with both formal and informal options. *Negotiation Journal,* pp. 161–171.

Rowe, M. (1997). An effective, integrated complaint resolution system. In B. R. Sandler & R. J. Shoop (Eds.), *Sexual harassment on campus*. Needham Heights, MA: Allyn and Bacon.

Rowe, M. P. (1991, October). The ombudsman role in a dispute resolution system. *Negotiation Journal*, 353–362.

Rule, C. (1993). *Planning and design of a student-centered collegiate conflict management system*. Amherst, MA: National Association for Mediation in Education.

Rule, C. (1994). Collegiate mediation programs: A critical review. *Fourth R, 50*, 36–37.

Ryor, A. (1978, June–July). Who killed collegiality? *Change, 11*.

Sander, F. (1995). The obsession with settlement rates. *Negotiation Journal, 11*, 329–331.

Schein, E. (1975). Changing role of the personnel manager. *Journal of College and University Personnel Association, 26*, 14–19.

Schein, E. (1987). *Process consultation, Volume II: Lessons for managers and consultants*. Reading, MA: Addison-Wesley.

Schneider, A. (1998, Mar. 27). Insubordination and intimidation signal the end of decorum in many classrooms.

Schwarz, R. M. (1994). *The skilled facilitator: Practical wisdom for developing effective groups*. San Francisco: Jossey-Bass.

Schwing, A. T. (1994). *Open meetings laws*. Anchorage, AK: Fathom.

Shadish, W. R., Cook, T. D., & Leviton, L. C. (1991). *Foundations of program evaluation: Theories of practice*. Thousand Oaks, CA: Sage.

Shonholtz, R. (1984). Neighborhood justice systems: Work, structure, and guiding principles. *Mediation Quarterly, 5*, 3–30.

Silbey, S., & Merry, S. (1986). Mediator ideology and settlement strategies. *Law and Policy, 8*, 7–32.

Sisson, V. S., & Todd, S. R. (1995). Using mediation in response to sexual assault on college and university campuses. *NASPA Journal, 32*(4), 262–269.

Slaikeu, K., & Hasson, R. (1998). *Controlling the costs of conflict: How to design a system for your organization*. San Francisco: Jossey-Bass.

Slaton, C. (1994). *Community mediation service: A model for teaching democracy and conflict resolution*. Paper presented at the Annual Meeting of the American Political Science Association, New York.

Stamato, L. (1989). Making mediation work for disadvantaged students: A project of Rutgers University. *Conflict Resolution Notes, 7*(1).

Stamato, L. (1992). *The campus as community*. New Brunswick, NJ: Rutgers Center of Negotiation and Conflict Resolution.

Stern, L. (1990, Fall). 1990 ombudsperson survey. *UCOA Newsletter*.

Stroup, H. (1966). *Bureaucracy in higher education*. New York: Free Press.

Stulberg, J. B. (1987). *Taking charge/managing conflict*. San Francisco: Jossey-Bass.

Symposium on dispute systems design. (1989). *Negotiation Journal, 5*, 357–407.

Syracuse University. (1991). *Campus Mediation Center Organizational Structure and By-Laws*. Syracuse, NY: Syracuse University.

Tidwell, A. (1997). Problem solving for one. *Mediation Quarterly, 14*(4), 309–317.

Tierney, W. G. (1988). Organizational culture in higher education: Defining the essentials. *Journal of Higher Education, 59*(1), 2–21.

Tinto, V. (1987). *Leaving college: Rethinking the causes and cures of student attrition*. Chicago: University of Chicago Press.

Tyler, T. (1989). The quality of dispute resolution procedures and outcomes: Measurement problems and possibilities. *Denver University Law Review, 66*, 419–436.

University and College Ombuds Association. (1995). *The ombuds handbook: A practical guide to establishing and operating an ombuds office on a college or university campus*. Boulder, CO: University and College Ombuds Association.

University and College Ombuds Association. (1999). *UCOA ethical principles.* Available from: http://www.colorado.edu/Ombuds/UCOA/ethics.html.

Ury, W. L., Brett, J. M., & Goldberg, B. (1988). *Getting disputes resolved: Designing systems to cut the cost of conflict.* San Francisco: Jossey-Bass.

Volpe, M. (1994). An urban university-based conflict resolution program. *Education and Urban Society, 27,* 22–34.

Volpe, M. (1998). Using town meetings to foster peaceful coexistence. In E. Weiner (Ed.), *Handbook of interethnic coexistence.* New York: Continuum Books.

Volpe, M., & Witherspoon, R. (1992). Mediation and cultural diversity on college campuses. *Mediation Quarterly, 9*(4), 341–351.

Waldo, M. (1989). Primary prevention in university residence halls: Paraprofessional-led relationship enhancement groups for college roommates. *Journal of Counseling and Development, 67,* 465–470.

Warters, W. (1991). Mediation on campus: A history and planning guide. *Fourth R, 45,* 4–5.

Warters, W. (1995a). Researching campus conflict management culture(s): A role for ombuds? In R. Wilson (Ed.), *The journal—1995.* Asilomar: California Caucus of College and University Ombudsmen.

Warters, W. (1995b). Conflict management in higher education: A review of current approaches. In S. Holton (Ed.), *Conflict management in higher education.* New Directions in Higher Education, no. 92. San Francisco: Jossey-Bass.

Warters, W. (1998a). *Campus Mediation Resources Web Site.* Detroit, MI: Wayne State University. Available at: http://www.mtds.wayne.edu/campus.htm.

Warters, W. (1998b, May 8). *The history of campus mediation systems: Research and practice.* Paper presented at the Reflective Practice in Institutionalizing Conflict Resolution in Higher Education, Georgia State University, Atlanta.

Warters, W., & Hedeen, T. (1991). *Campus-based mediation programs survey.* Syracuse, NY: Syracuse University.

Warters, W., & Sherman, B. (1991). *Annotated campus mediation bibliography.* Syracuse, NY: Syracuse University Campus Mediation Center.

Weber, M. (1947). *The theory of social and economic organizations* (Anderson, A. M., & Parsons, T., Trans.). New York: Oxford University Press.

Weddle, C. J. (1992). The case for "structured negotiation" in sexual misconduct cases. *Synthesis: Law and Policy in Higher Education, 4,* 291–292.

Weick, K. E. (1976). Educational organizations as loosely coupled systems. *Administrative Science Quarterly, 21*(1), 1–19.

Wilson, R. (1997, August 1). Colleges get psychological help for dysfunctional departments. *Chronicle of Higher Education,* p. A10.

Wing, L. (1994). Multicultural conflict resolution team/University of Massachusetts at Amherst. *Fourth R, 48,* 25–26.

Young, P. D., & Gehring, D. D. (1973). *The college student and the courts.* Asheville, NC: College Administrations Publications.

Zdziarski, E. L. (1998). Alternative dispute resolution. In B. Paterson & W. Kibler (Eds.), *The administration of campus discipline* (pp. 233–248). Asheville, NC: College Administration Publications.